DUNCAN
RAY BRANNAN

THE

SOLDIER CODE

ANCIENT WARRIOR WISDOM FOR
MODERN-DAY CHRISTIAN
SOLDIERS

All Scripture quotations, unless otherwise indicated, are taken from The English Standard Version. Text Edition 2016. Copyright © 2001, Crossway Bibles, a publishing ministry of Good News Publishers.

Scripture quotations marked GW are taken from The GOD'S WORD Translation. Copyright © 1995, 2003, 2013, 2014, 2019, 2020, God's Word to the Nations Mission Society. All rights reserved.

Scripture quotations marked NLT are taken from The New Living Translation. Copyright © 1996, 2004, 2015, Tyndale House Foundation. All rights reserved.

Scripture quotations marked NLT, 1996 are taken from The New Living Translation. Copyright © 1996, Ibid. All rights reserved.

Scripture quotations marked NIV are taken from The New International Version. Copyright © 1973, 178, 1984, 2011, Biblica, Inc. All rights reserved.

Scripture quotations marked MSG are taken from The Message. Copyright © 1993, 2002, 2018, Eugene H. Peterson.

Scripture quotations marked GNT are taken from The Good News Translation. Copyright © 1992, American Bible Society.

Scripture quotations marked CEV are taken from The Contemporary English Version. Copyright © 1995, American Bible Society.

Scripture quotations marked AMPC are taken from The Amplified Bible, Classic Edition. Copyright © 1954, 1958. 1962, 1964, 1965, 1987, The Lockman Foundation.

Scripture quotations marked EHV are taken from The Evangelical Heritage Version. Copyright © 2019, Wartburg Project, Inc. All rights reserved.

Publishing Services provided by Paper Raven Books, LLC

Printed in the United States of America

First Printing, 2022

Paperback ISBN= 978-1-7378858-2-5

Hardback ISBN= 978-1-7378858-1-8

To Jesus
—My Lord, Champion, & Friend:
Thank You for loving, saving, and making me yours.
Come quickly!

To Ralana
—My Love, Fair Princess, & Shield-Maiden:
Thank you for trusting the Lord,
Supporting me, and believing in this.
I love you forever!

TABLE OF CONTENTS

ACKNOWLEDGMENTS

So many fingerprints are on these pages, but I'll start here.

When Ralana asked what God was showing me about my next season one day, I said: "Bringing together what's only been shared in pieces with different parts of the Lord's Army over the last twenty-plus years. It's time to write the book for the whole Body of Christ." She knew exactly what I was saying and agreed, and we both knew it would take sacrifices to make it happen. Two-and-a-half years later, what you now hold is just as much hers because she held down the fort, allowing me to focus like never before.

Next come my dearest man-friends, my "Warriors Three": armor-bearer—Dave Grover, "XO"—Jeff Roberts, and anchorman—Hershel Reid. Men, thank you for battling for and beside me and mine all these years, for every soul won and every life changed.

Ralana and I also wish to send out a special nod to that phalanx of godly men and women throughout our story—pastors, friends, and fellow ministers who've fed, encouraged, and walked with us. You are too many to mention. But Father knows your names, and you've earned many rewards through your ministry to us. May He repay your kindness!

Last, thank you to the band of brothers who gave up their time to read through my manuscript, provide amazing feedback, and help shape this work: J. David Thayer, Sean McGowan, Justin Davis, Hershel Reid, Craig Beaman, and my pastor—Matt Oxley.

Fellow soldiers, I love you all "with deadly intensity"!

PROLOGUE

SUN TZU & SPIRITUAL WARFARE

The general who understands war is the minister of the people's fate and arbiter of the nation's destiny.

—Sun Tzu, *The Art of War*

A shrewd general can take a city defended by strong men, and destroy the walls they relied on.

—King Solomon, Proverbs 21:22, GNT

An ancient Chinese proverb states, "The journey of a thousand miles begins with a single step."[1] Mine began more than twenty years ago as I entered a Barnes & Noble bookstore. Passing its military history section, I sensed the Lord prompting me to stop. Walking over, I found myself before a copy of Sun Tzu's classic *The Art of War*. I bought it, and from its first maxim was taken by its relevance to the Christian soldier's warfare: "War is a matter of vital importance to the State; the province of life or death; the road to survival or ruin. It is mandatory that it be thoroughly studied."[2]

As followers of the Lord Jesus Christ, we groan with all creation for His return—when swords will be beaten into plowshares and spears into pruning hooks, when we will at last lie down in safety, and war will be studied no more (Isaiah 2:1-5). Yet we find ourselves in perilous times (2 Timothy 3:1-5). We have witnessed those we know and don't know setting aside the clear teaching of Scripture to placate secular and anti-religious culture, abandoning the Faith to follow deceiving spirits and doctrines of demons (1 Timothy 4:1-2).[i] Trojan horse attacks weaponized with "another Jesus, another spirit, and another Gospel" populate virtually every street corner (2 Corinthians 11:3-4).[ii] Research reveals masses claiming Christian faith yet leading wholly contradictory lives (Matthew 7:15-27).[iii,3] Social activists, ignorant of the powers they tamper with, have even adopted the devil as their mascot while others invoke the souls of the dead in attempts to influence political outcomes (Deuteronomy 18:9-14).[iv] Now, more than ever perhaps, the Church of Jesus Christ must return to the study of spiritual warfare—the saints' ongoing battle with sin, Satan, and the sway of this fallen world (Romans 6:13).[v]

My off-the-beaten-path quest quickly proved more than an exercise in comparative history. As I read further, Sun Tzu's call for discipline, strategy, intelligence (knowledge of one's foe and other factors), the concept of *total war* (all resources engaged to achieve victory), and the parallels between

---

i   *2 Timothy 4:3-4*
ii   *Galatians 1:8-10*
iii   *2 Timothy 2:19; Titus 1:16*
iv   *2 Corinthians 11:14-15*
v   *Ephesians 6:11; 1 John 2:16*

earthly warfare and the Christian soldier's heavenly one astounded me. I shook my head frequently, responding aloud as I pored over the text. Even greater, without realizing, this parabolic approach (comparing the natural with the spiritual) freshly sharpened my mind on scriptural truths and verses I'd learned years ago.

Mind you, my belief in essential Christian doctrine did not change, as the rest of this work will attest. God's existence and sovereignty, Scripture's inspiration and inerrancy, man's creation and fall, Christ's deity and redemption…all I knew to be biblical orthodoxy ("right belief") from years of study and sound interpretative principles remained precisely the same. What changed was my earnestness, discernment, daily conduct, and approach to spiritual warfare. Truth remained truth, but now it held more weight, color, and clarity.

Within days, I devoured the Art of War, but one nagging question remained: "Does this principle of parallels between earthly and heavenly warfare apply to other warrior cultures?" "Sun Tzu hails from Chinese history. If I study the Japanese samurai, for example, will I find other similarities?" I asked God in prayer one day. I'd love to tell you, "The clouds parted and a great voice thundered from on high!" But it was more of an impression that I received, that our Heavenly Father was looking down with a knowing gaze and a smile peeking from the corner of his mouth. Proverbs 25:2 says, "It is the glory of God to conceal things, but the glory of kings is to search things out." So, like a king, I searched.

My exploration into martial culture soon branched into other fields: archaeology, philosophy, religion, mythology, and more. In all of these various digs, however, one captivating fact continually surfaced: every major warrior tradition of the world contained a code—an ethos instantly separating soldiers from civilians. It demanded the dearest of sacrifices and drove them to the most daring exploits. It unleashed their passion and power in wartime and restrained them in peacetime. It punished them when violated and praised them when venerated. It hardened warriors into the fiercest opponents on the field while making them the tenderest of servants off of it. Most of all, every code embodied an archetype, the ideal of a master soldier.

In my studies, a handful of martial cultures emerged at the forefront of history: the samurai of Japan, the Spartan of Greece, the Roman legionary, Europe's medieval knight, the Norse Viking, and Rome's second addition: the gladiator. Certainly, other historians could emerge with a different list—longer or shorter. But, I suspect that many of these iconic figures would make the cut. Each culture highlighted a different chief virtue. However, like a samurai's lamellar breastplate or Roman legionary's *lorica segmentata* body armor, I found that these martial virtues did not conflict but overlapped like protective plates, fitting together and complementing each other from one tradition to the next.

Each culture also brought its own set of lessons, which proved to be most encouraging to my faith at times and deeply convicting at others. Every area of my life grew, ministry retreats developed, men and women became empowered and equipped, and scores went on to launch various Kingdom missions. My first, small step in a thousand-mile journey with God proved to be a giant leap for many others, and it's my earnest prayer that in the following pages the Lord of Heaven's Armies will consecrate new soldiers for the good fight of faith, stir up veterans, sharpen dull weapons, and restore to the weak and wounded a loving, heavenly war cry in Jesus' mighty Name. Amen.

Introduction

THE SOLDIER STONE

Men have divided the world into heathen and Christian, without considering how much good may have been hidden in the one, or how much of evil may have mingled with the other. They have compared the best part of themselves with the worst of their neighbors, the ideal of Christianity with the corruptions of Greece or the East. They have not aimed at impartiality but have been contented to accumulate all that could be said in praise of their own and in dispraise of other forms of religion.

—Benjamin Jowett, *Sermons on Faith & Doctrine*

And he made from one man every nation of mankind to live on all the face of the earth, having determined allotted periods and the boundaries of their dwelling place, that they should seek God, and perhaps feel their way toward him and find him. Yet he is actually not far from each one of us, for "In him we live and move and have our being"; as even some of your own poets have said, "For we are indeed his offspring."

—The Apostle Paul, Acts 17:26-28

I n July of 1799, French army engineer Pierre-Francois Bouchard received a commission from Napoleon Bonaparte that would change the world. Northeast of the city of Rosetta, Egypt stood the tattered Fort Julien, a former stronghold of the Ottoman Empire now under the French army's control. Bouchard's commission was simple: rebuild that fortress to strengthen the French position against an Ottoman siege. As work began, with soldiers collecting stones to fortify the walls, Lieutenant Bouchard came face-to-face with a most puzzling one—a large, gray, granite-like fragment measuring almost four feet tall, two-and-a-half-feet wide, one-foot thick, and weighing a little less than one ton. Most peculiar of all were three distinct inscriptions covering its face: Ancient Egyptian hieroglyphs, Egyptian demotic script, and Ancient Greek. Bouchard knew instantly the monument or *stele* held great value. Not until it fell into English hands, however, resting in London's now famous British Museum, would the world come to know the Rosetta stone: the key that unlocked Egyptian hieroglyphics.

Today, we employ the term "Rosetta stone" for any object used to decipher encoded information, and a work which takes a fresh approach to an old subject like this necessitates one. I, for one, don't know of any book on spiritual warfare which takes this path around the proverbial barn. Exploring military history and ethics, archaeology and liturgy, mythology, and religion in order to better understand and apply biblical principles may seem a strange endeavor. Thus, this chapter centers on giving my fellow soldiers a "Rosetta stone" to decipher this work.

After all, some within or without the religious pale may ask, "Are we, perhaps, treading dangerous ground, maybe even militarizing Christian faith by this kind of teaching approach? Remember, Jesus was a man of peace, not war. Is there a biblical foundation to support this type of comparative methodology? What could those who wielded carnal weapons against flesh and blood possibly teach Christians about warring with evil spirits (2 Corinthians 10:3-5; Ephesians 6:10-18)? Do we taint God's sacred Word by placing it beside things of this world?" These and similar questions are not unreasonable.

So, let's take some time to address them and carve out our soldier Rosetta. As we do, I'll provide you with biblical references and other important information in parentheses and footnotes. We begin with the God of Scripture Himself.

I. God's Soldier Names & Image

One of the most misunderstood or entirely overlooked attributes of the biblical God remains His soldier image. At numerous moments in history, God revealed this facet of Himself through titles, miracles, prophecies, and the Person of Jesus, then conveyed those revelations to subsequent generations through the Holy Scriptures. After God shattered slave-master Egypt with ten plagues and swallowed Pharaoh's army in the Red Sea to liberate Israel, Moses sang, *"Yahweh ish Milchamah; Yahweh semow"*—"the Lord is a man of war; the Lord is His Name (Exodus 15:3)!" Before Israel's Canaan conquest, Joshua fell prostrate before a preincarnate appearance of Jesus as *Sar Tsaba Yahweh:* "Prince of the Lord's Army (Joshua 5:14)." 1 Samuel 1:11 introduced God's soldiers to the title *Yahweh Sabaot:* "The Lord of Armies." Finally, David in the Psalms, along with Isaiah and Jeremiah in their prophecies, refer to God as *Gibbor*—the "Warrior" or "Mighty One" (Psalm 24:8).[i, 1]

Dr. Robert Hicks, former professor of pastoral theology at Bethel Seminary of the East, points out that the messianic title *El Gibbor* ("Mighty Warrior God") in Isaiah 9:6 occurs right beside others like *Abiad* ("Eternal Father") and *Sar Shalom* ("Prince of Peace"). Thus, being the Mighty Warrior in no way contradicts being God, Eternal Father, or the Prince of Peace.[2] Further, Isaiah's prophecy of God's Messianic Warrior-Son points us directly to the New Testament. Here, we see Jesus clash with Satan and demons (Matthew 4)[ii]; confront cold religion standing in the way of His Gospel (Matthew 23); cleanse God's Temple of corruption with a whip to minister healing to the blind and lame (Matthew 21:12-14)[iii]; chivalrously stare down a stone-brandishing mob while gently lifting up a shamed, adulterous damsel (John 8:1-11); and obey the Father's charge, suffering the most humiliating and agonizing of deaths to redeem a lost world (Matthew 26-27). Likewise, Revelation and other parts of Scripture promise us Christ's second coming: his bodily return to earth on a white

---

i   *Psalm 45:3; Isaiah 9:6; 10:21; 42:13; Jeremiah 20:11*

ii   *Matthew 8-9; 12*

iii *John 2:13-17*

The idea of protecting those we love, standing on moral principles, championing those with no voice, and fighting evil... originates from God's own fierce, unrelenting love...

horse leading Heaven's army to slay His foes and establish an everlasting kingdom (Zechariah 14:1-4).[iv, 3]

The main point here is that the biblical God differs drastically from the cheap knockoffs of Hollywood pop-culture and half-baked Christian theology. The genuine article has never been passive and weak, nor savage and uncaring. The idea of protecting those we love, standing on moral principles, championing those with no voice, and fighting evil and injustice in their various forms originates from God's own fierce, unrelenting love which, in turn, was perfectly modeled by Jesus Christ and His Cross. As beings created in God's image then, man and woman also share in His soldier image (Genesis 1:26-27). The reason we passionately "battle disease, attack problems, combat drugs, struggle with ignorance, fight fires, and make war on poverty" is because the apple never falls far from the Tree.[4] Like it or not, embrace it or reject it, soldiery remains an inherent trait of the masculine and feminine design, each sex bearing specific attributes of God's own soldier heart. To shun this image is to deny an entire facet of our Creator and ourselves clearly revealed in Scripture and repeatedly confirmed in history.

II. History: The Sovereign God's Sermon

History has always played a central role in communicating God's message. The Old Testament centers on His dealings with ancient Israel and records His personal military operations as He manifests in *direct* confrontations with those threatening His people, like His fiery presence fending off Pharaoh's army then utterly consuming them in the Red Sea (Exodus 14:19-25) or the angel of the Lord smiting 185,000 Assyrian warriors (2 Kings 19:35). The Old Testament also chronicles the Lord's *indirect* yet sovereign work through prophets, judges, priests, kings, and soldiers leading Israel into battle, such as Saul's clash with Ammon (1 Samuel 11) or David's champion warfare with Goliath (1 Samuel 17). Like all Scripture, though, God's Spirit breathed out each word of these accounts (2 Timothy 3:16-17).

---

iv   *Acts 1:11; Revelation 19:11-21*

As we come to the New Testament, the Lord of Armies picks up these tales of natural warfare to train His saints for spiritual combat. Bolstering Jewish Christians for mounting persecution, the author of Hebrews cites Gideon, Barak, Samson, Jephthah, David, Samuel, and the prophets "who through faith conquered kingdoms, enforced justice, obtained promises, stopped the mouths of lions, quenched the power of fire, escaped the edge of the sword, were made strong out of weakness, became mighty in war, [and] put foreign armies to flight (Hebrews 11:32-34)." Writing to embattled Jewish believers, the apostle James notes Job's Satan-ravaged life as a model of faith, saying, "Behold, we consider those blessed who remained steadfast. You have heard of the steadfastness of Job, and you have seen the purpose of the Lord, how the Lord is compassionate and merciful (James 5:11)." In summary, we learn that the history of God's people "was written for our instruction, that through endurance and through the encouragement of the Scriptures we might have hope (Romans 15:4)."

But what of the rest of human history? Has God confined His teaching ministry to the Scriptures in what we call *revealed religion*? If we study man or nature, the stars or other sciences (biology, genetics, physics, etc.) or philosophy, and so on, can we discover proofs of God's existence, power, and attributes? The Bible answers, "Yes!" David writes in Psalm 19:1-4, NLT, "The heavens proclaim the glory of God. The skies display his craftsmanship. Day after day they continue to speak; night after night they make him known. They speak without a sound or word; their voice is never heard. Yet their message has gone throughout the earth, and their words to all the world...." In Romans 1:20, NLT, Paul agrees, declaring, "For ever since the world was created, people have seen the earth and sky. Through everything God made, they can clearly see His invisible qualities—His eternal power and divine nature. So they have no excuse for not knowing God."

This secondary means by which God reveals Himself through reason and experience, versus miracles or other supernatural means, we call *natural religion* or *natural theology*. Rather than shy away from it, God encourages us to study it, saying, "Instead, ask the animals and they will teach you. Ask the birds, and they will tell you. Or speak with the earth, and it will teach you. Even the fish will relate the story to you. What creature doesn't know that the Lord's hands made it (Job 12:7-9, GW)?"

Notice how the passage touches various sciences: animals (zoology), birds (ornithology), earth (geology), and fish (marine biology). The Holy Spirit, who Jesus said would lead us into all truth, doesn't stop here (John 16:13). He also beckons, "Ask the people of past generations. Find out what their ancestors had learned. We have only been around since yesterday, and we know nothing. Our days on earth are only a fleeting shadow. Won't their words teach you? Won't they share their thoughts with you (Job 8:8-10, GW)?" The Lord of history calls us to study history because not knowing it can prove costly. As Sir Winston Churchill warned, "Those who fail to learn from history are condemned to repeat it."[5] Dr. Inazo Nitobe—educator, diplomat, and devout Christian—bemoaned the arrogance and ignorance of early missionaries to Japan, revealing:

> One cause of the failure of mission work is that most of the missionaries are entirely ignorant of our history—"What do we care for heathen records?" some say—and consequently estrange their religion from the habits of thought we and our forefathers have been accustomed to for centuries past. Mocking a nation's history?—as though the career of any people—even of the lowest African savages possessing no record—were not a page in the general history of mankind, written by the hand of God Himself. The very lost races are a palimpsest [a manuscript page which has been cleaned off and reused] to be deciphered by a seeing eye. To a philosophic and pious mind the races themselves are marks of Divine chirography [handwriting]....[6]

In other words, if the biblical God has penned the whole of history, not just the parts we so easily grasp or readily adore, who are we to tear a page from *His story* and exclaim, "This means nothing?" Our generation comprises a mere drop in history's bucket. As Job 8:9a said, "We have only been around since yesterday, and we know nothing." The idea then that the history of other people—lost or saved, whose existence eclipses ours by hundreds or thousands of years—cannot enlighten us seems a tad conceited. Any thoughtful, thorough examination of another's past should leave us with a sobering, penitent pause on how we're living in the present. We should arise humbler, wiser, more prayerful, and far more grateful.

If we ever emerge with a sense of self-righteousness, some "holier-than-thou" attitude over those we have studied, it's because we have changed history from a mirror into a window, from a place of self-examination into a throne of judgment. We haven't just missed the point. We've missed the boat! When we truly study history, like

If we ever emerge with a sense of self-righteousness, some "holier-than-thou" attitude over those we have studied, it's because we have changed history from a mirror into a window...

a reflection, it studies us right back. It cross-examines us like a prosecutor, questioning our motives, words, and deeds.

More than statistics and hard facts, history is people: how they lived and loved, what they believed and dreamt. It's marked by their birth, progress, and triumph; colored by their blood, sweat, and tears; underscored by their joy, rage, and anguish; and eulogized by their defeat, disease, and death. It's beginning, end, and all that happens in between. It's truth and lies; reflective prose and romantic verse; crime against humanity and poetic justice; the telling of what has been because of human nature and forewarning of what will be because that nature has not changed. We study history because *we are history* and were meant to learn and grow from it!

One of the primary reasons Christians neglect the study of secular history or religion lies in the fact that we unwittingly compare our redeemed position to another's unregenerated one, which is most foolish because God saved us, not we ourselves (Ephesians 2:8-9). Furthermore, we will continue to wrestle with our own flesh till we see Christ face-to-face (Romans 7:14-25). We must be wary then of the pride Jesus presaged in the parable of the publican and tax collector: "God, I thank you that I am not like other people—robbers, evildoers, adulterers—or even like this tax collector. I fast twice a week and give a tenth of all I get," the Pharisee boasts as he stands praying (Luke 18:11-12, NIV). Similarly, Anglican cleric and Oxford theologian Benjamin Jowett pointed out:

Men have divided the world into heathen and Christian, without considering how much good may have been hidden in the one, or how much of evil may have mingled with the other. They have compared the best part of themselves with the worst of their neighbors, the ideal of Christianity with the corruptions of Greece or the East. They have not aimed at impartiality but have been contented to accumulate all that could be said in praise of their own and in dispraise of other forms of religion.[7]

Any kindergarten Christian can point out the hedonism of Rome, polytheism of Greece, or mysticism of the East, Jowett notes. It takes a mature, Spirit-led believer like Paul, however, to look at a Roman legionary and see lessons in spiritual warfare or gaze upon Athenian idols and discern a way to preach the "unknown god" (Ephesians 6:10-18).[v, 8] God's prophets and apostles had no problem separating secular chaff from spiritual wheat to evangelize and equip. It's time then for modern-day Christians to recognize and reclaim the sermons our Sovereign God has preached in history and places like martial culture.

III. Martial Culture: The Holy Spirit's Training Camp

Hand in hand with history, the Bible uses vivid martial imagery in Old and New Testaments to arm saints. In the medieval knight's chapter, we'll explore David's warfare in the Psalms, their role in the birth of European chivalry, and how present-day believers can tap their vast arsenal for wisdom, courage, and victorious prayer. One of the Old Testament's most intriguing uses of martial culture, however, comes with Jeremiah's call to prophetic ministry. Invoking militant language, the Lord says, "Today I have put you in charge of nations and kingdoms. You will uproot and tear down. You will destroy and overthrow. You will build and plant (Jeremiah 1:10, GW)."[9] The original Hebrew *nathats*, rendered as "tear down," traces back to Israel's divine charge in the Canaan conquest to "tear down their altars, crush their sacred stones, and cut down their poles dedicated to the goddess Asherah (Exodus 34:13, GW)."

Moving forward in Scripture, the Spirit uses this term to refer to both Israel's call to destroy idols (Deuteronomy 7:5)[vi] and siege warfare against her foes (Judges 8:9, 17).[vii, 10] The Hebrew *haras* translated above as

---

v   *Acts 17:16-34*

vi   *Judges 2:2; 2 Kings 10:27; 2 Chronicles 31:1*

vii   *2 Kings 25:10; Jeremiah 52:14; Ezekiel 26:9, 12*

"overthrow" bears similar usage—for the overthrow of physical idols and, hence, dethroning of false spiritual gods (Exodus 23:24)[viii], and the overthrow of fortress cities in siege (2 Samuel 11:25).[ix, 11] As the apostle Paul confronts idolatrous cultural and philosophical barriers affecting the Corinthian church, he takes up the siege-craft metaphor, saying, "We use God's mighty weapons, not worldly weapons, to knock down the strongholds of human reasoning and to destroy false arguments. We destroy every proud obstacle that keeps people from knowing God. We capture their rebellious thoughts and teach them to obey Christ (2 Corinthians 10:4-5, NLT)."

In mobilizing the New Testament Church, the apostolic writers frequently use military vernacular but none more than Paul, who wrote almost half of the New Testament.

In mobilizing the New Testament Church, the apostolic writers frequently use military vernacular but none more than Paul, who wrote almost half of the New Testament. Paul's references to Greco-Roman athletic and military traditions, which number about seventy-seven in all, offer more than enough foundation for any work of this sort.[12] The Roman Legion's renowned discipline and ingenious cultivation of military art and science were powerful illustrations only waiting for an insightful teacher to brandish. Paul, moved by the Spirit, seized them and, as previously noted, penned two of the Bible's most profound exhortations on spiritual combat: the armor of God (Ephesians 6:10-20) and siege warfare (2 Corinthians 10:3-5). He only expanded, though, upon the armor of God metaphor. Isaiah had fashioned it by the Spirit seven hundred years before, prophesying yet again of God's messianic Warrior-Son (Isaiah 59:16-21).

Paul's use of the Greek athletic *agón*, which forms the basis of our English word "agony," holds great heft in this discussion also. *Agón* in its noun and verb forms occurs nineteen times in the New Testament.[13] Strong's Concordance sums it up as "a gathering, contest, [or] struggle," but such a brief definition leaves vital cultural and archeological data on the editing room floor.[14] Thomas F. Scanlon, professor of classics at the University of California, Riverside,

---

viii   *Judges 6:25; Ezekiel 16:39*
ix   *2 Kings 3:25; 1 Chronicles 20:1; Ezekiel 26:4, 12*

relates that *agón* was the term for the most brutal contests of the Panhellenic festivals, which consisted of the Olympic, Isthmian, Pythian, and Nemean Games. These contests included chariot racing, boxing, wrestling, and their ancient equivalent of mixed martial arts.[15] All four took place at Corinth's Isthmian Games. Reliefs and writings from the era depict *agón* bouts with bloody punches, broken limbs, genital strikes, dislodged eyes, and disembowelment—an almost no-holds-barred showdown in honor of the gods.

Unlike today, ancient Greek boxing held no rounds, time limits, corner men, hydration, or weight classes. Matches featured two nude men fighting with sharp-edged, rawhide leather–strapped fists called *oxys*. To make things more interesting, when Romans began governing the games (146 B.C.), "the boxers inserted inch-long metal spikes between the straps."[16] Matches ended only when one fighter raised an index finger in submission or died. Many contestants chose death, however, because of the tremendous shame which came with surrender. With blood, bone, and death mingled throughout, Greeks esteemed the *agón* events most pleasing to their pantheon and, in the Olympic games, they heralded them with a dash to a thirty-foot altar of Zeus "made entirely from the ashes of sacrificed animals."[17]

Now, with all this in mind, read Paul's exhortation in 1 Corinthians 9:26-27, NIV: "Therefore I do not run like someone running aimlessly; I do not fight like a boxer beating the air. No, I strike a blow to my body and make it my slave so that after I have preached to others, I myself will not be disqualified for the prize." Think about it: at the Holy Spirit's inspiration, Paul used a graphic, cultural pastime to train Christians to discipline their bodies (which had been given to all kinds of sexual immorality), subjugate their flesh (which was running wild at the time of his writing), and endure hardship to fulfill God's will. The same Lord who said, "Be holy, for I am holy," had no qualms in using a barbaric blood sport to make His point, showing Christian soldiers then and now that spiritual warfare is brutal and, at times, relentless (Leviticus 11:44).

If I were loosely paraphrasing from the original Greek and seeking to tease out all the cultural nuances in these verses, I would word it something like…

I don't run around like some aimless fool, chasing after all this world has to offer. I run straight for the finish line where the One True God's altar, not Zeus', awaits me. Moreover, the sacrifice I'm taking to that altar is not an animal; it's me, my own body, which has been totally set aside for God's glory, not my own. When it comes to dealing with my flesh, I don't "spar." My aim—no different than a boxer at the games—is to beat my opponent silly, buffet my God-hating flesh until it raises its little finger in submission. I do this so I don't disqualify myself in the eyes of a spectating world, having failed to practice what I preached.

Does that give you some extra insight into this verse? Does the unveiling of the culture bring greater clarity and conviction? This is just one of twelve *agón* references in Paul's letters. Think about the impact this had on Corinthian believers. This was their world, and Paul didn't cast it aside because it wasn't rated "G." To the contrary, He used it to confront and coach a selfish, immature church into Christ's overcoming life.

This is also just one example of the Bible's striking use of culture. Time fails us to ponder a host of others in the Greek New Testament, from athletic ones like *athleó* (contend), *dromos* (race), *gumnazó* (training), *palé* (wrestling), *stádion* (stadium), *stephanos* (crown), and *trechó* (run) to militaristic ones like *anthistémi* (resist), *histémi* (stand), *hoplizó* (to arm), *hoplon* (weapon), *ochuróma* (stronghold), *machaira* (sword), and *strateia* (military campaign). One quickly sees the origins of many English words here, and we'll explore some of these terms later. The point once more, though, is that God engages worldly culture to teach in Scripture, and the Master Teacher, Jesus, remains the best example.

IV. Parables: The Master Teacher's Pointer

In each warrior culture's chapter, we'll follow a sort of *a-b/a-b* rhythm, that is, a parable-then-explanation, another parable-then-explanation literary flow. A few questions called "tactical takeaways" will close the chapter, helping identify key themes and truths. The parable will come in the form of a survey of some important era, event, or aspect of ancient to roughly late-modern martial history. Following this, I'll share insights for the Christian's warfare from original biblical language, context, and culture. Behind this "rhyme" or pattern lies great reason.

From the beginning, Jesus proved to be a different kind of teacher. He dined with outcasts, spoke with authority, challenged hypocrisy, drew hard lines for disciples, and taught using odd and frequently provocative stories called "parables." Dictionary.com defines a parable as "a short allegorical story designed to illustrate or teach some truth, religious principle, or moral lesson."[18] Being moved by God's Spirit, the Old Testament prophets employed parables throughout Israeli history (Hosea 12:10).[19] What's so haunting about Christ's use of them, however, is not only that He never spoke to crowds without one, but why (Matthew 13:34).

This is why I speak to them in parables, because seeing they do not see, and hearing they do not hear, nor do they understand. Indeed, in their case the prophecy of Isaiah is fulfilled that says: "You will indeed hear but never understand, and you will indeed see but never perceive. For this people's heart has grown dull, and with their ears they can barely hear, and their eyes they have closed, lest they should see with their eyes and hear with their ears and understand with their heart and turn, and I would heal them. (Matthew 13:13-15)

Almost a thousand years before Christ, the Psalmist Asaph predicted His parable-laced ministry. "I will open my mouth in parables; I will utter dark sayings from of old," Psalm 78:2 says in the *Septuagint*—the Greek translation of the Old Testament. Jesus came to reveal the secrets of the Kingdom of Heaven, but as His ministry began He faced a huge problem: a spiritual plague among God's people. The word which He chose to describe it was not politically correct. The New Testament's original Greek, rendered above as "dull," means "fat, thick, stupid, dull, and unfeeling."[20] That's not a good report! The people of Jesus' day had grown spiritually dim. They grew up around Scripture, heard it on the streets and in synagogues every Sabbath. Pharisees purposefully wore oversized phylactery boxes and lengthened their garment fringes to broadcast how many verses they knew (Numbers 15:37-39).[x] Thousands more of Israelite men could recite entire Scripture books by heart, yet theirs had grown calloused and their spiritual eyes closed.

So, God led His Son to speak to the public in parables, using material

---

x   *Deuteronomy 6:8; 11:18; Matthew 23:5*

examples from their familiar, earthly culture to convey spiritual truths of His foreign, heavenly one. The purpose of this was twofold: a.) to *trip up* hard-hearted foes looking only for a chance to destroy Him, and b.) *stir up* sincere seekers to think, thirst, and search for God. Eugene Peterson's paraphrase of Jesus' words from Matthew 13:13-14 in *The Message,* captures this latter purpose well: "That's why I tell stories: to create readiness, to nudge the people toward receptive insight. In their present state they can stare till doomsday and not see it, listen till they're blue in the face and not get it. I don't want Isaiah's forecast repeated all over again...."[21] I bear a similar burden for God's army in this hour and believe He led me to this type of parable-then-explanation pattern for three reasons:

A.) Parables Sharpen Discernment. Biblical ignorance has become the spiritual pandemic of our day, within and without the Church. In coming chapters, we'll examine troubling statistics in this area. Part of the divine purpose of parables, though, lies in their ability to stir sleeping hearts and sharpen dull minds, as Jesus Himself hinted (Matthew 13:13). Parables give us a mental workout, engaging our imaginations and exercising our faculties by taking us out of our world with its comforts, distractions, and undesirable circumstances and placing us in a new, fascinating one. Without thought, we move from "uh, yeah, Jesus" to "I'm all ears, Lord!"

B.) Parables Give Permission. In these new "parable worlds," these ventures into imagination, we have zero attachments. They provide sterile, nonthreatening environments where our minds can weigh and test hard matters; wrestle with good and evil, truth and lies; and reach righteous conclusions without consequence. It's perfect! Even more, when parables end and their imaginary environments dissolve, the truth, which came cleverly packaged within them, remains. Then, slowly, quietly, our thoughts drift back to our own lives, where applying these uncomfortable truths suddenly proves more palatable.

Parables possess a sort of God-given blessing, it seems. They slip past our amygdalae, those two little trigger-happy guards at the base of our brains which produce the "fight-or-flight" response and often hijack our ability to respond in a calm, rational manner. The amygdalae do not allow us to *consider;* they just *react* with anxiety, aggression, and fear. Parables almost seem to tell our amygdalae, "At ease, boys! Take five."

C.) Parables Offer Perspective. The last thing parables offer is a fresh look at an old subject, one which may have become too familiar. Such is the case here. Too often, when someone utters the term "spiritual warfare," instead of ears perking up, eyes glaze over. A casual, even cavalier attitude unknowingly takes over, which says, "Oh, spiritual warfare? Been there. Done that. Got the T-shirt. Tell me something I don't know." Yet again, the data we'll examine in this work tells a different story. What we witness, in too many places, is not the steady advance of a counterculture on pagan society or the sturdy combat of an occupying army taking ground from the legions of hell. It's more akin to the diffused, legalistic throes of one more worldly religion or meaningless trend passing into the pages of history.

What has happened to the army of God and the good fight of faith (1 Timothy 6:12)? Where is the shout of a king in our midst (Numbers 23:21)? Could our enemy be so brilliant as to attack us at the "well"—the source from which we draw our strength, wisdom, purpose, and power? Would the devil dare to attack us where we'd never expect it?

I submit that, somewhere between the lusts of our lower nature and the wiles of our ancient foe, our understanding of spiritual warfare has been corrupted in key places; our martial codes and spiritual weaponry—how we define and wage warfare—swapped out for religious hype and diluted with devilish wisdom (James 3:13-18). Satan knows our celestial armor is impervious when in place, and the Church invincible when unified and standing on God's Word (Psalm 133).[xi] No weapon he forms will overcome these (Isaiah 54:17). But, if he can substitute God's purposes and instruments with fake ones, well, as Sun Tzu said, "To subdue the enemy without fighting is the acme of skill. Thus, what is of supreme importance in war is to attack the enemy's strategy."[22] The English Puritan William Gurnall identified this same satanic scheme in *The Christian in Complete Armor,* writing:[23]

The Christian's armor which he wears must be of divine institution and appointment. The soldier comes into the field with no arms but what his general commands. It is not left to every one's fancy to bring what weapons

---

xi   *Matthew 16:18; 2 Corinthians 10:3-5; Ephesians 6:11*

he please; this will breed confusion. The Christian soldier is bound up to God's order; though the army be on earth, yet the council of war sits in heaven; this duty ye shall do; these means ye shall use. And [those who] do more, or use other, than God commands, though with some seeming success against sin, shall surely be called to account for this boldness....

I submit that, somewhere between the lusts of our lower nature and the wiles of our ancient foe, our understanding of spiritual warfare has been corrupted in key places...

Therefore, I beseech you, look to your armour. David would not fight in armour he had not tried, though it was a king's.... Bring your heart to the Word, as the only touch-stone of thy grace and furniture; the Word, I told you, is the tower of David, from whence thy armour must be fetched; if thou canst find this tower stamp on it, then it is of God, else, not. Try it therefore by this one scripture-stamp. Those weapons are mighty which God gives his saints to fight his battles withal.[24]

So, hear me, fellow soldier: in this book I'm not offering a different armor than what our King has supplied or setting forth another stamp beside His Word. My only aim is to refresh our understanding of spiritual warfare and, where necessary, reform our practice. My approach will mimic our Master Teacher by using parables, a set penned by the God who not only breathed out Scripture but sovereignly wrote human history. And if the Lord of Hosts, in His own Word, trains hands for war through fact and fiction and teaches spiritual fingers to fight by physical examples; if Jesus thought that the religion, history, philosophy, and culture of Jew and Gentile held so many acceptable illustrations for His, His prophets' and apostles' teaching ministries, I contend that the cultures of the samurai, Spartan, Viking, gladiator, and others can help freshly uncover forgotten truths in our warfare, unlock a martial code desperately needed in this hour, and unleash Christian soldiers in powerful ways for God's glory. Join me now as we venture into the Valley of Soldiers. Our trek begins in the Far East.

BOOK I

WAY OF THE SAMURAI

A man is a good retainer to the extent that he earnestly places importance in his master.... Sagara Kyuma was completely at one with his master and served him as though his own body were already dead. He was one man in a thousand.... The fact that a useless person often becomes a matchless warrior at such times is because he has already given up his life and become one with his lord.... For a warrior there is nothing other than thinking of his master.

—Yamamoto Tsunetomo, *Hagakure*, The Samurai Book of Wisdom

Listen carefully: Unless a grain of wheat is buried in the ground, dead to the world, it is never any more than a grain of wheat. But if it is buried, it sprouts and reproduces itself many times over. In the same way, anyone who holds on to life just as it is destroys that life. But if you let it go, reckless in your love, you'll have it forever, real and eternal. If any of you wants to serve me, then follow me. Then you'll be where I am, ready to serve at a moment's notice. The Father will honor and reward anyone who serves me.

—The Apostle John, John 12:24-26, MSG

S omewhere in the distant past, shrouded by the sacred mists, the fire god Izanagi stood upon the Bridge of Heaven. Gazing down into the formless, watery void below, he drew his gem-bladed sword and plunged it into the primordial chaos, churning it like a cauldron. At last, withdrawing its blade, he watched as tiny drops fell from its tip and formed the first island of Japan.[1] So goes the creation myth of the land that spawned the world's most feted warrior. No other figure in antiquity so clearly stands as the archetype. Why? Was it the samurai's unbending devotion to a chivalric code or his peerless skill in the martial arts, his terrifying intensity in battle or dauntless tranquility in death? To answer, we must steal a glimpse into the samurai's war-torn age. There, we shall also find wisdom for battles raging in our own.

Like his deadly *katana* sword, the knight of the East emerged as the gleaming, razor-sharp result of the most incendiary epoch in Japanese history. Back and forth, across a thousand years, he went from prolonged trials in war's fiery furnace to brief reprieves in peacetime's tempering waters, each successive era folding and hardening him into the mythical steeled image. His roots reach deeply into the country's fabled past, from conscripted peasant armies and elite cavalries in the eighth century A.D. to an emerging warrior caste in the ninth. As the nation fell to economic decline, pandemic, and starvation, the ensuing lawlessness and rebellion heated his proverbial forge, underscoring the need for a warrior class.

Equally, as China's imported influences of Zen Buddhism, Confucianism, and Taoism collided with Japan's native religion, Shintoism, ("the way of the gods"), all the doctrines which would form the samurai's mystical blend of spirituality shifted into position like tectonic plates. Not until the tenth century, though, would the world first hear the name *samurai* applied solely to the warrior.[2] The eleventh century narrowed samurai ranks into noble bloodlines. No longer would just any warrior serving a lord and battling in his behalf bear the sacred title. Finally, from the ashes of the twelfth century's great Gempei War (A.D. 1180-85), the essential samurai elements arose like the legendary phoenix. Samurai specialist Dr. Stephen Turnbull explains:

> The Gempei War is fundamental to understanding samurai history. First, the battles that took place...created benchmarks for samurai excellence

that were to last for the whole of samurai history. Heroic tales and works of art logged the incidents in the Gempei War as a verbal and visual catalogue of heroism that would show future generations the most noble, brave and correct ways of being a samurai. Nearly all the factors that were to become indelible parts of samurai culture have a reference point somewhere within the Gempei War.[3]

From savagery to chivalry, the way of the sword to the way of tea, ritualized suicide to its eulogistic poetry, almost all the virtues and practices soon to comprise samurai culture began merging. Still, a greater forge was needed to finish the work. So came the Age of War.

The Age of War

In 1465, a dispute erupted at the country's highest seat of government, the *shogunate*. Factions formed. War escalated into the streets. Twelve years later, the capital was wasted.[4] Japan disintegrated into a patchwork quilt of states led by *daimyo* ("great names") and for almost 150 years these feudal lords baptized the land in the blood and fire of civil war. Sending forth *kashindan* ("call to arms")—letters with status, orders, and supply needs—masters summoned their samurai to the field. Sieges slaughtered entire garrisons.[5] Clashes consumed up to 72 percent of armies.[6] Battlefields became mass graves.[7] The Battle of Nagashino claimed 16,000 souls.[8] Nagashima's Third Siege: 20,000.[9] Kawanakajima's Fourth Battle: 25,000.[10] Sekigahara, the era's final battle: 40,000.[11]

These are the casualties of just four, one-day battles in a century-and-a-half of over one hundred. By the end of the period, death tolls ranged into the millions with tens of thousands dying in a single day, including women and children. Additionally, these numbers do not even factor for lifestyle-related deaths off the field like duels, assassinations, ritual suicide for defeat, honor code violations, homage to a fallen lord, or protesting injustice. When we consider all the data for the Age of War, we face a lament of biblical proportions. This seething era forged the samurai, heating and hammering his soul until it produced a paradigm shift in thought: warfare was no longer an event but a way of life. Master Taira Shigesuke wrote in his *Bushido Shoshinshu*, "The Way of the Warrior for Beginners":

For warriors it is essential to keep the spirit of combat in mind twenty-four hours a day, whether walking, standing still, sitting down, or reclining, never forgetting it…. It is related that a famous warrior known as the Master Archer used to have a sign on his wall with four words he applied in everyday life: "Always on the battlefield." I note this for the edification of novice warriors.[12]

History's forge completed its work. Like metallic dross, the fatal mindset confining warfare to the field or certain seasons had been skimmed away. Never knowing when his master would call or enemy would come, the samurai stood ready to serve at a moment's notice.

The Christian's Call to Arms

As we ponder these truths in the light of Scripture, we find that, like the samurai, the Church of Jesus Christ arose from a crucible of combat. The New Testament world was a hotbed of false religion, sexual immorality, political corruption, and syndicated violence. Within her first three hundred years the Church faced ten vehement persecutions under the Roman Empire (A.D. 64-313). At the hands of rulers, mobs, gladiators, and beasts, millions of Christians were beaten and beheaded, trounced and torn apart for their faith. New believers were like sheep among wolves, grappling with supernatural forces they could not comprehend. Someone needed to make sense of it all and arm them for war.

In many respects, the apostles' letters came like a *kashindan*, a call to spiritual arms from the *Daimyo of daimyos*, the "Great Name above all names"—Jesus. Replete with military terminology traceable from Classical Greek to first-century Roman warfare, they addressed Christians as soldiers, issued orders with imperative language, laid out spiritual armament, drew battles lines, identified the foe, and explained his tactics. With great insight into the Christian warfare, Paul charged Gentile (non-Jewish) believers across Asia Minor:

Like the samurai, the Church of Jesus Christ arose from a crucible of combat.

Finally, be strong in the Lord and in the strength of his might. Put on the whole armor of God that you may be able to stand against the schemes of the devil. For we do not wrestle against flesh and blood, but against the rulers, against the authorities, against the cosmic powers over this present darkness, against the spiritual forces of evil in the heavenly places. Therefore, take up the whole armor of God that you may be able to withstand in the evil day, and having done all, to stand firm. (Ephesians 6:10-13)

Paul called the Church to battle formations, barking out martial lingo like an old general. The term "whole armor" (Gk., *panoplía*), its description later in the chapter (helmet, shield, sword, etc.), and the commands "take up," "stand," and "withstand" (respectively, *analambáno, histémi,* and *anthistémi*) were native military equipment and vernacular.[13] And, one could have heard a pin drop when Paul described a personal, tactical devil, his well-organized legion, and then contrasted Greek wrestling (*palé*) with hand-to-hand combat. "This is not an Olympic wrestling match where you compete for a leafy crown then everyone goes home," he related. "This is life-and-death combat with creatures who hate you with paranormal passion, strategize constantly on how to gut your life, and will do it the first chance they get!"

James, a veritable drill sergeant of the Early Church, boldly called out Jewish Christians, saying, "You adulterous people! Do you not know that friendship with the world is enmity with God? Therefore whoever wishes to be a friend of the world makes himself an enemy of God.... Submit yourselves therefore to God. Resist the devil, and he will flee from you (James 4:4, 7)." Confronting Jewish Christians for their spiritual infidelity, James ordered them to "submit" to God, meaning "to place or rank oneself under."[14] "Fall in and knock it off!" he commanded. "You're so busy fighting among yourselves you've forgotten your commander and mission. Get your eyes off the world, obey your God, and get back to fighting the REAL enemy!"

Peter sounded an alarm to churches across the western Mediterranean, declaring "Be sober-minded; be watchful. Your adversary the devil prowls around like a roaring lion, seeking someone to devour. Resist him, firm in your faith, knowing that the same kinds of suffering are being experienced by your brotherhood throughout the world (1 Peter 5:8-9, NKJV)." The old fisherman cautioned Christ followers that Satan actively hunted them.

On every page, Scripture shouts: "Spiritual warfare is not an event but a way of life!"

"Prowl" and "devour" were rated "R" imagery, likening Satan's bloodthirsty tactics to a lion stalking, ambushing, and devouring its prey—right down to lapping up its blood and licking the bones clean![15] "Be vigilant" meant: "Keep watch, stand post like a sentry."[16] Like Paul and James, Peter also closed with the military charge: "Resist," which we will discuss more in our study of the Spartan.

Finally, John taught Christians that the evil one actively warred against them on numerous battlefronts, wielding a variety of sinister strategies. He wrote:

> The great dragon was hurled down—that ancient serpent called the devil, or Satan, who leads the whole world astray. He was hurled to the earth, and his angels with him. When the dragon saw that he had been hurled to the earth, he pursued the woman who had given birth to the male child. Then the dragon was enraged at the woman and went off to wage war against the rest of her offspring—those who keep God's commands and hold fast their testimony about Jesus. (Revelation 12:9, 13, 17, NIV)

Many truths can be drawn from Revelation. We'll focus on two here: 1.) John mentions the devil thirty-two times, enough to cover each day of our longest calendar months.[17] 2.) His warnings of Satan's ruthless warfare with the saints occur *post* Christ's resurrection. Satan is also not consigned to the abyss (off the earth) until Christ's Millennial Reign (Revelation 20), which has not occurred. Thus, all living saints are engaged in "The Great War of the Ages." Like the samurai, every believer is always on the battlefield—walking, standing, sitting, or reclining. On every page, Scripture shouts: "Spiritual warfare is not an event but a way of life!"

Yes, Jesus won the ultimate battle on the Cross, crushing sin, Satan, and death (John 12:31-32).[i] But the war rages on until His return. Solomon said, "For everything there is a season, and a time for every matter under heaven...a time to love, and a time to hate; a time for war, and a time

---

i   *Colossians 2:13-15; Hebrews 2:14-15; 1 John 3:8*

for peace (Ecclesiastes 3:1, 8)." Christians live in the Age of War, but too many of us live like it's the "Age of Peace." The fatal, civilian mindset which threatened the samurai has infiltrated the Church and is costing us dearly. Statistics of pastoral and church health are alarming.

Pastoral Health:

- 35 percent of pastors struggle with depression.[18]
- 42 percent wish they'd spent more time with their children.[19]
- 50+ percent view pornography regularly.[20]
- 53 percent believe seminary did not adequately equip them.[21]
- 54 percent feel overworked.

Church Health:

- From 2008 to 2017, the number of born-again believers fell from 46 to 31 percent.[22]
- Since 1993, weekly church attendance plummeted from 45 to 29 percent.[23]
- 40 percent of adult churchgoers feel no connection to their faith.[24]
- 51 percent of attendees have never heard of The Great Commission.[25]
- 89 percent of Christians cannot respond to questions about faith.[26]

Do these numbers break your heart? These are the sieges slaughtering our "garrisons"—our families and local churches. One third of pastors suffer psychologically. Half stand morally compromised, and more than half feel stressed out, ill-equipped, or just lonely. The Church at large shrinks annually while members are missing monthly, detached spiritually, or ill-equipped missionally. Endless material distraction blunts our influence. A steady IV drip of secular media numbs us to the dangers of a depraved culture. Spiritual bondage abounds, marriages and families struggle, and many soldiers have gone A.W.O.L. ("absent without leave")—drawn away from lives of virtue, discipline, and sacrifice to compromise, ease, and self-absorption.

The Church stands at a crossroads, and the prophet Jeremiah's words ring with fearful warning: "Thus says the Lord: 'Stand by the roads, and look, and ask for the ancient paths, where the good way is; and walk in it, and find rest for your souls...(Jeremiah 6:16).'" We must rediscover the ancient paths blazed by those who trusted God, followed Him into the fray,

If Christians are to survive and take new ground in the Age of War, we need a revival of the soldier spirit in Scripture.

and held fast till answers came. If Christians are to survive and take new ground in the Age of War, we need a revival of the soldier spirit in Scripture. Perhaps the samurai can help us find it.

Live with Deadly Intensity

An era of political upheaval and unspeakable violence brought a lethal edge to samurai skill and thought. "Step from under the eaves and you're a dead man. Leave the gate and the enemy is waiting," said the *Hagakure,* the samurai book of wisdom whose name means "found among the leaves."[27] When death's cold gaze falls on a man, it changes him in one of two ways: he either plays the fool, burying himself in denial and dissipation, or plays the man, rethinking and re-aiming his life. The samurai chose wisely, and something beautiful happened: from the ashes of war and death arose maxims of life and peace.

At *dojo*, their school of the martial arts, samurai practiced with curved wooden swords. Occasionally, masters would call for *shinken shoubu* ("real sword fight"). Down went blunted wood; up came razor-sharp steel. To lose focus now was to lose one's head! In time, this practice term became a proverb for all of samurai life: *shinken shoubu*—"live with deadly intensity."

In an Age of War, life proved too fragile to be lived without focus. Samurai began seizing every moment for reflection. The most mundane activity became imbued with sacredness, purpose, and gratitude—from savoring incense (*kodo,* "the way of fragrance") to arranging florae (*kado,* "the way of flowers"), practicing calligraphy (*shodo,* "the way of beautiful writing") to savoring a cup of matcha (*chado,* "the way of tea"). Life's frivolous things fell among the leaves. Reality's cold steel had trained samurai to savor each breath as a divine gift. Similarly, Paul exhorted the Early Church: "So be careful how you live. Don't live like fools, but like those who are wise. Make the most of every opportunity in these evil days (Ephesians 5:15-16, NLT)." Again, however, Paul only echoed the cry of an old prophet.

The Lament of Moses

Like the Age of War, the backdrop of Psalm 90 sobers us. Its superscription identifies it as the only Psalm written by Moses, and it sadly chronicles

God's judgment on the rebellious Exodus Generation. To lay out the context, in Numbers 13-14 Israel arrives at the oasis of Kadesh-Barnea—the edge of their promised land, Canaan. At God's command, Moses sends twelve men to spy out the land. Forty days later, they return and report of a land flowing with milk and honey, just as God said. But ten spies raise an evil report: the inhabitants are too powerful; the Israelis look like grasshoppers in comparison; they cannot take the land. Only two spies believe God will deliver on His word: Joshua and Caleb.

Fear and unbelief sweep the crowd like nerve gas. The people breathe in the ten's faithless report and exhale bitter murmuring—again. Moses, Aaron, Joshua, and Caleb try to reassure them, but the fuming mass calls for their stoning. After miraculous deliverance from slavery by ten plagues that wasted Egypt, culminated with the parting of the Red Sea and the annihilation of Pharaoh's army, the children of Israel treacherously turn and tempt God for the tenth time. The long-suffering Lord is done and decrees that none of this generation, from twenty years old and up, shall see the promised land, except Joshua and Caleb.

The wilderness becomes a cemetery. Over the next thirty-eight years, approximately 1.2 million people die.[28] Everyone Moses knows from Egypt, including his siblings Aaron and Miriam, falls at a rate of 31,579 fatalities per year. "You sweep them away as with a flood; they are like a dream, like grass…in the morning it flourishes and is renewed; in the evening it fades and withers," Moses pens in Psalm 90:5-6. Life's brittleness and brevity batter his soul. His thinking changes. He writes: "The years of our life are seventy, or even by reason of strength eighty; yet their span is but toil and trouble; they are soon gone, and we fly away (v. 10)." With some 2,632 people dying each month, Moses' prayers also change: "So teach us to number our days that we may get a heart of wisdom (v. 12)."

Moses watches the weeping and wailing of some eighty-eight funerals a day. Broken, he cries: "Let the favor of the Lord our God be upon us, and establish the work of our hands… (v. 17)." In layman's terms, "Dear God, make our lives count! Let our works have eternal impact." A forty-year lament has its way, changing how Moses thinks, prays, and lives. Like the samurai, he learns to number his days. But, years after Japan's Age of War, something happened.

Keeping Death In Mind

As the sound of war drums faded into the distance of peacetime, samurai focus faltered. *Shinken shoubu*, the deadly intensity once applied to all of life, dwindled. Warrior skills waned. Idleness and ease weakened bodies. Distractions and drunkenness followed. To fix the problem, a practice of daily meditation on death was invoked. Master Tsunetomo wrote in the samurai book of wisdom: "Meditation on inevitable death should be performed daily.... And every day without fail one should consider himself as dead."[29] Master Shigesuke elaborated on the practice:

> One who is supposed to be a warrior considers it his foremost concern to keep death in mind at all times, every day and every night, from the morning of New Year's Day through the night of New Year's Eve. As long as you keep death in mind at all times, you will fulfill the ways of loyalty and familial duty. You will also avoid myriad evils and calamities, you will be physically sound and healthy, and you will live a long life. What is more, your character will improve and your virtue will grow.

> Here are the reasons for that. All human life is likened to evening dew and morning frost, considered something quite fragile and ephemeral.... If people comfort their minds with the assumption that they will live a long time, something might happen, because they think they will have forever to do their work and look after their parents—they may fail to perform for their employers and also treat their parents thoughtlessly. But if you realize that the life that is here today is not certain on the morrow...you will have the sense that this may be the lasttime....[30]

With the Holy Spirit's deadly intensity, James bore a similar message to the Church:

> Come now, you who say, "Today or tomorrow we will go into such and such a town and spend a year there and trade and make a profit"—yet you do not know what tomorrow will bring. What is your life? For you are a mist that appears for a little time and then vanishes. Instead you ought to say, "If the Lord wills, we will live and do this or that." As it is,

you boast in your arrogance. All such boasting is evil. So whoever knows the right thing to do and fails to do it, for him it is sin. (James 4:13-17)

Credited by God as the wisest man to ever walk the earth (1 Kings 3:12), Solomon said: "Better to spend your time at funerals than at parties. After all, everyone dies—so the living should take this to heart. Sorrow is better than laughter, for sadness has a refining influence on us. A wise person thinks a lot about death, while a fool thinks only about having a good time (Ecclesiastes 7:2-4, NLT)." The Hebrew root for "wise" in this passage and "wisdom" in Psalm 90:12 refers to a sage, one who is shrewd and skillful.[31] Think you might become more skillful at living for God if you stared death in the face? As we've seen, samurai did not invent meditation upon death. Under God's inspiration, Moses and other scriptural sages recognized it would hone them, propel them toward Kingdom purposes, and keep them from many evils.

Messianic Jewish scholar Dr. Arnold Fruchtenbaum, whose research on Psalm 90 influenced this chapter, suggests an exercise: Begin by assuming you have the minimum amount of time to live noted in Psalm 90:10— seventy years. Subtract your current age from that number. Assume that is the number of your remaining years. Now, break that number down into days. You've just numbered your days. Sobering? What if you observed this practice daily, moving forward toward your seventieth birthday?[32] How might it refine you?

Would you rise early to study and pray? Take stock and refocus on building God's kingdom instead of yours? Could it embolden you to reach out to that estranged friend or relative, ask a cashier to church, or invite a neighbor to dinner? Would you stop making excuses, write the book, or launch the mission? What divine passion would this ancient warrior practice awaken in you? Might you become a bit more samurai?

The Way of Desperation

Not surprisingly, this daily rite of meditation had profound effect, rekindling passion, focus, and desperation in the samurai heart. Daimyo Nabeshima

Think you might become more skillful at living for God if you stared death in the face?

Naoshige described how desperation animated the warrior toward the uncommon and courageous:

> The Way of the Samurai is in desperateness. Ten men or more cannot kill such a man. Common sense will not accomplish great things. Simply become insane and desperate. In the Way of the Samurai, if one uses discrimination, he will fall behind. One needs neither loyalty nor devotion, but simply to become desperate in the Way. Loyalty and devotion are of themselves within desperation.[33]

What does desperation look like to you? Better yet, what does it look like in Scripture? In the life of Jesus, we find some desperate imagery: crying lepers defying Mosaic Law and reaching toward Him with withering limbs (Luke 5:12)[ii]; naked and bloody demoniacs screeching as they fall at His feet (Matthew 8:28-29); a bleeding woman pressing through a multitude to touch His garment (Mark 5:25-27); blind men crying out from the roadside to stop Him (Matthew 9:27); people literally tearing the roof off a house to place a paralytic at His feet (Mark 2:4). Behold, God's definition of desperation!

In this fresh Gospel light, I submit: most Christians don't know the meaning of the word. We live in a cozy bed lined with self-sufficiency, draped by common sense, and wrapped in complacency. Too many of us who name Jesus as Savior have never been desperate for anything, and that's precisely why we don't see Him move like He did for the Early Church. Theologians can say what they will about God's eternal purpose, but only the unread would fail to make a connection between the miracles in Acts and the desperate love of the disciples. They passionately pursued their risen Lord day by day in the Temple, fellowshipping from house to house and breaking bread (Acts 2:46), preaching in public squares and on hilltops (2:14).[iii] They told phony religious leaders trying to silence them where they could get off (4:19-20)[iv], worshiped when they were beaten (5:41), asked God to make them bolder (4:29), and engaged in round-the-clock prayer when leaders were arrested (12:5).

---

ii   *Luke 17:12-13*

iii   *Acts 5:20, 42; 17:22*

iv   *Acts 5:29*

In the heart of the Early Church roared a passionate flame, longing for God's Presence and prayerfully aching for Heaven to touch Earth. Consequently, they saw Him do what most believers only read about. When God's absence becomes painful, His people become desperate and rise from the bed of religious complacency. The problem for most Christians today is that God's absence is not painful enough. Listen to the Shulamite in the Song of Solomon 3:1-4 from *The Message*:

Too many of us who name Jesus as Savior have never been desperate for anything, and that's precisely why we don't see Him move like He did for the Early Church.

Restless in bed and sleepless through the night, I longed for my lover. I wanted him desperately. His absence was painful. So I got up, went out and roved the city, hunting through streets and down alleys. I wanted my lover in the worst way! I looked high and low and didn't find him. And then the night watchmen found me as they patrolled the darkened city. "Have you seen my dear lost love?" I asked. No sooner had I left them than I found him, found my dear lost love. I threw my arms around him and held him tight, wouldn't let him go until I had him home again, safe at home beside the fire.

That is desperation, and this stirring allegory is a type for the unbridled passion Jesus, the Bridegroom, desires from His Bride—the Church (Ephesians 5:32). From the moment of our creation, God has longed for a love from us that consumes our whole being. "You shall love the Lord your God with all your heart, with all your soul, with all your strength, and with all your mind, and your neighbor as yourself (Luke 10:27)." It's no mistake that before mentioning the Christian's armor in Ephesians 6, Paul prayed that the Church would become rooted in the extravagant dimensions of God's love in chapter 3: "And I pray that you, being rooted and established in love, may have power, together with all the Lord's holy people, to grasp how wide and long and high and deep is the love of Christ, and to know this love that surpasses knowledge—that you may be filled to the measure of all the fullness of God (3:17b-19, NIV)."

Paul understood that God's love, coursing through her veins, would make the Church an unassailable fortress in persecution and unstoppable force in battle. In the first Roman persecution (A.D. 64), when the maniacal Emperor Nero set Rome ablaze, blamed Christians, then squealed as they were sown into animal skins and thrown to the dogs, clothed in wax shirts and set ablaze to light his gardens, it was God's love that proved inextinguishable.[34] In the fourth persecution (A.D. 162), when Emperor Marcus Aurelius scourged Christians till muscle and sinew were exposed and forced them to trod barefoot over thorns, nails, and sharp shells, that same love struck hell's gates like a battering ram.[35] And when Emperor Diocletian sought to finish the job in the tenth persecution (A.D. 303), burning homes and families, building a column over a charred Bible and declaring, "The name of the Christians is wiped out," God's love prevailed again—for by A.D. 380, Christianity was the state religion of the Roman Empire!

> Hang my locket around your neck, wear my ring on your finger. Love is invincible facing danger and death. Passion laughs at the terrors of hell. The fire of love stops at nothing—it sweeps everything before it. Flood waters can't drown love, torrents of rain can't put it out. Love can't be bought, love can't be sold—it's not to be found in the marketplace.... (Song of Solomon 8:6-7, MSG)

The Shulamite's declaration of love became the Early Church's war cry. Christ's unquenchable love swept the Roman Empire. And, though their devotion was to an earthly master and their affections were often misused by him or misplaced by themselves, the samurai also understood that a reckless love marked the greatest of warriors. Nowhere is this more evident than the samurai ethos, *bushido* (Jap., "the way of the warrior"), which framed *jin*, typically translated as "benevolence," as a chief virtue. Dr. Inazo Nitobe, a pre–World War II Christian, scholar, diplomat, and descendant of the samurai, fleshed out its meaning in his book on the samurai code. It should ring familiar to anyone who's read the New Testament:

> Love, magnanimity, affection for others, sympathy, and pity, were ever recognized to be supreme virtues, the highest of all the attributes of

the human soul…. "The bravest are the tenderest, the loving are the daring." *Bushi-no-nasake*—the tenderness of a warrior—had a sound which appealed at once to whatever was noble in us…. Benevolence to the weak, the downtrodden or the vanquished was ever extolled as peculiarly

To this day, love—not spiritual gifts or armor—remains THE most dangerous weapon in the Christian arsenal.

becoming to a samurai…. Tenderness, pity, and love were traits which adorned the most sanguinary exploits of a samurai.[36]

Behind the ferocious war mask and lamellar armor lay a soft kimono of love—the sacrificial heart of the samurai code. In the Age of War, it made the samurai one of the deadliest soldiers on earth. In the Era of Martyrs, it made the Christian the most dangerous one in the heavenlies. To this day, love—not spiritual gifts or armor—remains THE most dangerous weapon in the Christian arsenal. Paul described this love and its limitless power, saying:

> Love is patient and kind; love does not envy or boast; it is not arrogant or rude. It does not insist on its own way; it is not irritable or resentful; it does not rejoice at wrongdoing, but rejoices with the truth. Love bears all things, believes all things, hopes all things, endures all things. Love never ends…. So now faith, hope, and love abide, these three; but the greatest of these is love. (1 Corinthians 13:4-8a, 13)

Thank God that, after praying for the Church to be filled with Christ's love, Paul took the time to describe it (Ephesians 3:14-21)! In the midst of our modern, media-soaked society, no word is more abused. So many evils are executed under the banner of a demonically twisted counterfeit of love, not the divine love Scripture extols. True love—God's kind of love—is holy, righteous, and good; devoted to Him, His Word, and His Kingdom. Etched into Christ's commands and enshrined in the samurai code, love is a devoted, desperate, and driving force in all of life. But driving toward what? That is the next question.

To Be Samurai

In *The Last Samurai*, a movie romanticizing the samurai's Satsuma Rebellion against the Meiji government's modernization of Japan, American Cavalry Captain Nathan Algren asks, "What does it mean to be samurai?" His question also holds great significance to the Christian warfare. At the core of our existence lies an epic struggle with evil spiritual forces for the souls of men. Thus, how we define the term "soldier" stands paramount to our success—for the definition always determines the approach. Are we approaching the lost world as a judge or ambassador, God's flock as a shepherd or hireling?

In his journaling, Algren ponders the way of the samurai: "I am surprised to learn that the word samurai means 'to serve.'" So are many others who embark upon the soldier path. To make a slight correction, it's the Japanese verb *saburau* which means "to serve." *Samurai* means "those who serve." It is a noun, an *identity* drawing its meaning from an accompanying action. Again, Dr. Nitobe fleshes this out, saying: "Nevertheless, as far as the doctrine of service—the serving of a cause higher than one's own self, even at the sacrifice of one's individuality; I say the doctrine of service, which is the greatest that Christ preached and was the sacred keystone of His mission—so far as that is concerned, Bushido was based on eternal truth."[37]

In bushido, to be samurai was to serve, and this concept—the servant-warrior—stood as their model and that of virtually all preeminent, oath-bound warrior cultures in history. *Samurai*, for example, is the Japanese sister for the English term *knight*. "Knight" is derived from the Anglo-Saxon root *cnicht* and the Germanic *knecht*, which both mean "servant." In Scandinavia, as far back as the ninth century, the name *húskarl*, the Viking bodyguards for kings and nobles, meant "house man" or "manservant."[38] The simple fact is that, whether discussing the *equitus* cavalier of Rome, the *hippeus* guardian of Greece, mounted *chevalier* of France, or *rhide* of the Celts—all native terms for "knight"—the purest, most primitive sense of the word was always "servant."

This scarlet thread also extends throughout Semitic warrior culture (Hebrew, Arabic, Aramaic) from the time of Moses to David, carries into the Middle Ages as we saw above, and in Scripture appears in the chivalrous context of warrior-to-king relationship, warrior-to-warrior, and warrior-to-God

Himself.[39] It's no coincidence that the Hebrew *tsaba*, from which the Lord draws His war name *Yahweh Sabaot* ("Lord of Armies"), not only means "army" and "war" but "service" and "waiting upon" another.[40] The most beautiful voicing of this servant-warrior ideal, though, may come from the mouth of a Philistine—the commander of six hundred elite Gittite

In bushido, to be samurai was to serve, and this concept—the servant-warrior—stood as their model and that of virtually all preeminent, oath-bound warrior cultures in history.

warriors who followed David back to Israel after his service to the Philistine King Achish. During the revolt of his son Absalom, as King David evacuates his court, he basically says to the commander Ittai, "This is not your fight. Go back and may the Lord bless you!" But Ittai replies, "As the Lord lives, and as my lord the king lives, wherever my lord the king shall be, whether for death or for life, there also will your servant be (2 Samuel 15:21)."

As Jesus approached His final hours and spoke of His coming death, He used this same turn of phrase to challenge His followers, saying: "If anyone serves me, he must follow me; and where I am, there will my servant be also…(John 12:26)."[41] Throughout His ministry, Christ drilled this principle into His disciples, that service to others is God's mark of greatness.

> And Jesus called them to Him and said to them, "You know that those who are considered rulers of the Gentiles lord it over them, and their great ones exercise authority over them. But it shall not be so among you. But whoever would be great among you must be your servant, and whoever would be first among you must be slave of all. For even the Son of Man came not to be served but to serve, and to give His life as a ransom for many." (Mark 10:42-45)

From samurai to Saxon, Semite to Scripture, the scarlet thread of history's soldier codes and its Greatest Soldier remains "one who serves." The antithesis is the *mercenary-warrior*.

Way of the Ronin
One of the great tsunamis the Age of War sent hurtling into feudal Japan

was a multitude of masterless samurai. Thousands of daimyo lords were slain in battle. Thousands more, shamed by defeat, took their lives in ritual suicide. And, following the era's final battle, still more were weakened by laws limiting their number of samurai retainers to ensure power remained with the newly established government. The result was wave upon wave of samurai set adrift into a peacetime culture, and their trouble was just beginning.

Back home, segregation laws and social customs punished discharged samurai for no clan affiliation. They were unwelcomed at inns, denied service by merchants, frowned upon by locals, and joked about by their working fellows. Scores of decorated, highly skilled warriors wandered about homeless, aimless, and friendless. Tossed back and forth by society, they came to be called *ronin* ("men of the waves"), and with no lodging, land, or lord, the forgotten frequently forgot who they were. Ronin became known for drunkenness, fighting, incessant dueling, bullying merchants, and terrorizing entire villages. They were the outcasts, and by the end of the Age of War the country was filled with these orphan-warriors.

It saddens me now to bring us to our application for this allegorical venture. You see, we in Christendom have created our own brand of ronin, commonly referred to in church metrics as the "dechurched." These individuals were once connected to a local assembly but have now abandoned it, and many because they were deeply wounded by those entrusted with guarding their souls (Hebrews 13:17). In a recent study of twenty American cities over a period of seven years, the percentages of dechurched ranged from 38 percent to as high as 47 percent—almost 1 in every 2 people![42] That is the tsunami we've sent hurtling into our society. Millions of decorated, highly skilled Christian soldiers wander the countryside emotionally wounded, spiritually homeless, and missionally aimless. I know this not just because of my work as a seasoned pastor, but because my wife and I almost became a statistic.

In a period of five years, Ralana and I were betrayed by leaders we had trusted; attacked by members we had served; slandered by ministers we had respected; hired by a senior pastor to produce dramas for his sermons; fired by a committee under the same roof because they didn't want dramas in church; and abandoned by another church as my father fought for his life and we for our marriage. To say we were *wounded* would be an understatement. We were devastated—humiliated beyond words and feeling as valued as a lame horse taken out back and shot. We wanted to leave the local church forever, stay at home, lick our wounds, study the Bible, and use our gifts on our own terms as full-tilt, spiritual ronin.

In a recent study of twenty American cities over a period of seven years, the percentages of dechurched ranged from 38 percent to as high as 47 percent—almost 1 in every 2 people!

Thankfully, I had a teaching commitment for an upcoming men's retreat, and Ralana would have some time away with her father and mother, a bastion of God's love and strength. I got alone and wept before the Lord, asking Him, "Please, release me from this commitment. I've got nothing left. I'm hurting and empty!" *"I want you to go,"* God whispered. "What do you mean you want me to go? Have you not been listening? How on earth can I do this now?" But the Lord answered softly, *"Trust Me. Go. I will speak to you there."*

Now, I was fuming. "Trust you?! I did trust you, and I'm a bloody mess because of it!" I shouted with tears streaming down my face. He didn't answer me right away this time. He waited. I could feel His Presence all around me. I was enfolded in Him—in the "shadow of the Almighty," the "cleft of the rock" (Psalm 91:1, 4).[v] Then, He took my breath away. I felt God weep. I sensed the Holy Spirit grieving with me over all that had happened—the lies, the betrayals, the pettiness.... His tenderness broke my hardness (Ephesians 4:30). This went on for I can't say how long. Finally, He whispered again, *"Trust Me. Go."*

All I mustered was a quick nod and a reluctant, "Okay." Like an obedient samurai, I went, but I was still shaking my head like a ronin at this God who wouldn't let me off the hook. Little did I realize that something amazing had already happened: my anger was gone. It wasn't till after the retreat that I recognized what He'd so quietly done in that moment: the "Sun of Righteousness" had risen with healing in His wings (Malachi 4:2)—Miracle #1.

In that week away, some things happened I never expected. While serving and fighting for the hearts of broken men, the Lord gave me back

---

v   *Exodus 33:22*

mine—Miracle #2. Never underestimate the blessing behind obeying one word from God. Still, that wasn't the end of it. On that retreat, my Heavenly Friend gave me one of the best friends I've ever had: a flank man, a yoke fellow—my friend Jeff—Miracle #3. When I returned home, Ralana had received some wonderful ministry from her parents; my shield-maiden had her second wind—Miracle #4. With our new strength, we rose from the ashes and started looking for a new church home.

In time, we found one, along with a great pastor—Miracle #5. I'll never forget when he first met us and took us for coffee after service one day. As Ralana and I sat down and began to ask about where he wanted us to serve, Pastor Jeff Little replied: "I just want to get to know you guys, want you to get to know us, and to give you both permission to lay down your plows and take a rest." Ralana and I sat stunned. Who was this guy taking such interest in our well-being, who wanted to know us *personally*—not just put us to work? Where was he five years ago? And, how did he get into our emotional mailbox? (We knew the answer to that last question.)

Over the next eight years, that shepherd showed us the heart of the Good Shepherd. He made time for us, helped us connect with new faces, made room for our spiritual gifts, provided great platforms for their use leading to hundreds of salvations, counseled us on decisions, and even invested in my seminary education. Jeff didn't just preach about "God's Family." He lived it, built a church on it, and that family served us like a clan of spiritual samurai, helping restore our faith in the Church.

Perhaps you are teetering at that same threshold we were. Or, maybe you've already joined the ranks of the *dechurched ronin*, wandering the spiritual countryside, callouses covering a once tender heart. You were serving God, laying it all on the line for the Kingdom, only to be beaten down and left for dead. Now, you've thrown in the towel, maybe crawled into some false comforts. Ralana and I did on an occasion or two.

But, as you stand before your valley of dry bones, can you sense God's Spirit hovering and asking, "Can these dry bones live?" I'll wager that your answer is just as noncommittal as Ezekiel's and ours was: "Lord, You know!" But would you dare to take one more step of obedience, trust God again like we did—say a prayer, utter a prophecy commanding your scattered soul and skeletal circumstances to rattle, receive breath, be clothed with sinew and skin, and stand up like a mighty army once more (Ezekiel 37:1-14)?

My fellow soldier, I come to you now with tears and as an ambassador of our Lord—not a judge. On behalf of those who wounded you, I ask for your forgiveness. I'm sorry for the hell you went through; that your kindness, labor, and sacrifices were repaid with ingratitude, hypocrisy, and deceit. I'm sorry that those called to represent Christ failed you. I'm sorry you were not valued as a priceless creation and child of our King.

But, I tell you the truth: The Lord never left you (Hebrews 13:5). He's been here the whole time. It was fallen humanity who wounded you—not our Father who purchased you with the blood of His Son, forgave your sins, and made you His child. You are not an orphan. You are loved, wanted, and still greatly needed in the fray. Christ's Body has been weakened by your absence. There *is* a spiritual home that will love you as a family, make room for your vision, passion, and gifts and give you a place to serve.

Today, we're going to shut the enemy's lying mouth. How? I'm going to expose his scheme against you, the age-old tactic he used against Ralana and me. This wisdom comes from the most famous ronin in Japanese history. Miyamato Musashi was one of the many disenfranchised samurai following the Age of War. He became an independent teacher of the martial arts, roamed the countryside as a professional dueler, and spent the rest of his days perfecting his art. In dueling, he taught students the principle of "knocking out the heart." Listen:

> When you fight with an adversary and appear to win…your opponent may still have ideas…still inwardly refuse to acknowledge defeat. Knocking the heart out is for such cases. This means that you suddenly change your attitude to stop the enemy from entertaining any such ideas; so the main thing is to see that adversaries feel defeated from the bottom of their hearts…. When your enemies have completely lost heart, you do not have to pay attention to them anymore.[43]

My friend, has the enemy knocked out your heart? If so, by God's grace, let's get it back! No more wandering or believing hellish lies. Micah 7:8 says, "Rejoice not over me, O my enemy; when I fall, I shall rise; when I sit in darkness, the Lord will be a light to me." Today, we're picking up that sword, knocking the rust off, and retooling the blade. We're brushing off the dust of unfaithful people and throwing off the chains of unbelief and bitterness. If this speaks to you, here's what I want you to do: in accordance with 1 John 1:6-9, confess your sins to God and ask for His forgiveness. Stop and do it right now. Pick the book back up when you're done.

Next, realign with Christ's command in Matthew 6:12, 14-15 and Ephesians 4:31-32: forgive those who wronged you. Apart from this, there is no moving forward. If it seems difficult, pause, weep if you need to, and breathe. The Lord will walk you through this. Ask Him for grace, and to maybe remind you of some things He's forgiven you of. When we freshly taste mercy, it's much easier to give it! Stop. Do this now. Then, return.

Third, fall in line with James 5:13-16. Reach out to a faithful friend today—a strong, trusted brother or sister in Christ. If possible, meet face-to-face and get some healing prayer. Ask God whom you should call, listen, and go to it. You know the drill already. Do it now.

Last, mark the pattern in the Book of Acts, the epistles, and some very clear admonitions in Scripture:

1.) Recognize we cannot fight the good fight alone. "Woe to him who is alone when he falls and has not another one to lift him up," Solomon warned (Ecclesiastes 4:10b). We need brothers and sisters in this fight—encouragement, support, and prayerful agreement (Matthew 18:19-20). Enlist it. Fighting alone works in movies, not spiritual warfare.

2.) Remember, we were designed for spiritual family, to be rooted in God's House. David couldn't shut up about this in the Psalms. "God sets the lonely in families; he leads out the prisoners with singing; but the rebellious live in a sun-scorched land (68:6, NIV)," he said. Just substitute the word "rebellious" with ronin there. "The righteous flourish like the palm tree and grow like a cedar in Lebanon. They are planted in the house of the Lord; they flourish in the courts of our God. They still bear fruit in old age; they are ever full of sap and green," promises Psalm 92:12-14. Finally, he declares, "I was glad when they said to me, 'Let us go to the house of the Lord (122:1)!'"

The rest of Scripture forbids going ronin also. "And let us not neglect our meeting together, as some people do, but encourage one another, especially now that the day of his return is drawing near (Hebrews 10:25,

NLT).” (No, "meeting together" doesn't mean sipping a beer with a few buddies who swore off church.) From Acts to the epistles, God's blueprint anchors believers in a *local church*—a weekly, committed fellowship with God-ordained elders in government, five-fold ministry workers teaching and equipping, and gifted, passionate people plugged in to sharing Jesus with the world.

Now, the meeting place might be a home, school, renovated storefront or otherwise. That's not important. What's critical are the above ingredients and a clear call of God on that fellowship. Anything less is a fake, and when storms come it will show. So, take time. Visit around. Let the Spirit lead you, minister healing, and rebuild your family's trust. Ask God to confirm what you sense. He'll help you find your spiritual family.

Rescuing the Ronin

On the other hand, if you're a healthy "samurai" rooted in a local church, there's work for you here also. Do you know a ronin, one who left Father's house because of an offense or was drawn away by sin? The Word is clear: "Dear brothers and sisters, if another believer is overcome by some sin, you who are godly should gently and humbly help that person back onto the right path. And be careful not to fall into the same temptation yourself. Share each other's burdens, and in this way obey the law of Christ (Galatians 6:1-2, NLT)."

The tragic stats of the dechurched aren't merely because of offenders and the offended, but a sore lack of mediators. Too many Christians have done nothing when a brother or sister disappeared from the fold. This should not be. In state penal codes, we have "Good Samaritan" laws. The term comes from a parable where Jesus showed disdain for a priest and Levite, two of God's servants, who were too busy to stop and render aid to a wounded man (Luke 10:25-37). The story's hero turned out to be "the kid from the wrong side of the tracks," a man Jewish society had written off—a Samaritan. (Samaritans were despised in Jesus' day because as ancient Jews, they intermarried with their Assyrian captors.)

See, in Christ's code we're all ministers of reconciliation and our brother's keeper (2 Corinthians 5:18; Genesis 4:9). Restoring the fallen is every believer's job—not just pastors. Hear me: in God's eyes, it's just as ronin to ignore a fallen soldier as it is to go A.W.O.L. If the Good Shepherd has laid

Restoring the fallen is every believer's job—not just pastors.

someone on your heart, be a servant-warrior: go fight to win that person back. That is spiritual warfare; that is samurai. Now, let's put a tip on this spear.

Following in Death

We have learned that the samurai's identity sprung from his daimyo-lord. His master was to be first in all—every thought, desire, and action measured against the ideal of total allegiance. At this point, the parallels between the samurai and the Christian soldier are blatant. Consider Tsunetomo's call to the samurai in the *Hagakure*:

> A man is a good retainer to the extent that he earnestly places importance in his master.... Sagara Kyuma was completely at one with his master and served him as though his own body were already dead. He was one man in a thousand.... The fact that a useless person often becomes a matchless warrior at such times is because he has already given up his life and become one with his lord.... For a warrior there is nothing other than thinking of his master.[44]

Now, compare these words with Christ's charge to His soldiers in *The Message*:

> Listen carefully: Unless a grain of wheat is buried in the ground, dead to the world, it is never any more than a grain of wheat. But if it is buried, it sprouts and reproduces itself many times over. In the same way, anyone who holds on to life just as it is destroys that life. But if you let it go, reckless in your love, you'll have it forever, real and eternal. If any of you wants to serve me, then follow me. Then you'll be where I am, ready to serve at a moment's notice. The Father will honor and reward anyone who serves me. (John 12:24-26)

The way of the samurai, as it came to be called, was found in reckoning himself dead to follow his lord. The way of the Christian soldier is no different. And, because the life of a samurai was so entwined with his daimyo, traditionally, at his master's death, the samurai took his own in ritual disembowelment (*seppuku*). Called *junshi* ("following in death"), it was the pinnacle expression of samurai love and service.

Now, the Bible never endorses suicide or self-mutilation. It does, however, with some gruesome metaphors, command God's soldiers to follow Him in death to our fleshly nature. "If your right eye causes you to lust, gouge it out and throw it away.... And if your right hand causes you to sin, cut it off and throw it away. For it is better that you lose one of your members than that your whole body go into hell (Matthew 5:29a-30)." The word "gouge" (Gk., *exaireó*) is the root for our English medical term "excise," as in excising a tumor. The *Life Application Bible Commentary* notes: "The act of surgically cutting sin out of our lives should be prompt and complete.... Believers must get rid of any relationship, practice, or activity that leads to sin."[45]

Like Jesus, Paul did not mince words here. "So put to death the sinful, earthly things lurking within you. Have nothing to do with sexual immorality, impurity, lust, and evil desires (Colossians 3:5, NLT)," he said. Christians often assert the devil is our greatest foe. In these and other passages, though, the New Testament reveals the deeper combat lies with evil desires lurking in our hearts—sins we continue philandering with long after we've named Jesus as Lord. These desires,

Our obedience or disobedience to follow Christ in death to our flesh remains the crux of our warfare.

James said, lead us into temptation and bondage (James 1:13-15); Satan only exploits what we refuse to put to death (Romans 6:12-14).[vi] Our obedience or disobedience to follow Christ in death to our flesh remains the crux of our warfare. Where many of us falter is building relationships with those who can help us win this fight.

The Companion

Samurai suicide or *seppuku* ("belly-cutting") was bloody business. In its thralls, one could lose heart or find himself unable to finish. For this reason, he sought a *kaishakunin* ("company-ward-man"). From the time he knelt,

---

vi   *Romans 7:14-25; 8:13; Galatians 5:16-24*

opened his robe, and grasped the *tanto* dagger, the kaishakunin's eyes never left his friend. Quietly, he watched with ready sword. If the dying samurai could not complete the belly cut, he leaned forward exposing his neck. The kaishakunin then drew his sword and severed the head.

This is a grim illustration, but bear with me. The truth is: in dealing with our own sins, we are often unwilling to follow Jesus in death. Killing pride and fleshly desires remains the Christian soldier's "bloody business." But it demands two things: "baring our belly" in gutsy confession to God, then exposing that sin's "neck" to a trusted, mature brother or sister who acts as our kaishakunin to "cut off its head" while guarding our honor. Let's break this down:

1.) Confession to God. 1 John 1:9 assures us, "If we confess our sins, he is faithful and just to forgive us of our sins and to cleanse us from all unrighteousness." So, we confess sin to God first, for only He can forgive it (Luke 5:20-25). Earthly priests cannot pardon sin; they can't even handle theirs (Hebrews 5:1-3)![vii] Only Jesus, God's perfect sin-offering, can do this (Luke 5:20-25).[viii]

2.) Confession to a Brother or Sister. If we wish to be healed of a sin's hold on us, Jesus instructs, "Therefore, confess your sins *to one another and pray for one another*, that you may be healed. The prayer of a righteous person has great power as it is working (James 5:16, italics mine)." "Healed" refers to God's supernatural healing of diseases, physical and spiritual.[46] (Sin, by nature, is addictive and disease-like in effect, body and soul.) Though God provides healing, He prescribes a path to it *through* His Body: praying with His people. This, in turn, heals us of sin's isolating guilt and builds trust and relationship.

Do you have some "bloody business" to conduct with sin? Do you need a spiritual kaishakunin? A samurai needed help to follow his master in death. So do we. It takes a deep love to take up the tanto knife of God's Word and gut the treasonous flesh holding us back (Ephesians 6:17).[ix] It takes a samurai spirit to repent of a civilian mindset and live as a soldier: dying to self, redeeming the time, loving recklessly, serving others, and

---

vii   *Hebrews 7:26-28; 10:11*

viii   *John 1:29; 14:6; 1 Timothy 2:5; Hebrews 7:22-28; 9:11-12; 10:11-12*

ix   *Hebrews 4:12*

following Jesus. The line between samurai and ronin is now drawn. Which one are you?

Tactical Takeaways

1. The Age of War taught samurai: *"Warfare is not an event but a way of life."* Scripture teaches the same (Ephesians 6:10-20).[x] How have you viewed and approached spiritual warfare? Does your mindset need to change? If so, how?

2. Endless war taught samurai to redeem the time. Wilderness trials taught Israel this lesson. Read Psalm 90:10-12. Number your days: start with 70 years, subtract your age from that, and multiply the difference by 365. How many days do you have left? What good works has God told you to finish before you die (Ephesians 2:10)?

3. Three striking parallels between the samurai and Christian soldier were: *love* as the highest virtue (Matthew 22:37-40)[xi]; *service*, the highest call (Mark 10:42-45)[xii]; and *sacrifice*, the highest honor (John 15:12-14).[xiii] The Christian soldier's struggle here centers around subduing our flesh and following in our Lord's footsteps. Where do you struggle most and why? Respond to the Lord in prayer.

4. *Junshi* ("following in death") and the *kaishakunin* (assistant) served as types for the Christian soldier dealing with hidden sins through accountability. Do you walk with someone in this way? If not, pray and seek one out. Is there an ensnaring sin you need to deal with?

---

x   *2 Timothy 2:3-4; Revelation 12:9, 13, 17*
xi   *John 13:34-35; 1 Corinthians 13:4-8*
xii   *Galatians 5:13*
xiii   *Ephesians 5:25; 1 John 3:16-18*

BOOK II

LAW OF THE SPARTAN

No one was allowed to live after his own fancy; but the city was a sort of a [military] camp, in which every man had his share of provisions and business set out and looked upon himself not so much born to serve his own ends as the interest of his country.... So much beneath them did they esteem the frivolous devotion of time and attention to the mechanical arts and to moneymaking.... He bred up his citizens in such a way that...they were to make themselves one with the public good, and...devoted wholly to their country.

—PLUTARCH, *LIFE OF LYCURGUS*, 24.1, 3; 25.3

Share in suffering as a good soldier of Christ Jesus. No soldier gets entangled in civilian pursuits, since his aim is to please the one who enlisted him. An athlete is not crowned unless he competes according to the rules. It is the hard-working farmer who ought to have the first share of the crops. Think over what I say, for the Lord will give you understanding in everything.

—THE APOSTLE PAUL, 2 TIMOTHY 2:3-7

The land called Lacedaemon stood as a phenomenon, and her credit for casting the Spartan, one of antiquity's most devout soldiers, traces back to one man shrouded in mystery. From his first mention in the *Histories* of Herodotus to Plutarch's *Parallel Lives*, history leaves us a table of puzzling pieces forming the legendary lawgiver Lycurgus. So conflicting are accounts, in fact, that Plutarch's biography begins with the disclaimer, "Nothing can be said which is not disputed,"[1] while historian Paul Cartledge dubs him "a mixture perhaps of George Washington— and Pol Pot."[2] But whatever the qualms with the ancient record, no one disputes Lycurgus as Sparta's founding father and the savior of the state.

Lycurgus the Lawgiver

In the mid to late eighth century B.C., seeing his home sliding into a pit of decadence and corruption, the philosopher took to the sea. After surveying civilizations from Crete to as far as Spain and India in some reports and climaxing with the fortune-telling Oracle at Delphi, he returned and convinced his countrymen to institute a series of laws changing Sparta forever—the *Megále Rhêtra* ("Great Sayings").[3] No sooner had his reforms taken root than the lone lawgiver disappeared into the sunset. The Greek historian and soldier Xenophon describes Lycurgus' most daring renovation: "At Sparta Lycurgus banned all free men from the pursuit of wealth and prescribed that their sole concern should be with things that make cities free. Lycurgus demanded that provisions should be contributed on an equal basis and the way of life be uniform, thus doing away with self-indulgent passion for wealth."[4] The biographer Plutarch adds:

> No one was allowed to live after his own fancy; but the city [Sparta] was a sort of a [military] camp, in which every man had his share of provisions and business set out and looked upon himself not so much born to serve his own ends as the interest of his country.... So much beneath them did they esteem the frivolous devotion of time and attention to the mechanical arts and to moneymaking.... He bred up his citizens in such a way that... they were to make themselves one with the public good, and...devoted wholly to their country.[5]

By law, Lycurgus forbade worldly entanglements, setting aside citizens for service to the state. He codified an ideal: worldly entanglements were beneath Spartans; Spartans were born for a higher pur-pose. I submit that a Lawgiver and Sayings

Worldly entanglements were beneath Spartans; Spartans were born for a higher purpose.

higher than these consecrate the Christian soldier: "Share in suffering as a good soldier of Christ Jesus. No soldier gets entangled in civilian pursuits, since his aim is to please the one who enlisted him (2 Timothy 2:3-4)."

Throughout his ministry, Paul accessed martial culture to instruct the Church. Here, he aimed to sharpen his protégé's mind to a subtle form of psychological warfare. The original Greek of verse 4 reads: "No one *serving as soldier*...." The phrase in italics is the verb *strateuomai* and refers to a soldier waging war.[6] Paul stressed that all Christians stand on the frontline, directly engaging with demonic forces. But a more sinister danger lurks under the radar, stealthy and camouflaged, and the gates of many Christian soldier hearts open freely to it because the threat appears as a Trojan horse, a gift—a welcomed assassin.

The word "entangled" (Gk., *empléko*) indicates something acting subtly upon the soul. Picture an anaconda slowly, silently entwining unsuspecting prey, crippling movement, constricting respiration, and finally consuming it.[7] Worldly entanglements work their way into the Christian life in like manner. Calling becomes blurred, judgment impeded, and integrity compromised. God forbids entanglements because they sabotage us and our mission. Clearly, though, Christians must still live in this world—making a living, carrying on duties as spouses, parents, citizens, etc. Such a strong warning then, demands further consideration.

Entanglements & Idols

In the parable of the sower, Jesus exposed two lethal entanglements (Matthew 13:1-9, 18-23). He explained that the seed sown among thorns symbolizes one who hears God's Word, but worldly cares and the deceitfulness of riches choke it out, and it becomes unfruitful (v. 22). "Cares" originates from a Greek root meaning "a part, separated from the whole."[8] Jesus warned that earthly ambitions, commitments, and pressures not only distract from our God-given purpose but create stress and anxiety, "dividing and fracturing a person's being into parts."[9]

Consider the multitude of diversions consuming Christian soldiers' time, energy, and income each week: gluttonous media saturation, excessive extracurricular activity, unequally yoked relationships, inordinate job demands, unrealistic personal goals, ungodly dreams and desires. According to Nielsen research, American adults spend more than eleven hours each day reading, watching, listening to, or "generally interacting with media."[10] Media consumes eleven out of sixteen waking hours—69 percent of each day! Further research reveals that the average person spends seven years and eight months of life watching television and five years and four months on social media.[11] Together, television and social media devour a staggering thirteen years of our existence!

The incessant blast of media disrupts actual, personal communication between people and drowns out God's still, small voice (1 Kings 19:11-12). Believers of this age repeatedly confess, "I can't hear God." No wonder: the noise is deafening. In war, cutting off an enemy's communications ensures quick defeat. What joy Satan must take as he watches us do it to ourselves—daily!

The "deceitfulness" of riches proves equally dangerous to the Christian soldier. Jesus cautioned against wealth's power to dull and delude our minds. Interestingly, *ploutos* ("riches" in v. 22) also appears in ancient Greek mythology as the god of wealth. Coincidence? I think not, for Jesus elsewhere commanded His disciples:

> Do not lay up for yourselves treasures on earth, where moth and rust destroy and where thieves break in and steal; but lay up for yourselves treasures in heaven, where neither moth nor rust destroys and where thieves do not break in and steal. For where your treasure is, there your heart will be also.

> The lamp of the body is the eye. If therefore your eye is good, your whole body will be full of light. But if your eye is bad, your whole body will be full of darkness. If therefore the light that is in you is darkness, how great is that darkness! No one can serve two masters; for either he will hate

the one and love the other, or else he will be loyal to the one and despise the other. You cannot serve God and mammon. (Matthew 6:19-24, NKJV)

Matthew captured our Lord's most potent admonition on greed and materialism, along with a call to unquestionable allegiance. The Christian soldier must ask: "Where is the majority of my time, energy, and talent spent?" Jesus taught that wherever our heart dwells (heaven or earth), we inexorably seek the native "treasure." Regardless of what we say, *treasure measures heart*. Quite literally, the pursuit of earthly treasure lies beneath a heavenly citizen. Our constant focus should be the business of heaven for "our citizenship is in heaven (Philippians 3:20)." "Seek those things that are above" and "set your minds" on them, Paul urged (Colossians 3:1-2).

Jesus also divulged that a bad or greedy "eye" leads to a soul filled with darkness. He exposed covetousness as a spiritual black hole which draws in, traps, and crushes the "matter" of our thought, time, energy, and talent. Whatever darkness the Christian tolerates poses danger. As the abode of sin and the demonic, it never remains *static* but gradually invades and overcomes the soul, for that is its consuming, mentally deceiving, and heart-hardening nature (Hebrews 3:13). Hence, Paul's stern charge: "Cast off the works of darkness," "put on the armor of light," and "make no provision for the flesh, to gratify its evil desires (Romans 13:12, 14)."

In the Bible, the Holy Spirit employs personification to awaken readers not only to God's sovereign work but Satan's invisible operations. Christ's discussion of mammon struck a dissonant chord with his audience and prods us toward reflection and repentance also:

A.) Lordship. It's striking that Jesus spoke of both God and mammon saying, "No one can serve two *masters* (Gk., *kúrios*)." *Kúrios* was a lord or master with complete ownership rights.[12] Jesus bore this same title in the New Testament and used it to address His Father. In the *Septuagint* (the Greek version of the Old Testament), *kúrios* is the sister for the Hebrew *adonai*, a title for God from Genesis to Malachi.[13] Remember that *ploutos* ("riches") was also the name of the Greek god of wealth. Unquestionably, Jesus unmasked a false god worshiped by many names and by many people for centuries.

B.) Contrast. The Master placed *mammon* opposite of the Person of God, uncovering its wholly contrary nature—malevolent versus benevolent; cruel instead of caring; enslaving not liberating. Jesus indicated that those who serve *mammon* won't find the happiness and security they seek, but the exact opposite.

C.) Slavery. By using the verb *douleuó* ("serve"), Christ also warned of the slave relationship we can develop with *mammon* through greed, extravagance, and debt. This insidious exchange unfolds like the sly work of a quick-change artist at a cash register. Before realizing it, the Christian has handed over God-given liberty for chains.[14] Like human slavery, mammon slavery humiliates us, drives us to exhaustion, and still demands more. It is a torturous master!

D.) Enmity. The Lord stressed that, like the opposing natures of these two masters, we also have a polar response: loving and devoting ourselves to one; hating and scorning the other. Now, no professing Christian in the bonds of greed says, "I hate the Lord!" But Jesus taught that our actions reveal our hearts. James 2:18 confirms this, stating that our works prove our faith.

Though heartbreaking, we must recognize: idolatry in our relationship with God is like marital infidelity. If we profess to love Him, yet refuse to deal with an idol, we're no longer walking in love (John 14:15). We're acting as the unfaithful partner who brings another lover into the bedroom. We contradict ourselves and insult our Beloved who bought us with His blood. When the Holy Spirit exposes an entanglement, we must repent. Healing and freedom only come as we come clean.

Spiritual Inspection

What must we do to free and guard ourselves from these adulterous bed-fellows, these civilian entanglements? To begin, we must open our lives to relationship and accountability. In the armed forces, drill instructors conduct routine inspections to teach soldiers discipline, safeguard their lives, and ensure they never lose missional focus. Inspections are simply pass or fail, and smart soldiers prepare for them because battlefield failure comes with harsh consequences. Repercussions for Christian soldiers range from dulling our biblical knowledge and discernment to being unfit for ministry opportunities or unprepared for enemy attacks. Long-term ramifications

can include damage to vital relationships; loss of credibility; and forfeiture of personal support, financial provision, or ministry office. Worst of all, entanglement draws public scorn to Christ's name and Church (2 Samuel 12:14).[i]

Idolatry in our relationship with God is like marital infidelity. If we profess to love Him, yet refuse to deal with an idol, we're no longer walking in love (John 14:15).

Yes, Christians live under God's covenant of grace. But people, especially those of the world, frequently prove unforgiving. Thus, the disgrace and damage of entanglement can be severe, even permanent. We must set ourselves into intimate relationships and regularly gather with mature Christ followers. Within these good ties, loving "Holy Spirit inspection" naturally occurs as caring people share life as God intended. We meet over coffee while purposefully devoting time for important questions. "So, how is the thing we talked about last time? Have you made any adjustments since then?" Meeting often also helps catch "weeds" in the bud and guards our soul against guilt, despair, and ungodly sorrow in the wake of bad choices.

God-breathed inspection in Scripture, by the way, never exposes or condemns someone (Romans. 8:1). The Lord's atmosphere, even in the toughest moments, like the woman caught in adultery (John 8:3), always exudes grace to the humble and broken. In that encounter, we see such amazing care on Jesus' part to lift up her downcast soul and show her dignity as a creation. We also see great patience and wisdom as He responds to her accusers. Finally, after running off the bloody-thirsty throng, He gently corrects and calls her into a new life.

Think also on God's wise and compassionate approach to mankind's Fall in Genesis 3. The Lord knew what happened yet humbled Himself to ask questions. He didn't blaze in shouting, "Come on out! I know what you did!" Instead, He opened with, "Where are you?" He then asked Adam, "Who told you that you were naked? Have you eaten of the tree of which I commanded you not to eat?" On and on, the Father questioned, shepherding His children into confession and repentance (Genesis 3:9-13).

---

i   *Nehemiah 5:9; Ezekiel 36:20; Romans 2:23-24; 1 Corinthians 9:27; 2 Peter 2:2.*

Yes, there were consequences, but they came as the natural result of sin and God's just response—not retribution. Then came the Gospel, the first animal sacrifice to make clothes and cover their nakedness and, with that, the promise of a future sacrifice, which would one day remove God's wrath so we could reap His mercy (Genesis 3:14-24). Accountability then should model the pattern the Lord sets in Scripture, always aiming at healing, freeing, and restoring us to God's original purpose. Don't tolerate abuse of any kind because you made a mistake. Submit *only* to relationships with trustworthy Christ followers who will fight for you.

Above all, hold on to these promises: By the Holy Spirit's power, we are reborn for a higher purpose. By the Son's blood, we have become citizens of Heaven. And, by the Father's Great Sayings, we are consecrated for Kingdom service. Let's free ourselves then of earthly entanglements and allow our Lawgiver to raise us into a more "Spartan" way of life.

The Raising

The most radical installment in the Lycurgan reform package made every Spartan male a *citizen-soldier*, a guardian of the state. The *agôgê*, which in this context means "a 'raising,' as of cattle" or an "upbringing," was a compulsory military schooling designed to produce the superior warrior.[15] The state *paidonómos* ("trainer-in-chief") took every boy from his child-hood home on his seventh birthday, placed him into a common barracks, and rigorously trained him the next thirteen years in the arts of war, the social compact, and Spartan-Homeric values such as *andreía* ("manliness"), *aristeía* ("martial excellence"), and *kléos* (immortal "glory" or "renown"), which a warrior achieved through the preceding virtues.

The Raising was ruthless, exposing students to the elements, forcing them to go barefoot and barely clad in winter, lashing them to posts for ritual beatings, and underfeeding them to promote hunting, endurance, high pain tolerance, and hone the survival instinct.[16] In a word, the *agôgê* beat self and civilian out, state and soldier in, compelling pupils to maturity, warriorhood, and a mindset centered on god and country. Those deserting or dying in process were deemed unworthy of citizenship and unfit for Sparta.

By the first century and writing of the New Testament, this Spartan warrior-training term had become a household word. Greeks used it to describe those who led extraordinary lives marked by uncommon discipline, exceptional training, and perseverance in the face of hardship. Inspired by the Holy Spirit, Paul used this term in 2 Timothy 3:10-17 as he rounded out Timothy's training and, subsequently, that of other Christian soldiers:

> But you know all about my teachings, my way of life, my purpose, my faith, my patience, my love, and my endurance. You also know about the kind of persecutions and sufferings which happened to me in the cities of Antioch, Iconium, and Lystra. I endured those persecutions, and the Lord rescued me from all of them. Those who try to live a godly life because they believe in Christ Jesus will be persecuted. But evil people and phony preachers will go from bad to worse as they mislead people and are themselves misled.

> However, continue in what you have learned and found to be true. You know who your teachers were. From infancy you have known the Holy Scriptures. They have the power to give you wisdom so that you can be saved through faith in Christ Jesus. Every Scripture passage is inspired by God. All of them are useful for teaching, pointing out errors, correcting people, and training them for a life that has God's approval. They equip God's servants so that they are completely prepared to do good things. (2 Timothy 3:10-17, GW)

Agôgê is rendered above as "way of life." Notice Paul's *agôgê*-type focus on hardening Timothy's spiritual body—the same way the Spartan *agôgê* hardened a warrior's physical body. This timid lad never would have become the man, pastor, and spiritual force he proved to be apart from Paul's intensive training. In this hour, the Church needs to apply this same wisdom, creating comprehensive systems to harden modern-day Christians into citizen-soldiers of God—Kingdom guardians known for love, integrity, discipline, and skill in the Faith. The typical church growth track cannot provide these

The Church needs to apply this same wisdom, creating comprehensive systems to harden modern-day Christians into citizen-soldiers of God....

Trial acts as our Trainer-in-Chief's rod to beat sin and self out, Spirit and Scripture in, and it remains the inescapable path to fulfill our mission.

essential supplements, nor should it. The widespread demographics of age (physical and spiritual) in weekend services make this goal untenable. We simply can't outfit saints for the fierce warfare of our time through these typical conventions.

We require spiritual "raisings" which rouse saints with the testimonies of the Christian martyrs and root them in Early Church history; we need to connect with who we are historically, not just presently. We're also dying for a theological outfitting that doesn't merely indoctrinate but equips believers to make biblically based decisions in relationships, family, career, ethics, and civics; we must hit Christians where they live with the Bible's incisive wisdom, passion, and force. Lastly, our times demand training that teaches Christ followers to think critically in the culture and to intelligently defend the Faith with evidence beyond Scripture. "Because the Bible says so" will not do. We need forges producing superior soldiers, prides birthing lions of the Faith instead of ignorant, crowd-following sheep.

Paul also wielded his trials in an instructive and empowering way to Timothy, speaking here and elsewhere of his sufferings and hardships. Likewise, our teaching must toughen today's Christians to face trials with faith and courage, to stop dropping their shields the moment things get rough. Our retreat from life's hardships shows weakness to the world, not Christ's overcoming strength. Our surrender, when we come under persecution, tells people our faith is conditional and fake. And our compromise on key Christian battlefronts costs us dividends.

The Bible reveals trial not as a random occurrence, but a sovereignly orchestrated test of faith and true citizenship (1 Peter 1:6-7). Trial presses us to move from spiritual infancy to maturity, an earthly focus to a heavenly, mere citizenship to soldiership (Romans 5:3-5).[ii] It washes away sandy, self-centered doctrine and settles us on the rocky foundations of God's Word (Matthew 7:24-27). And, according to James 1:2-12, it burns off spiritual fat and builds a durable, muscular faith. Trial acts as our

---

ii   *Colossians 3:1-3; Ephesians 6:10-20*

Trainer-in-Chief's rod to beat sin and self out, Spirit and Scripture in, and it remains the inescapable path to fulfill our mission. We must, therefore, take our share (2 Timothy 2:3).

Paul touching on Timothy's raising in the Scriptures from infancy (Gk., *brephos*) also bears significance as Greeks used specific terms to mark various life stages from childhood to adulthood. Plutarch notes that Spartan midwives washed a newborn (*brephos*) in wine instead of water, believing it tempered healthy babies like steel and strengthened their frames.[17] In His ministry, Jesus likened skillful, Scriptural teaching to old and new wine. (See Matthew 9:16-17.)[iii] As Paul rounded out Timothy's training, was he intimating that the young soldier's grandmother Lois and mother Eunice, like Spartan midwives, had bathed him in the wine of God's Word (2 Timothy 1:5)? One can only speculate, but Paul's coupling of these terms, along with his incomparable schooling in the Mosaic system and marks of Classical Greek training in his epistles, make his references more than coincidental to this author.[18]

In the *Sh'ma Israel* prayer, which Paul knew by heart and is the foundation of the traditional Jewish education and training, Moses said:

> So love the Lord your God with all your heart, soul, and strength. Memorize his laws and tell them to your children over and over again. Talk about them all the time, whether you're at home or walking along the road or going to bed at night or getting up in the morning. Write down copies and tie them to your wrists and foreheads to help you obey them. Write these laws on the door frames of your homes and on your town gates. (Deuteronomy 6:5-9, CEV)

In this appeal, God ties a parent's love for Him with training their children to memorize Scripture and saturate the home in biblical training. Have you made this vital connection in your home and preparing your children for spiritual warfare?

Years ago, Father brought this passage and 2 Timothy 3:10-17 to mind while I was praying and fasting before the birth of our first daughter. I

---

iii   *Also, Matthew 13:51-52*

resolved then that I would employ these models with her and any other child He gave Ralana and me. Every night I leaned over Ralana's tummy, prayed, spoke Scripture, and sang a special song God had given me just for Kaydra.

Throughout Kaydra's infancy, I read the Bible and recited verses aloud to her as I held or fed her. One day her Mimi said, "Duncan, she can't understand what you're saying." I replied, "Her spirit can," and went right back to it. At age three, Kaydra and I began nightly devotions. Every evening we sat on the bed, sang some children's worship songs, then one more to the tune of "The More We Get Together" to introduce our Bible reading. "Oh, we love to pat the Bible, the Bible, the Bible. Oh, we love to pat the Bible. It's God's holy Word," we would sing as we patted her little children's Bible. Then, it was story time. When she got older, the tune became "Oh, we love to read the Bible." Kaydra loved this time and would shout, "Oh, boy!" when I called her. When we finished, she always requested one more "dong"—her adorable baby speak for "song."

At age four, I started teaching her memory verses, putting together twenty verses on basic points of faith: creation, salvation, Christ's birth, worship, prayer, forgiveness, and so on. When she was ready for a new verse, I'd ask the Holy Spirit to help me set it to a tune. Right there, as we sat on her bed, it would come. All her childhood memory verses were set to music, and her Mimi and Pawpaw learned them too as they practiced them with her when she slept over. In fifth grade, I introduced Kaydra to critical thinking (about the Bible and our world) and in middle school added basic Christian apologetics on God's existence, Creation, the inspiration of Scripture, Christ's Deity, and moral dilemmas.

Finally, for her eighteenth year, I put together another set of memory verses focusing on themes of womanhood, leadership, virtue, and other topics, along with an eight-month study program culminating in a rite of passage. I repeated this process for our second daughter, Karlisa. From our little arrows' formation to their release, Ralana and I labored to give them an *agôgê*-type raising, bathing them in the wine of biblical teaching and the pure water of God's Word to help them become strong young women with a sturdy faith in Christ.

As a children's pastor, I used this same template in ministry, setting Scripture memory to music, sharing basic evidences for faith, and endeavoring to constantly wash children through the systematic teaching of the Word. As a college and career pastor, I recalibrated, used similar tools, and ditched the cute music. Over the years, Ralana and I have seen hundreds of

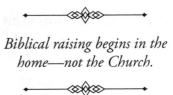

Biblical raising begins in the home—not the Church.

children come to Christ and awaken as little Christian soldiers. We also witnessed college students finding Jesus, healing, freedom, becoming secure in their spiritual identity and as bold as lions on campus. They were not moved when professors railed on Christianity or fellow students mocked their faith. They were ready. They shared the Gospel, challenged people on issues, and invited them into relationship and church. And, as they began families, they used many of these same tools.

What if you took up these tools as a parent—mommas bathing your babies in biblical "wines" to temper their frames and feeding them the pure milk of the Word (Proverbs 1:8)?[iv] Fathers, what if you raised your children in a spiritual *agôgê* fashion, "in the discipline and instruction of the Lord (Proverbs 22:6)"?[v] Biblical raising begins in the home—not the Church. As one who's pastored students young and old, I can tell you: this principle remains the most neglected in Christian homes. Consider carefully, if your child attends public school like ours did, he/she receives forty-plus hours of secular instruction each week. If your child goes on to a state-sponsored university like ours, he/she will face routine bombardments against faith and morality in class and elsewhere.

What are you doing now to biblically immunize your babes against the diseased world system? Are you training little hands for war (Psalm 144:1)? Will you send lambs to slaughter or lions to battle? God calls parents to train children in the way they should go, and men to guide and guard the home because we are the walls (Proverbs 22:6)[vi]

The Walls of Sparta

The "Wolfish Worker" (the meaning of Lycurgus' name) had looted Lady Sparta's coffers and robbed her of her cubs. His next act, however, was

---

iv   *2 Timothy 1:5; 3:15; 1 Peter 2:2*

v   *Ephesians 6:4; 2 Timothy 3:10-17*

vi   *Nehemiah 4:14*

a wrecking ball. During his travels, a destructive pattern in walled cities disturbed the reformer. In hallowed isolation, cultures tended to turn inward, degenerating into ease, idleness, and indifference toward the outside world. Citizens began trusting in fortress walls to protect them, rather than a singular social vision and military readiness to meet the enemy. "This will never suffice," Lycurgus thought. With the *agôgê* system in place, building mentally and physically fortified men from the ground up, the lawgiver ordered Sparta's fortress walls be torn down.

With civilizations routinely attacked and overthrown in days, understandably, inhabitants must have thought Lycurgus mad. Plutarch records Spartan society's reaction and Lycurgus' challenging reply: "When they asked how they could ward off an invasion of enemies, he answered: 'By remaining poor, and by not desiring to be greater the one than the other.' And when they asked about fortifying their city, he answered: 'A city will be well-fortified which is surrounded by brave men and not by bricks.'"[19]

Lycurgus had dreamt of a day where inhabitants saw themselves as citizens, where they stopped looking to the state for welfare and started being the state by serving it, where minds were set not upon reaching the top but reaching out. Most of all, he'd envisioned an age where men assumed their role as consecrated guardians—the principled walls of society and gatekeepers of the home. The fact that Plutarch's account ends here may indicate the men could not refute Lycurgus' point.

Far from whitewashing, at every turn Lycurgus razed and rebuilt Sparta's entire social structure. Like a campaigning general, he laid siege to the cultural psyche, battering bulwarks of apathy and indulgence, tearing down ramparts of rank and towers of greed, rounding up selfish ambition and publicly executing emasculating ideals. The destruction of the city's fortress walls only stood as an outward sign of those being torn down in the people's minds.

Two centuries later and eight hundred miles away, another fiery reformer wasn't tearing down walls, but rebuilding them. With the holy city still in charred heaps years after the Babylonian siege (586 B.C.), governor Nehemiah called the men of Israel to action: "You see the trouble we are in, how Jerusalem lies in ruins with its gates burned. Come, let us build the wall of Jerusalem, that we may no longer suffer derision (Nehemiah 2:17)."

As construction began, though, old enemies appeared, taunting weakened Israel like jackals and threatening to devour her. Rallying fearful hearts, Nehemiah exhorted the men, "Do not be afraid of them. Remember the Lord, who is great and awesome, and fight for your brothers, your sons, your daughters, your wives, and your homes (4:14)." At a near fatal moment, God's wise wall builder paused to rebuild Israel's true walls, her shaken men and their crumbling faith. Nehemiah roused hearts under the banner of the "great and awesome" God, ancient code language from Deuteronomy 7. Here, Moses charged Israel upon settling in her Promised Land and facing new foes, "Do not be terrified by them, for the Lord your God is among you, a great and awesome God (v. 21)!"

Nehemiah reached way back, digging deeply into ancient Israel's bedrock foundations to ensure her spiritual walls would not waver. Applying Deuteronomy 7:21's wisdom, He gave men a reset by turning their fearful eyes from themselves and their foes, back onto the God of their glorious history, the Warrior-God who had promised to fight their battles (Exodus 14:14).[vii] Then, he took it one step further by reminding warriors of those they were fighting for—brothers, wives, children, parents, and the land they'd grown to love. Arrayed in battle formation, with sword in one hand and trowel in the other, Israel's spiritual wall of fighting men pressed forward and finished her physical wall (Nehemiah 4:17). Lycurgus wasn't the only reformer who understood that fortress walls are made of brave men, not bricks.

God Seeks Men

Leading up to her destruction, exile, and Babylonian captivity, Israel wrestled in the throes of moral collapse. At that time, the Lord spoke to the prophet Ezekiel: "The people of the land have used oppressions, committed robbery, and mistreated the poor and needy; and they wrongfully oppress the stranger. So I sought for a man among them who would make a wall,

---

vii   *Deuteronomy 1:30; 7:22-24; Joshua 10:25; 2 Chronicles 20:17; Nehemiah 4:20*

and stand in the gap before Me on behalf of the land, that I should not destroy it; but I found no one (Ezekiel 22:29-30, NKJV)."[20]

Going back further in biblical history, to another time of social upheaval, when the wickedness of Sodom and Gomorrah flooded neighboring cities…

> The Lord said, "Shall I hide from Abraham what I am about to do, seeing that Abraham shall surely become a great and mighty nation, and all the nations of the earth shall be blessed in him? For I have chosen him, *that he may command his children and his household after him to keep the way of the Lord* by doing righteousness and justice, so that the Lord may bring to Abraham what he has promised him." Then the Lord said, "Because the outcry against Sodom and Gomorrah is great and their sin is very grave, I will go down to see whether they have done altogether according to the outcry that has come to me. And if not, I will know." So the men turned from there and went toward Sodom, *but Abraham still stood before the Lord. Then Abraham drew near and said, "Will you indeed sweep away the righteous with the wicked?"* (Genesis 18:17-23, italics mine)

With civilizations on the brink of destruction, how does the Triune God respond? Does He shut the throne room doors and take counsel solely within Himself? Does the King of kings hold court and make unilateral decrees? He would certainly be right in doing so. In the Bible, though, something else happens. The Almighty looks down locally into the earth and takes a stroll to share His concern for ailing society with faithful *men*. But why?

In the economy of God, man stands uniquely accountable for the welfare of the home and social fabric. When either are threatened, the Lord calls men to battle. This model of masculine leadership (protection, provision, nurture, and admonition) stands as a fundamental axiom of warfare throughout Scripture. It begins in Eden with God's command to Adam and follows with God questioning him *first* after the Fall (Genesis 2:15-17; 3:8-13). The revelation proceeds through the Old Testament with God calling and moving through patriarchs, prophets, priests, judges, and kings. Finally, in the New Testament, it concludes with the apostles' instructions to husbands and fathers (Ephesians 5:22-33).[viii]

The reason Sparta's men could not contend with Lycurgus that fateful day was because God's Law, which is written on the human heart from creation, had confronted them—not man's. In the beginning, God made men the walls of society and gatekeepers of the home. Little did the

In the economy of God, man stands uniquely accountable for the welfare of the home and social fabric. When either are threatened, the Lord calls men to battle.

Wolfish Worker know, though, that his application of this sacred principle (c. 750 B.C.) would prepare Sparta to meet a deadly foe at the gates almost three hundred years later.

The Hot Gates

The movie *300* romanticizes the historically decisive Battle of Thermopylae, which in Greek means the "Hot Gates." Geographically, the "gates" were a small, cliffside corridor situated between the mountainous Kallídhromon massif and the Gulf of Maliakós. Spartan authority Paul Cartledge relates that the Hot Gates were "scarcely wide enough for two chariots or wagons to pass each other comfortably."[21] Strategically, he adds that the gates stood as the northern entryway for an invading force intending "to destroy the armies of Athens and Sparta, and their allies in southern Greece."[22] Mythologically, just as the gods dwelled on Mount Olympus, Thermopylae marked the home of Hades, lord of the dead and demonic underworld. Known for its sulfur springs, the Hot Gates allegedly became hot when the demi-god Heracles dove into the waters to wash off the poison from his deadly encounter with the multiheaded hydra.

In 480 B.C., at this intersection of mountain and sea, mythology and reality, three hundred handpicked Spartans and a few thousand local citizen-soldiers faced a Persian army of over one million under King Xerxes I.[23] With the enemy marching toward them and a religious festival underway, Sparta stood at a crossroads. By law, she could not go to war. Philosophers, politicians, clergy...all of her statesmen stood idle as

---

viii Ephesians 6:1-4; Colossians 3:18-21

destruction approached—all but one. King Leonidas I, knowing the law yet seeing the threat, assembled a team of Sparta's finest, an ancient Delta Force. A powerful scene in the movie *300* depicts this moment of destiny.

On the outskirts of the city, a group of Sparta's social elite approach to remind the troubled king of their law, the festival, and decrees of their prophets. Leonidas, aware of their inflexibility, turns and with laconic wit replies, "I'm here just taking a stroll, stretching my legs. These three hundred men are my personal bodyguard. Our army will stay in Sparta." "Where will you go?" a politician asks. "I hadn't really thought about it. But, now that you ask, I suppose I'll head north," Leonidas smirks. The men look at one another knowingly. "The Hot Gates," the politician answers. Leonidas nods as thunder cracks in the darkening sky behind him.

"Move out," a captain barks in the background. The warriors turn to depart as the idle statesmen stare at one another. An elder asks, "What should we do?" The politician, seeing Leonidas' resolve, responds, "What can we do?" Marking their indifference, Leonidas replies, "What *can* you do?" Then, he turns and heads for the Hot Gates.[24]

Biblically and historically, gates served as hallowed places of public assembly,[25] courts of civic justice,[26] platforms of divine proclamation,[27] and sites for religious offering.[28] Thus, gates also stood as prophetic symbols of decision, destiny, and sacrifice. With divine judgment at Sodom's gates then, Abraham didn't remain quiet. He interceded. When apostasy struck Israel's gates, Ezekiel didn't just weep. He prophesied. As Jerusalem's gates lay in heaps, Nehemiah didn't just survey the damage. He rebuilt. And, as Persia headed toward the Hot Gates, three hundred Spartans didn't politicize, pontificate, or play stupid. They marched. That is what real men do. They act because they are the gatekeepers, because they are the wall.

The Phalanx

Lycurgus' vision of a wall of men found its fullest expression in a tactical military formation called the *phálanx*. By the Battle of Thermopylae, Sparta had honed this deadly art to razor-sharp perfection. In this ancient fighting style, heavy-infantry soldiers stood shoulder to shoulder with overlapping shields. Each sturdy, multilayered shield was held in the left hand to guard his fellow soldier's right hand, the vulnerable flank and spear arm. The tightly packed phalanx typically ran eight columns deep. When bracing for an enemy charge, each row pressed their shields against their brother-warriors' backs while the first three rows poised their eight-to- nine-foot *dory* spears over the shield tops, minimizing danger in a synchronized wall of men and maximizing damage with a serrated fence of spears.

To maneuver effectively, Sparta instituted fifes along with the *paen* ("war song"), which soldiers sang as they marched. The music unified the phalanx like one massive war engine—in effect, an ancient armored tank. The lyrics bolstered morale, reminding soldiers of who they were and what they were fighting for, which they desperately needed for the coming clash. Conflict ensued when the invading army advanced. Drawing closer, they charged, approaching like a massive tidal wave of gleaming metal and screaming flesh. The ultimate test of courage, strength, and sheer will for the defending phalanx had begun.

Spartan law forbade retreat or surrender, however. Soldiers dropping their shields, exposing comrades, and fleeing the line faced unending disgrace at home and possible death. Such a fearsome sight and sound as a charging phalanx, though, could give unseasoned soldiers second thoughts, which is why the strongest, most-skilled warriors occupied the first three rows *and* the last. Comprised of older veterans, the back row pressed forward, keeping the unit tight and speaking over the shoulders of all to steady, encourage, and, if necessary, prevent frightened upstarts in rows four through seven from retreating as blood began to fly.

With the enemy almost on them, the defending phalanx captain shouted again and again: *Stéte*—"Stand [your ground]!" (The same martial lingo Paul barked out in Ephesians 6:13-14.) Every man tightened his grip, set his feet, and leaned forward. Those on the front line depended entirely on faithful brothers behind them pressing in tightly to help absorb the force of the impending collision. If the phalanx failed to stand together, only death lay ahead.

Then, IMPACT! Row upon row of armored flesh and blood crashed against the defending shield wall with some charging bodies flying straight over the top and onto the vertically pointed spears of rows four through seven. Other foes sometimes slid under the feet of the phalanx wall where they were stabbed by a dory spear's butt spike. Now, the *othismos* ("the shoving match") began—kingdom versus kingdom, shield on shield pressing relentlessly against one another. The defending captain shouted: *Antistéte*—"Resist" (again, the same command issued by Paul, Peter, and James). With this order, the unit lunged forward as one man, seeking to drive the enemy line backward. Rows one through three thrust over shield tops with their spears, stabbed with long, tip-weighted swords (*xiphos*), or hacked at exposed limbs with short, curved ones (*kopis*). The goal: draw blood, create a gap, and collapse the enemy column.

This wall welcomed Xerxes and stopped his army cold at the Hot Gates for three days as Greek city-states evacuated and made other preparations. Paul and the apostles employed these terms and illustrations under God's inspiration, bringing insight and urgency to the Christian's warfare. Study of these principles packs power for our battles in these dark modern times.

Years ago, I was studying this very history when danger appeared at the gates of our home. Lying in bed one night, casually bantering, my fair flank-woman unveiled a wounded heart—a heart I had wounded over the course of our marriage. Ralana and I came from different family trees. Hers resembled that titanic oak in TV insurance commercials—godly parents, a rich spiritual heritage, and healthy, well-educated children. Mine looked like Charlie Brown's Christmas tree—spiritually lost, dysfunctional relationships, divorced parents, and an abusive environment with alcohol addictions and others. I left home deeply wounded and unprepared for marriage or life. When God saved me in college at twenty-one, my heart changed in many ways: purpose, dreams, desires.... I wanted to live for Christ and spend my life sharing Him.

But salvation did *not* change numerous lies my mind believed over the years or heal all the wounds my soul had incurred. The Bible reveals that deeply entrenched beliefs and behaviors can take years to unravel, like the siege of a fortress (2 Corinthians 10:3-5). Bible-based weapons like fasting, prayer, worship, counseling, Scripture memory, and meditation are highly effective, but the process takes time. (See this footnote to explore some scriptures on this issue.[29])

Getting back to our story, Ralana and I met shortly after I became a Christian, fell in love, married a year later, and started our family. As the pressures of parenting and providing began to squeeze, my wounds bled out on those who never cut me. When the stress of life touched those "lesions" of abuse, fear, pain, and anxiety inside me, I reacted like a wounded animal. I never physically or sexually abused Ralana, Kaydra, or Karlisa. Nor did I belittle and curse them as I had experienced. But I got upset and loud—yelling, slamming doors, hitting walls, and storming around in a cloud, leaving everyone on edge till I cycled out.

Over time, these forms of verbal/emotional abuse proved just as harmful inwardly to Ralana and the girls as physical abuse can be outwardly. The pain pouring out of me created in them beliefs, fear, isolation, coping mechanisms, secrecy, and compounded wounds Ralana had received from her father growing up, wounds neither of us even knew of yet.

Life wasn't all bad, of course. Ralana and I enjoyed many amazing times, laughing with one another, raising two beautiful girls, and doing all the fun activities families do between school, sports, church, and whatnot. We constantly ministered, too, saw God save thousands of people, and all kinds of cool things. See, we hadn't entered marriage with secrets. We'd shared everything with each other, every hairy experience growing up and each regret from bad decisions we'd personally made. We knew it all, had accepted, embraced, fought for, and committed to loving each other—no matter what this world or hell threw at us.

We also weren't living in a religiously hypocritical or hyper-spiritualized form of denial. When things happened, we worked through them—with the tools we had *at the time*. The simple fact was: we were young and inexperienced, too unlearned to recognize this other type of abuse, much less deal with it, and make connections between my hard past and our sometimes horrible present. The two Christian counselors I saw, in two separate seasons, provided no ultimate help because they lacked the necessary knowledge and skill. They treated symptoms, not causes.

So, we did what every Christian couple is called to do: we kept seeking God, loving each other, and believing for a miracle neither of us could fully articulate. When I melted down, I apologized sincerely. Ralana forgave freely. I prayed fervently. She pressed forward continually. I tried harder to be gentle and kind. She tried harder to be patient and merciful. Above all, we clung to our wedding vows, which we had both meant. Retreat or surrender was not an option.

Fast-forward thirteen years now. Repeat that cycle many times over: Ralana stood emotionally numb; me, spiritually blind. When she opened her heart that night, I knew the situation was critical. We were in over our heads. We needed a phalanx! So, I reached out to our church elders and some trusted soldier-friends for prayer, ministry, accountability, resourcing—whatever they could offer. We went into counseling and got raw and real about everything. I committed to doing whatever it took to change, heal, save our marriage, and help my family find the same. Early on and quite reasonably, though, Ralana stood unsure about part of that equation.

Over the next few years, my best friend, Jeff, and Ralana's best friend, Angela, stood beside us like Spartan flank men, their unfailing love, prayers, and encouragement guarding our vulnerabilities. Before us marched a crack team of Kingdom soldiers—shepherds, teachers, and counselors who'd already won the same battle at their gates or helped others overcome. Their sturdy faith, lined with powerful testimonies, biblical wisdom, spiritual discernment, and brazen determination, helped shield us and extinguish Satan's fiery arrows. Behind us, constantly steadying and assuring, pressed the hearts and hands of Ralana's amazing family and a few others. Before we realized it, our Captain had hemmed us into a heavenly phalanx.

In the battle for our marriage came critical moments of decision, destiny, and sacrifice. My first came in the beginning, when I determined, regardless of whether I got fired from my ministry job or not, to do it God's way, going to our church elders as James 5:13-16 instructs. As it turned out, I did lose my job. The church worked with us at first, graciously granting me a sabbatical. When the battle went longer than forecasted, though, they released me. A tough moment indeed, but Ralana and I would not change our decision to obey God and seek help, nor do we have any stones for our brothers. These godly people helped start our journey to healing, paying for a six-month sabbatical, all of our counseling at that time (including a three-day, out-of-state intensive with a world-class specialist), and a generous severance.

A second moment arrived months later. As we readied ourselves in the bathroom one morning, the future of our marriage came up. Unselfishly, Ralana then asked about a ministry endeavor I'd been working on for some time called "Bushido," after the samurai code. "What about your dream?

What about 'Bushido'?" Without hesitation, motioning back and forth to us, I said, "Babe, *this* is 'Bushido' right here. If we don't have this, nothing matters. Nothing else exists." Ralana searched my gaze and saw no flinch. I meant every word from the bottom of my heart and, when her walled-up one saw it, something cracked and began to give way.

On a third occasion, the battle was joined. In the midst of an argument (neither of us remembers what it was about), Ralana shouted, "That's it! I'm done!" She headed to her car with me close behind saying, "Honey, please, don't give up. Don't walk away. Please, don't quit!" She later recounted how those split seconds moved in slow motion. As she looked through her windshield at my pained face, the soldier within her arose and shouted, "No! I can't hurt him or the girls like this, and I will not hurt God!"

These fleeting moments marked our battle at the Hot Gates, and a phalanx of brothers and sisters bled with us for every square inch of ground. They ministered God's truth to us and wept with us as we sifted out Satan's lies. Lovingly, they challenged obstinate and wayward thinking. Tirelessly, they interceded and breathed life into our discouraged souls. Our "300" never stopped fighting for our home as if it was theirs. Four years later, our battle at the Hot Gates was won.

Either With Or On This!

Our choices to retreat or surrender in life never affect solely us. My parents' divorce sent shockwaves through the Brannan home still felt by sons, siblings, grandchildren, and great-grandchildren. To this day, I wish my parents had not given up at the gates. But, alas, they didn't have the godly support Ralana and I had; they didn't even know the Lord at that time. As a teacher, though, I fear that too many believers will lose their battle at the Hot Gates because of a critical flaw in their life strategy or plain old pride.

For years, it's been claimed that Christian and non-Christian divorce rates are the same. The claim originated with a 2008 Barna Research Group study.[30] Author and social researcher Shaunti Feldhahn not only exposed this as false, however, but unveiled an even greater truth.

Partnering with George Barna, Feldhahn reexamined the data pertaining to the divorce rate among Christians and found that the numbers were based on survey-takers who identified as "Christian" rather than some other religion. Under that broad classification, respondents were as likely as anyone else to have been divorced. The "Christian" category included people who profess a belief system but do not live a committed lifestyle. However, for those who were active in their church, the divorce rate was 27 percent to 50 percent *lower* than for non-churchgoers. Nominal Christians—those who simply call themselves "Christians" but do not actively engage with the faith—are actually 20 percent *more* likely than the general population to get divorced.[31]

Notice the phrases "committed lifestyle" and "active in their church." In other words, those Christians who had a phalanx and anchored themselves in Christ's Body, their divorce rates were 27 percent to 50 percent lower. After thirty years of ministry, I can tell you: the majority of Christian divorces are avoidable through prayer, moral support, personal ministry, and counseling. Sadly, some believers are simply unwilling to pay the price to win at the Hot Gates. For them, "in sickness and in health, till death do us part" prove nothing more than meaningless prose when tested. (Many marriage ceremonies no longer include such language in their vows!)

Biblically, a marriage vow should bind us more than any outward ordinance or code. The Genesis God who instituted the marital covenant intended it to be irrevocable law written on the tablet of the heart (Genesis 2:24).[ix] In his *Sayings of Spartan Women*, Plutarch records that when Spartans departed for war, mothers placed their sons' shields in their hands with these words, "Either with or on this,"[32] basically meaning: "Come back carrying this shield in victory or being carried on it because you died valiantly." A Spartan returning with no shield signified he had dropped it and fled, exposing his flank man. The Higher Law governing our warfare dictates that we guard our spiritual flanks—spouses, children, Christian brothers and sisters—with our lives (Nehemiah 4:14).[x] It's time for God's soldiers to apply some Spartan law to their warfare, coming home with their shields because they broke through or being carried on them because they went down fighting for Kingdom ground.

---

ix   *Matthew 19:4-8; John 15:13-14*
x   *1 John 3:16*

Few people ever recognize how a single decision will impact their present world or ripple through the generations behind them. As the three hundred took up their shields that last day, they knew they were not coming home, nor would there be a man left to carry them. Did they understand, though, that their phalanx wall stood not only between a Persian horde and their homes but the

It's time for God's soldiers to apply some Spartan law to their warfare, coming home with their shields because they broke through or being carried on them because they went down fighting for Kingdom ground.

cradle of democracy resting in the heart of Greece? Do we comprehend not only what hellish sufferings we guard our homes from but what wondrous heavenly futures we set in motion—for family, faith, and the world—when we take an immovable stand at our Hot Gates?

When Xerxes' ordered the Spartans, "Hand over your arms," Leonidas (whose name means "born of the Lion") replied, "Come and take them!"[33] In an equal show of valor, on hearing that the Persian arrows raining down on them would be so vast as to blot out the sun, the Spartan Deineces replied, "So much the better—we shall fight them in the shade!"[34] Where is this thunder in Christendom today when hell threatens us or a fallen world presses against our shields? Why are we so ready to surrender? Have we forgotten the heavenly defiance that roared through Shadrach, Meshach, and Abednego at a hellish Babylonian dictator?

> O Nebuchadnezzar, we do not need to defend ourselves before you. If we are thrown into the blazing furnace, the God whom we serve is able to save us. He will rescue us from your power, Your Majesty. But even if he doesn't, we want to make it clear to you, Your Majesty, that we will never serve your gods or worship the gold statue you have set up. (Daniel 3:16-18, NLT)

That is a triple-braided cord not quickly broken—a faith that conquers kingdoms and obtains promises (Ecclesiastes 4:12).[xi] When we look back

---

xi   *Hebrews 11:33*

at our Hot Gates, what will the report be? Will it tell the world we took our stand or dropped our shields? Will it show our faith was not only a defense against Satan's arrows but a mighty weapon (Ephesians 6:16)?

You see, the Spartan shield's grip design strapped this three-foot bronze buckler around his forearm and steadied it in front with a handgrip. With a quick rotation of hips and shoulders in a discus-style swing, the shield became a blunt-force trauma weapon. Spartans were famous for cracking skulls and breaking necks with it. By the Spirit, that's what we do when push comes to shove for God's will! We wrap that most holy faith around our spiritual arms and, with a death grip on God's promises, bash in hell's face. When Hades' gates won't budge, we look to our Captain who assembles a phalanx of faith. Then, we crash them together (Matthew 16:18).

We heed the voice of the One crying, *"Stéte—stand your ground!"* and we do not retreat. We lock our shields in a wall of fellowship, absorb life's blows in a phalanx of brothers and sisters, and as one Body push back the darkness in the great shoving match. Then, we prayerfully stab, prophetically skewer, and scripturally hack our way to victory. And when any demon in hell tells us to lay down our spiritual arms, we who are born of the Lion of Judah roar from behind our shields, "In the Name of Jesus, come and take them!"

Tactical Takeaways

1. Lycurgus consecrated Spartans for state service and forbade civilian pursuits. Similar commands are found in Matthew 6:19-24, 33, Colossians 3:1-2, 2 Timothy 2:3-4, Hebrews 11:24-25, and 1 John 2:15-17. Read and list some of God's reasons for these commands.

2. On a scale of 1-10, "1" being "none" and "10" "severe," place a number beside each item to mark the degree to which these civilian pursuits distract you from a heavenly focus or hinder your Christian mission in some way. Pray and ask God to help you be honest in this exercise.

Debt (Credit Card, Loans, etc.)	Social Media	Apathy & Laziness
Lack of Education /Equipping	Personal Sin & Effects	Health Problems
Carnal Relationship	Pride & Vanity	Greed & Materialism
Arts & Entertainment (TV, Sports, etc.)	Anxiety & Fear (Fear of Loss, Failure, etc.)	Other (Whatever you believe is relevant)

3. In "The Raising" section, we explored Spartan *agôgê* training and how Paul used this term in his life and Timothy's training. I also shared how I prepared my daughters for release. Are you preparing your children? Do you need to make adjustments?

4. In the "Hot Gates" section and moving forward, we discussed strategic spiritual battles for believers and the need for a "phalanx." Are you in such a battle now? Do you have one?

Book III

VOW OF THE VIKING

All people and nations shall tell of the word I spake, yet being unborn, wherein I vowed a vow that I would flee in fear from neither fire nor the sword; even so have I done hitherto, and shall I depart therefrom now I am old? Yea withal never shall the maidens mock these my sons at the games, and cry out at them that they fear death; once alone must all men need die, and from that season shall none escape; so my rede is that we flee nowhither, but do the work of our hands in as manly wise as we may.

—King Volsung, The Saga of the Volsungs

Only be strong and very courageous, being careful to do according to all the law that Moses my servant commanded you. Do not turn from it to the right hand or to the left, that you may [act wisely] and have good success wherever you go. This Book of the Law shall not depart from your mouth, but you shall meditate on it day and night, so that you may be careful to do according to all that is written in it. For then you will make your way prosperous, and then you will have good success. Have I not commanded you? Be strong and courageous. Do not be frightened, and do not be dismayed, for the LORD your God is with you wherever you go.

—Joshua, Joshua 1:7-9

With the fury of their hammer-wielding storm god Thor, the barbarians of the north flashed into European history. According to the *Anglo-Saxon Chronicle*, in A.D. 789 three lightning-sleek warcraft appeared in the English Channel, heralding an era of terror from the high seas.[1] In thunderbolt fashion, ferocious warriors clad in bear and wolf skins and with painted faces began striking the coasts of Britain, Ireland, and Francia, leaving behind a wake of terror and destruction. In time, a term for the ruthless warfare and piracy practiced by these seaborne soldiers found its way onto stone and parchment, forever setting them apart in the world of warriors. To go *i viking* meant "to plunder," and one who did this was called a *vikingr.*[2]

Though Viking ranks primarily consisted of Scandinavians (Danes, Swedes, Norwegians, Faroese, and Icelandic), they were frequently flecked with Anglo-Saxons, Bretons, Franks, Irishmen, and Slavs.[3] And, though our study centers upon the warrior, it must be said up front that Vikings brought far more to the world than buccaneering and brutality. In their three-hundred-year voyage across the global stage they shaped language, art, technology, trade, design, and government. They also left a treasure trove of poetry, prose, and mythology. Above all, they pushed the boundaries of nautical theory and the known world. By A.D. 1100, the Vikings had spanned seas from the Caspian to the North Atlantic and settled lands from Russia to Newfoundland, earning their place among the most courageous explorers and pioneers of history.

A New Enemy

The first wave of Viking raids (A.D. 789-834) sent shockwaves across Europe, making it clear from commoner to king that a new enemy had landed, one unbound by conventional thought or religious tradition. In A.D. 793, the English cleric Alcuin of York recounted the Vikings' most shocking attack to date: the sack of Lindisfarne. "Never before has such an atrocity been seen...as we have now suffered.... Such a voyage was not thought possible. The church of St. Cuthbert is spattered with the blood of the priests of God, stripped of all its furnishings, exposed to the plundering of pagans—a place more sacred than any in Britain."[4]

Shedding more light on the massacre, Symeon of Durham, an English monk, recorded, "They killed some of the brothers; some they took away with them in fetters; many they drove out, naked and loaded with insults; and some they drowned in the sea."[5] Finally, expert on Dark Age Europe, Dr. John Haywood, adds: "When Alcuin wrote of the attack, 'it was not believed that such a *voyage* was possible,' he was not expressing surprise at some…seafaring ability on the part of the Vikings…but shocked that God and the saints had not intervened to prevent it happening. If somewhere as holy as Lindisfarne was not safe, nowhere was!"[6]

The monastery of St. Cuthbert lay on the tiny island of Lindisfarne, just off the northeastern coast of modern-day England. Built by a succession of devout Celtic monks, it stood as a most holy place—a stronghold of Christian evangelism throughout the region and crown jewel in the kingdom of Northumbria. Up until this time, no one dared attack a religious institution—no European anyway. Vikings held no such taboos. Consequently, they escalated the volume of European warfare to unprecedented levels. Haywood notes: "Even in Ireland, the most anarchic region of western Christendom, the Vikings brought a great increase in the scale of violence. In the period 831-919, Irish sources record only sixteen instances of natives plundering and burning, compared to 110 by the Vikings."[7]

Vikings also plunged warfare into unfathomable depths of violence. Haywood cites one of the Viking's most malevolent misdeeds—the "blood eagle":

It is also from Scandinavian sources that we know of the "blood eagle," the Viking practice of killing captives by hacking through the ribcage on either side of the spine and then tearing the victim's lungs out. This horrific act, of which some historians are oddly reluctant to believe the Vikings' capable, may have been performed as a sacrifice to the warriors' god Odin.[8]

As if this horror were not enough to contemplate, Viking poets (ON., *skalds*) celebrated these ghastly acts and asserted that deities like *Hel*, goddess of the dead and daughter of the devilish *Loki*, joined in the revelry: "The destroyer of the Scots fed the wolves. Hel trod on the eagle's evening meal [of corpses]. The battle-cranes flew over the rows of the slain; the beaks of the birds of prey were not free from blood; the wolf tore wounds and waves of blood surged against the raven's beaks."[9] Where hideous reality left off, hellish poetry painted in the details.

Plundering monasteries, slaughtering priests, enslaving old and young, sacrificing men, women, and children, this was but a day's work for a Viking.[10] And, upon returning to camp, warriors celebrated the work with hoots and hollers, mead and maidens. Little wonder why a ninth-century prayer circulated among European churches: "Our supreme and holy Grace, protecting us and ours, deliver us, God, from the savage race of Northmen which lays waste our realms."[11] In His good time and glorious way, God would answer this humble prayer.

God's Viking

Why, though, have we followed Viking lore to such a grim place? Two biblical reasons: First, Scripture teaches that man's heart can plummet into the darkest fathoms, where only divine grace can reach (Jeremiah 17:9-10).[i] Part of God's breathtaking beauty, though, lies in so doing. While the Viking goddess Hel revels in her violence, the God of Heaven revels in His mercy. The prophet Micah asks: "Who is a God like you, pardoning iniquity and passing over transgression for the remnant of his inheritance? He does not retain his anger forever, because he delights in steadfast love. He will again have compassion on us; he will tread our iniquities underfoot. You will cast all our sins into the depths of the sea (Micah 7:18-19)." Mercy, and delighting in its show, is the core of the Gospel and a critical pillar in our warfare.

When man has gone overboard, drowning in the depths of his sin, God revels to reach out with mercy. "Where sin increased, grace abounded all the more (Romans 5:20b)." Before Christian soldiers can be deployed with full effect for the Captain's "deep-sea operations," they must come to love mercy as He does. Micah 6:8, NKJV, says, "He has shown you, O man, what is good; and what does the Lord require of you but to do justly, to love mercy, and to walk humbly with your God?" What amazing feats we could accomplish if we only grasped the depths of God's mercy upon us! How much more would we freely offer it to others (Matthew 10:8)?

---

i   *Romans 1:18-32; 5:20-21*

The second reason for rummaging through Viking barbarism is this: the worst sinners often make the greatest missionaries. Exhibit A: Saul of Tarsus. Saul ravaged the Early Church like a Viking in a medieval monastery. A proud Pharisee, Saul sneered and watched the coats of a religious wolfpack as they stoned Stephen,

Before Christian soldiers can be deployed with full effect for the Captain's "deep-sea operations," they must come to love mercy as He does.

the Church's first martyr (Acts 7:58; 8:1; 26:10). Discontented with spectating, he then marched house to house across Jerusalem in Gestapo-like fashion interrogating witnesses, dragging Christians to prison, punishing them in the synagogues, compelling them to blaspheme, and casting his vote for their deaths (8:1-3; 26:10-11).

Still thirsting for blood, Saul petitioned the Jewish High Priest to deputize him and his secret police to go to the synagogues of Damascus and repeat the same satanic purge of the followers of "the Way (Acts 9:1-2)." A jealous God guarding His young Church, however, held other designs. On the road, the Lord appeared and knocked Saul from his horse, announcing Himself as the one Saul had persecuted. Striking him with blindness, Jesus then ordered the militant tormentor to wait in the city till He sent word (Acts 9:3-9). For three days, this Early Church terrorist sat in sightless terror of his own, God's Spirit exposing his murderous heart and shattering his religious pride. Saul prayed like never before, and the God who revels in mercy revealed the truth of His Son (Acts 9:11).[II]

The Lord spoke to one of his trusted warriors in a vision, a man named Ananias. He told Ananias where Saul resided, what had happened, and His plans for the newfound follower—using him to spread the Gospel. Ananias went his way, laid his hands upon Saul, restored his sight (Acts 9:17), and the news soon spread like wildfire throughout the churches, "The one who used to persecute us is now preaching the very faith he tried to destroy (Galatians 1:23, NLT)." Across the Mediterranean world, by road and sea, horse and ship, Saul went *i víking* for God!

Striking Satan's kingdom like a thunderbolt, the man who became

---

ii   *Galatians 1:15-16*

known as Paul cast demons out of diviners disrupting the mission (Acts 13:9; 19:18); blinded sorcerers barring others from the Good News (Acts 13:8-12); had handkerchiefs and aprons from his body placed on the diseased for healing and the demonized for deliverance (Acts 19:11-12); raised the dead (Acts 20:7-12); preached to Jewish authorities (Acts 23), Roman principalities (Acts 24), and Greek philosophers (Acts 17); and became a veritable *skald*-poet of Scripture penning almost half of the New Testament. Paul's name disseminated in demon dens like Viking deeds in a mead hall. "Jesus I know, and Paul I recognize, but who are you?" a demon taunted seven unsaved men (Acts 19:13-15). The Church's most violent persecutor had become hell's most violent plunderer.

From Violent Bloodshed to Violent Faith

Christ taught His disciples they would face great violence, saying, "From the days of John the Baptist until now the kingdom of heaven has suffered violence, and the violent take it by force (Matthew 11:12)." In these words, the Great Teacher imparted two invaluable truths to the Christian warfare using a double entendre. He first pointed out that God's Kingdom suffered at the hands of violent people and would continue to do so. The preaching of John the Baptist heralded God's Kingdom. He was soon jailed by King Herod, however, and eventually beheaded for reproving his adulterous marriage to his brother Philip's wife (Mark 6:17, 21-29).[III]

Jesus had already been threatened with violence as murderous Jews sought to throw Him off a cliff on one occasion and stone Him on two others (Luke 4:29-30).[IV] Still, the greatest suffering ever lay just ahead, as Jew and Gentile would band together to pummel His body beyond recognition and crucify Him as the worst of criminals (Isaiah 50:6).[V] Violent men sought to stop the advance of God's Kingdom through devilish deeds. This was the ugly part of Christ's twofold lesson.

The beautiful part lay in the fact that, from John's to Jesus' ministry, massive crowds pressed into God's Kingdom like a fortress under siege. They'd come to the Jordan River in thralls to be baptized by John (Matthew 3).

---

iii   Luke 3:19
iv   John 8:59; 10:31-32; 11:7-8
v   Isaiah 52:14; 53:4-5; Luke 22:63-70; 23

Now, they mobbed Jesus for healing (4:23-24), gathered on mountainsides to hear Him (5:1), and tore roofs from houses just to get at Him (Mark 2:4). Though trampled by uncaring crowds, they pushed through to touch the hem of His garment (5:27); though scolded by indifferent onlookers, they screamed for His attention (Matthew 9:27); and, though judged by cold religionists, they wept at His feet for forgiveness of sins (Luke 7:36-50). "The violent take it by force," Jesus said, speaking also of the emotionally violent response many experienced at His Gospel's revelation of mercy.

When Jesus opened his blind eyes, Saul reacted similarly, going "all-in" with a faith that ransacked hell. Being forgiven much of such evil and violence as he'd done to Jesus' followers, Saul, who became Paul, loved and followed with even greater abandon, just as the Lord once said to another sneering Pharisee (Luke 7:42-43). And Paul soon faced violence himself in whippings, beatings, stoning, imprisonments, shipwreck, and more (2 Corinthians 6:4-10).

The crazed and violent Gadarene demoniac also experienced an earth-shaking conversion when Jesus, in a moment, cast a legion of demons out of him, healing years of torment. The newly reborn and crushingly grateful man then turned at Christ's command and spread the Good News across ten neighboring cities (Mark 5:1-20)! Equally, the Samaritan woman at the well underwent mighty transformation as the Lord gently, prophetically unpacked her ravished life and offered a new one. Instantly, she forgot her water pot, ran to tell the entire city, led many to Jesus' feet, *and* paved the way for even more to come later (John 4:1-42).[vi]

Yes, Scripture proves that the greatest of sinners can become God's mightiest soldiers, and murderous Viking monarchs like Harald Bluetooth and Olaf Tryggvason would prove no exception to the rule.

Sagas, Signs, & Wonders

In his work *Heimskringla* (ON., "The Circle of the Earth") the thirteenth-century Icelandic poet and politician Snorri Sturluson recorded the *sagas* ("utterances") of Norwegian kings.[12] Relating the Viking King Harald Bluetooth's Christian conversion, he said:

---

vi   *Acts 8:4-8*

A saintly bishop, Poppo by name, preached the faith before Harald, and to show the truth thereof bare he a glowing iron in his hand, and Harald testified that the hand of the holy man was unscarred by the heated iron. Thereafter was Harald himself baptized with the whole of the Danish host that were with him.... So, the King sent a message to the Earl to come to him, and...compelled him also that he should be baptized. After this manner was the Earl made a Christian, and all his men with him. Thereafter did the King appoint him priests and other learned men and commanded him to cause all the people of Norway to be baptized into the faith....[13]

Just as Paul's miracles confounded the Corinthians and brought many to the Gospel, Poppo's "sign of the glowing iron" astonished Harald's mind and opened his heart (1 Corinthians 2:1-5).[vii] Viking King Olaf Tryggvason fell to the Faith in like manner. Following the death of his wife, Geira, Olaf set out to drown his sorrows in typical Norse fashion: he went *i víking*. Four years later, he landed on the Isles of Scilly, just off the southwestern tip of present-day England. Nicknamed "Crowbone" for his habit of reading the omens, Olaf became intrigued on hearing of a local monk's prophetic powers and decided to test them by sending someone disguised as himself.[14] When Olaf's man arrived and announced himself as the great king, the prophet answered: "A king you are not, but my counsel to you is be loyal to yours!" The would-be monarch returned, relayed the encounter, and King Olaf left to meet the unknown seer.

As they dined, the monk predicted that Olaf would go down in history as a "glorious king" and bring many to Faith. First, however, he'd face an assassination attempt, be borne back to his ship on a shield, recover after seven days, and be baptized. When the events unfolded as the prophet foretold, Olaf returned and asked, "Where did you get this wisdom?" The mysterious monk then preached of God and His "mighty works." Olaf and his men were baptized, stayed several months, "learned the true Faith," and left with a "train" of "priests and other learned men" to share the Good News.[15]

Christ's Gospel transformed Saul from the Church's violent persecutor

vii   *2 Corinthians 12:12*

80

into a light to the Gentiles, and it turned Harald Bluetooth and Olaf Tryggvason into beacons to the Scandinavians (Acts 13:46-48).[16] To Satan's dismay, the Norse invasion, which brought unprecedented hell to Europe, brought a heavenly invasion to Scandinavia, and it began when axe-brandishing Vikings encountered a lightning-fisted Christ through sign-wielding Christians.

A Duel of Deities

At the end of Mark's Gospel, Jesus commanded His disciples:

> "Go into all the world and proclaim the gospel to the whole creation. Whoever believes and is baptized will be saved, but whoever does not believe will be condemned. And these signs will accompany those who believe: in my name they will cast out demons; they will speak in new tongues; they will pick up serpents with their hands; and if they drink any deadly poison, it will not hurt them; they will lay their hands on the sick, and they will recover." And they went out and preached everywhere, while the Lord worked with them and confirmed the message by accompanying signs. (Mark 16:15-18, 20)[17]

As the disciples went out to preach, Jesus promised to confirm His Gospel through signs, wonders, and miracles (Acts 2:22).[VIII] This is precisely what we see in the Book of Acts, and when Vikings invaded Europe centuries later, the God of wonders had not left the business. Bishop Poppo's sign and the unknown monk's prophecy hold a valuable lesson modern Christian soldiers must not miss.

If these holy men had led with, "Hey, big guy! Jesus loves you, and His body was broken for you," they would've been met with a blank Viking stare or worse. "This God of yours was crushed and crucified by His foes? Ha! We have no need of your puny god, priest!" Strap on a Norseman's boots for a moment, which were routinely bathed in his foes' blood. What use would a plundering, skull-crushing Viking see for Christianity's pulverized Savior? But a red-hot iron not burning one's hand, a detailed prophecy

---

fulfilled—these signs would've held the same weight as a *hólmgäng*: a Viking duel to the death. Except, this was a dual between deities.

When first-century audiences wrestled over Christ's identity, His miracles often ended the debate.[18] John 6:14 notes: "When the people saw the sign that he had done, they said, 'This is indeed the Prophet who is to come into the world!'" The bishop's sign and the monk's fulfilled prophecy instantly scrapped the Norse pantheon for Harald and Olaf. Their hearts opened to hear of a Heavenly Father who could shatter All-Father Odin's spear with a glance (Psalm 46:8-9)[ix], an Only Son whose thunder would make Thor Odinson wet himself (2 Samuel 22:14-16)[x]; and a Risen Lord who'd stepped on Loki's neck, seized Hel by her throat, and snatched her keys (Colossians 2:15)![xi]

Signs and wonders won scores of first-century skeptics and Vikings from the ninth to eleventh centuries. By the mid-eleventh century, Christian churches were replacing pagan altars across Scandinavia, and not just because Vikings like King Olaf forced Christianity on the defeated as some have alleged. Dr. Peter Hammond of Frontline Fellowship notes:

> The Vikings came to be convinced that the Christian God is more powerful than all other gods. They saw how He answered the prayers of the Christians. They witnessed miracles. They saw how Christian kings and missionaries were able to destroy idols and defy the heathen gods and taboos—without suffering any ill effects. They saw their pagan gods were powerless before the all-powerful Jesus Christ. Christ was honored and worshiped as the mighty Warrior who had triumphed over the powers of death, hell, and the grave.... The prominence of the Cross in every Scandinavian flag serves as a dramatic testimony to the conversion of the Vikings.[19]

I wonder how many heathen altars would be overturned if our world witnessed the twenty-first century Church wielding power like the first-century one or Viking-era Christians? We must recognize that, no different than

---

ix   *Matthew 6:9; James 1:17*
x   *Matthew 8:26-27*
xi   *Hebrews 2:14; Revelation 1:18*

Vikings, many today must first meet the Mighty Warrior God before seeing their need for the Merciful Savior. They must learn, as Paul said, that "the kingdom of God is not a matter of talk but of power (1 Corinthians 4:20, NIV)."

It's time to be done then with religious excuses and half-baked theology that has left saints powerless before demons and anemic in a pagan culture.

The sign-working God of Scripture and Vikings lives still. He has not changed, nor did the completion of His Book spell an end to His miracle ministry (Malachi 3:6).[XII] The supernatural gifts seen in Acts and taught in 1 Corinthians 12 have not "passed away" because "the perfect" has not come; we have yet to see Christ "face-to-face" and "know fully, even as we are fully known (1 Corinthians 13:8-12)." It's time to be done then with religious excuses and half-baked theology that has left saints powerless before demons and anemic in a pagan culture.[20] As the Scottish theologian James S. Stewart once said, "[I]t is no use, in a day when spirit forces of passionate evil have been unleashed upon the earth and when fierce emotions are tearing the world apart, it is no use having a milk-and-water passionless theology: no good setting a tepid Christianity against a scorching paganism. The thrust of the demonic has to be met with the fire of the divine."[21] The primary problem is not that God didn't promise the Church of all ages power to witness (Luke 24:49).[XIII] He did! The issue is what once limited Jesus' own ministry: unbelief. One of the most stunning statements in the Gospels remains, "And he [Jesus] did not do many mighty works there, because of their unbelief (Matthew 13:58)." How many mighty works have we not seen because of ours?

Over the years, Ralana and I have seen many miracles—from dislocated limbs to torn ligaments, bursitis to arthritis, speech impediments to emphysema, manic depression to epilepsy, sexually transmitted disease to Lou Gehrig's disease, massive tumors to terminal cancer. Yes, there have also been many instances where God did not heal. We had to wrestle with disappointment, examine ourselves, and search the Scriptures like every

---

xii   Hebrews 13:8; 1 Corinthians 13:8-10
xiii   Acts 1:8

other believer. In all candor, our faith wasn't always as strong; we're sure there were times that hindered God's hand.

In the larger biblical view, though, we must recognize that, often, someone has simply reached the end of his days. Nothing can be done. Elisha was a mighty miracle-working prophet, but not even he could hold death at bay when his time came (2 Kings 13:14).[xiv] At other times, the Sovereign God holds a grander purpose than we can presently see. Occasionally, it's to heal at a later moment and unveil His glory in a greater way (Job 1-2; 42).[xv] In other cases, He withholds healing but gives willing receivers an extra measure of grace to bear up under it, along with a powerful testimony—like Paul, the New Testament's greatest miracle worker after Jesus Himself (2 Corinthians 12:7-10). Finally, sickness can come as a chastisement, by natural consequences or divine direction, and prod the afflicted toward wiser, holier living (John 5:14).[xvi]

Not one of these scenarios, however, excuses Christians from praying for healing in Scripture.[22] We need to come clean with God: many of us just don't ask because we're afraid His answer will be, "No" (John 14:13-14).[xvii] We have not because we ask not (James 4:2). Or, we ask once or twice but fail to persevere as Jesus taught (1 Kings 18:42-46).[xviii] We don't connect the biblical dots of praying months or years for breakthrough. Imagine how many miracles we would see if we enjoined extended fasts with our prayers, rather than create doctrines enshrining our unbelief (Isaiah 58).[xix] I prayed fervently for God to save my marriage; the answer came four years later. I prayed unceasingly for my father's salvation; he came to the Lord after fifteen years—one week before he passed! How glad I am for God's grace to fast and persevere in prayer!

So, our miracle discussion returns to square one: unbelief. When our faith falters, we need to strengthen it by meditating on God's Word. "Faith comes from hearing, and hearing through the word of Christ,"

---

xiv   John 11:4
xv   2 Kings 20:1-11; John 9:3; 11:4
xvi   Romans 1:27; 1 Corinthians 11:30
xvii   John 16:24; 2 Timothy 1:7
xviii Luke 11:9-12; 18:1-8; John 15:7; James 5:13-16
xix   Matthew 17:21

and faith is what He'll be looking for at His return (Psalm 1:1-3).[xx] If this stirs something within you, start memorizing verses on healing or others relating to your circumstances. You never know what mission God has in store or what miracle He waits to perform. His eyes scour the earth for brave, believing souls to be His shining lights and healing hands (2 Chronicles 16:9).[xxi] Has He called you as a light to a special people, to a work requiring a crazy, Viking-kind of faith? Then prepare to meet one of history's most dreaded soldiers.

The Kingdom Shock Trooper

A multitude of words coloring contemporary English come from the mouths of our crazy Norse brothers. Our word "berserk" originates from the most vicious of Viking warriors: the *berserkr*, their version of the modern-day *shock trooper*. Shock troopers play a vital role in military strategy. Possessing uncommon valor, skill, and more advanced training or equipment, a shock trooper's job is simple: make a way where none exists.

Like other Old Norse words, *berserkr* originates from multiple sources. It first comes from their word for "bear" (*bjorn*) and *serkr*, meaning "shirt" or "coat." The *berserkr* shrouded himself in bear's or wolf's fur and dark face paint, giving him a fierce, otherworldly appearance. Secondly, *berserkr* derives from the term *berserkrgäng*—a raging, bestial state sought before combat by drinking an unknown concoction of herbs and/or alcohol. *Berserkrgäng* augmented battle fury to seemingly superhuman levels, making warriors almost impervious to pain.

Finally, a *berserkr* fanatically followed Odin, head of the Norse pantheon and god of war, wisdom, death, and destruction. In accordance with his demands for costly sacrifice, the *berserkr* remained ready to lay down his life. In fact, he longed for a valiant battlefield death as it was the only way to *Valhalla*, the heavenly "Hall of the Fallen," where slain warriors joined Odin and other mighty ancients in revelry.[23] In Viking sagas, Odin shape-shifted into various creatures. Many Viking foes also believed that berserkers shape-shifted into beasts like the god they worshiped. The concept of the werewolf (a half-human, half-wolf) holds kindred ties here.

---

xx   *Joshua 1:8; Luke 18:8; Romans 10:17*
xxi   *Acts 9:17; 13:47*

One of the most terrifying soldiers to Satan's kingdom remains the Kingdom berserker—the man or woman of uncommon faith.

Combine these elements now and imagine whirling around on the field as you hear hair-rising howls behind you. You turn to catch sight of a horde of hulking, animal-like forms hurtling toward you with axes, spears, and swords. Your eyes search for faces, but all you see beneath furs of black, gray, and brown are gleaming white eyes. By the time you've braced, the pack of screaming banshees leap into your company's shields and blood begins to flow. Quite understandably, the shield-biting *berserkr* terrified his enemies.[24]

I now offer that one of the most terrifying soldiers to Satan's kingdom remains the Kingdom berserker—the man or woman of uncommon faith. In Scripture, this spiritual shock trooper is that one person crazy enough to trust God, to step out of the boat of the familiar and comfortable and make the sacrifice that brings breakthrough. This person's life often bears marks of valor, knowledge, life experience, or skill setting him/her into a unique class.

Kingdom berserkers understand the fear of failure and loss, but prayerfully push it aside with a powerful devotion to God, implicit trust in His Word, and a burning vision of some Kingdom-advancing exploit. It calls to them in the night (Acts 16:9). They talk of it, write about it—can't shut up about it because God's Spirit won't either. Like Jeremiah, fire is in their bones, and every fiber of their being screams, "They're made for this (Jeremiah 1:5; 20:9)."[xxii] If they don't heed the call, they'll be miserable.

Kingdom berserkers prayerfully "shape-shift" also, making serious sacrifices and adjustments to morph their lives around God's vision. They give up luxury and comfort.[25] They invest large sums of time, talent, and treasure for the call.[26] They're out to please God—not man—and won't allow selfish, carnal loved ones to hinder or kill a Kingdom work.[27] Most of all, berserkers deny themselves and will risk life and limb to win souls.[28] As Paul said:

---

xxii   *Romans 12:29; Ephesians 2:10; Philippians 2:13*

For though I am free from all, I have made myself a servant to all, that I might win more of them. To the Jews I became as a Jew…. To those under the law I became as one under the law…. To those outside the law I became as one outside the law…. To the weak I became weak…. I have become all things to all people, that by all means I might save some. I do it all for the sake of the gospel, that I may share with them in its blessings. (1 Corinthians 9:19-23)

Paul became more than a Kingdom Viking. He went full-blown ber-serker! Proverbs 11:30b says, "Whoever captures souls is wise," and Paul's soul-capturing wisdom displayed itself in a willingness to shape-shift his life, sacrificing whatever was necessary to save just one (Acts 20:24). Can we say the same? See, evangelism's greatest barrier lies not with the world or Satan's army but the Christian's unwillingness to adjust his/her life to follow God. It was to a believer insisting on his own way that Jesus said, "Get behind Me, Satan!"

From that time Jesus began to show his disciples that he must go to Jerusalem and suffer many things…and be killed, and on the third day be raised. And Peter took him aside and began to rebuke him, saying, "Far be it from you, Lord! This shall never happen to you." But he turned and said to Peter, "Get behind me, Satan! You are a hindrance to me. For you are not setting your mind on the things of God, but on the things of man."

Then Jesus told his disciples, "If anyone would come after me, let him deny himself and take up his cross and follow me. For whoever would save his life will lose it, but whoever loses his life for my sake will find it. For what will it profit a man if he gains the whole world and forfeits his soul? Or what shall a man give in return for his soul? (Matthew 16:21-26)

What are we willing to give up to become what God destined us to be? How far will we go to follow Him, fulfill

Evangelism's greatest barrier lies not with the world or Satan's army but the Christian's unwillingness to adjust his/her life to follow God.

Faith is the piston of the Christian life, transferring the Holy Spirit's power into action to drive God's Kingdom forward.

a heavenly vision, and reach the lost? One thing is certain: To go *i víking* with our Great Chief and plunder hell's coasts we must berserk, casting aside our fears and selfishness and "shape-shift" our lives in humility and faith.

The Driving Force of the Kingdom

Hebrews 11 records the Bible's greatest discourse on faith, and its first verse gives us a wonderful definition: "Now faith is the substance of things hoped for; the evidence of things not seen." It then tells us that it was by faith, by trusting God, that our biblical forefathers "obtained a good report"—His approval (v. 3). The Greek New Testament word for "faith" is *pistis*—where we derive our English "piston," the working cog in an engine cylinder which transfers the force of expanding gases to the crankshaft creating motion. Without a piston, there is no motion; and without faith there is no Kingdom action. Faith is the piston of the Christian life, transferring the Holy Spirit's power into action to drive God's Kingdom forward.

In terms of our Viking discussion, faith is Christian *berserkgäng*. Remember that *berserkgäng* came as the result of some unknown concoction of herbs and/or alcohol. Upon consumption, it plunged the Viking into a frenzy, fearlessly hurled him into enemy ranks, and rendered him virtually invulnerable. Similarly, faith floods the Kingdom soldier with a fiery passion to follow Jesus; imbues him with heroic courage to charge forward, trusting what God has said; and endows him with supernatural fury to fight hell and suffer well for God's purposes.

The rest of Hebrews 11, often dubbed the "Roll Call of Faith," remains one of Scripture's most inspiring passages, especially for embattled Christian soldiers. It reads much like an Icelandic *saga*, the Viking prose which recounted warrior exploits. Listen:

> How much more do I need to say? It would take too long to recount the stories of the faith of Gideon, Barak, Samson, Jephthah, David, Samuel, and all the prophets. By faith these people overthrew kingdoms, ruled with justice, and received what God had promised them. They shut the

mouths of lions, quenched the flames of fire, and escaped death by the edge of the sword. Their weakness was turned to strength. They became strong in battle and put whole armies to flight. Women received their loved ones back again from death.

But others were tortured, refusing to turn from God in order to be set free. They placed their hope in a better life after the resurrection. Some were jeered at, and their backs were cut open with whips. Others were chained in prisons. Some died by stoning, some were sawed in half, and others were killed with the sword. Some went about wearing skins of sheep and goats, destitute and oppressed and mistreated. They were too good for this world, wandering over deserts and mountains, hiding in caves and holes in the ground. (Hebrews 11:32-40, NLT)

In nine verses, God reveals His mystical concoction for transforming believers into heavenly berserkers. Faith enabled Kingdom soldiers of old to charge hell, save souls, free captives, and fell kingdoms. But, like the Viking sagas, faith didn't always lead to "happy endings." Often, faith manifested as a supernatural "No!" to renouncing Christ and to endure the hellish pain which followed—to be whipped but keep witnessing, to be spat upon yet continue serving, or face death without flinching. Faith believes God for the impossible but trusts Him, regardless of where the path leads.

The Deep and Uncharted Waters

Hebrews 11:6 says, "And without faith it is impossible to please him, for whoever would draw near to God must believe that he exists and that he rewards those who seek him." In the life of every Kingdom Viking who would dare to follow God in a heavenly vision (Acts 26:19), there comes a "shoving-off point"—a moment where one must choose to "berserk," to cut the mooring lines of common and comfortable and press out into faith's uncharted waters. Kingdom exploits are never accomplished by timid souls splashing around in the Christian kiddie pool. God works His wonders in the deep, where faith faces impossible odds and only He can save the day.

Some went down to the sea in ships, doing business on the great waters; they saw the deeds of the LORD, his wondrous works in the deep. For he commanded and raised the stormy wind, which lifted up the waves of the sea. They mounted up to heaven; they went down to the depths; their courage melted away in their evil plight; they reeled and staggered like drunken men and were at their wits' end. Then they cried to the LORD in their trouble, and he delivered them from their distress. He made the storm be still, and the waves of the sea were hushed. Then they were glad that the waters were quiet, and he brought them to their desired haven. Let them thank the LORD for his steadfast love, for his wondrous works to the children of man! (Psalm 107:23-31)

That is not the safe harbor of our cozy couch, the church's four familiar walls, "how it's always been done," or the aromatic atmosphere of the coffee shop. That is the impossible waters of faith, which translates to those following God experiencing distress, risk, the possibility of embarrassment, failure, loss, and death. This is the Christian berserker's job, and if we are to become vessels for the Master's use, we must reach the place where we embrace it like Paul.

So to keep me from becoming conceited because of the surpassing greatness of the revelations, a thorn was given me in the flesh, a messenger of Satan to harass me, to keep me from becoming conceited. Three times I pleaded with the Lord about this, that it should leave me. But he said to me, "My grace is sufficient for you, for my power is made perfect in weakness." Therefore I will boast all the more gladly of my weaknesses, so that the power of Christ may rest upon me. For the sake of Christ, then, I am content with weaknesses, insults, hardships, persecutions, and calamities. For when I am weak, then I am strong. (2 Corinthians 12:7-10)

Paul wrote from a place of profound vision, power, and revelation. But the Only Wise God coupled that with a place of weakness, pain, and hardship to keep him humble and dependent. This is the double-edged sword of the Viking call: the Christian who faithfully follows in obedience to a heavenly vision will experience a crow's nest height of intimacy with

God and miracles which make him/her shout His praise. This is the fun part! In His love and wisdom, though, God typically lashes that bliss to a set of sovereignly orchestrated circumstances, which keep the Christian soldier's nose pressed to the deck in prayer. This is the tough part, the sifting floor where the Lord separates fans from followers, Christian preschool from spiritual adulthood.

Anyone can hang out with Jesus, chitchat, and sip wine with Him while He heals broken lives or feeds the five thousand. It takes a berserking valor, however, to stay the course with Him to the Cross (Luke 9:10-27). God's Kingdom advances upon the shoulders of those willing to trust what He's said and sacrifice life and limb to see it through.

A Longship Faith

Let's round out our lesson now with one final illustration. Billowing the sails of Viking exploits was an ingeniously designed warcraft. Curved from stem to stern (front to back) like an archer's bow and constructed using their signature lapstrake technique of overlapping planks, the *langskip's* ("longship") hull was amazingly flexible, durable, lightweight, barely resting in the water.[29] *Langskip* sizes began around fifty feet, ranged up to approximately one hundred fifty in length, and stretched only some eight to eighteen feet wide—a long and lean build. Finally, the *langskip* employed the power of oar and sail. Together, these masterful strokes allowed the vessel to glide across the water, flex in rough seas, maneuver in tight and shallow channels, speed in stealthily for attack, and vanish before foes could respond. *Langskip* names then—like *Long Serpent, Oar Steed,* and *Surf Dragon*—made perfect sense. As author Jason Greenling pointed out, "No other civilization of the time could rival Viking shipbuilding."[30]

In the same way, the Kingdom soldier who wants to be used for God's berserking exploits of evangelism, healing, and freedom must also have a flexible faith, a lightweight life, and a durable devotion. We are of no use to God when we're so stuck in our own ways that we cannot try new measures to win souls; so weighted down with worldly cares and

God's Kingdom advances upon the shoulders of those willing to trust what He's said and sacrifice life and limb to see it through.

comforts that we can't follow Him onto the mission field; or so shallow that we give up because of hardship.

Hear me: I understand well the fear, risk, and pain which come with the Viking voyage—one you may be contemplating or recovering from right now. But, I'm here to tell you: it's worth it! Ralana and I would not trade a single thing we had to sacrifice over the years because we said, "Yes!" to God. Again, Paul said: "But whatever gain I had, I counted as loss for the sake of Christ. Indeed, I count everything as loss because of the surpassing worth of knowing Christ Jesus my Lord. For his sake I have suffered the loss of all things and count them as rubbish, in order that I may gain Christ (Philippians 3:7-8)."

The Greek word rendered "rubbish" means "thrown to the dogs," referring to everything from table scraps to excrement.[31] Paul said that anything placed next to knowing Jesus is trash or dung in comparison. Oh, if we could only catch a glimpse—or whiff—of the waste we clutch so tightly versus the glory which calls us! When we pass from this life, we'll take nothing with us but the good we've done in Christ and the souls we've won (Job 1:21).[xxiii] Yet we constantly allow fear, unbelief, and the most trivial things to moor us to the shore of status quo Christianity. In light of being purchased by Christ's blood, it's a disgrace.

God made us for a brave, adventurous faith, and there's unspeakable joy and peace when we follow Him into the impossible depths (Joshua 1:6-9).[xxiv] And, truly, we'll never find peace until we have the salt of the missional sea in our face because we finally obeyed and took the plunge. Nor will we ever see the "deeds of the Lord"—His power, miracles, and "wondrous works in the deep" until we're "doing business on the great waters (Psalms 107:23-24)." The uncomfortable, the unknown, the impossible—that is where God dwells, and where He beckons His vision-following Vikings.

A few years ago, God called Ralana and me back to the mission field. After attending a retreat where I taught on biblical manhood, a senior pastor friended me on social media. He began following my devotional-oriented posts, and I began reading his—watching all the happenings of his sweet congregation. As I headed to bed late one night, the Holy Spirit spoke to

---

xxiii *1 Corinthians 3:10-15; 1 Timothy 6:7*
xxiv   *Philippians 4:6-7; 1 Peter 1:7-9*

me, "Ask him if he needs help." Now, this man and I had never texted, talked on the phone, nor had he posted one thing on social media indicating a need for a new staff member. I knew Father was speaking to me, though (John 10:27). So, I obeyed, typed out a quick message, and went to bed.

The following morning my friend messaged me back, "Wow! I'm flattered that you would ask. Yes, as a matter of fact, we are looking for help. Let me touch base here, and I'll get back with you soon." Months later—after many phone calls, prayers, lunches, confirmations through visions, counsel from trusted friends, and daily Bible readings—the Lord made His will clear. To obey Him, however, required selling virtually everything we had, moving almost 150 miles, and starting over again at middle age. The house we'd intended to retire in one day—it had to go. Ralana's job and benefits she'd worked hard to achieve, my position with a ministry which had touched thousands—both went to the altar.
Following the Lord in this vision also meant moving away from our daughters, who were in college, other family members like Ralana's mother, a sister, a grandfather, and the city we were born in and loved. We had to find a new home for our chubby, gray kitty, funnel our lives from a two-story house into a small apartment, and take a heavy hit in income. We lived apart from each other for six months—Ralana, back home training a replacement and selling things; me, in a barn's efficiency apartment and starting the new job. Initially, after Sunday services, I commuted home to help pack. Later, we alternated as Ralana visited to help in the service. All of this happened as we waited for a new apartment to become available.

Finally, after having served as a children's, men's, interim worship, creative arts, college and career, and small groups pastor, what was God's assignment? Was it a senior pastorate or some other executive role? No. It was children's pastoring again. I say this because, through man's carnal lens of career and accomplishment, that's a demotion. "Why, one is supposed to climb the ladder of wealth, position, and power—not stoop to wipe noses, sing songs, and tell Bible stories!" That, my friend, is the mindset Jesus confronted in Peter when He said, "Get behind Me, Satan! You're a hindrance to Me...(Matthew 16:23)." God does not see as man sees (1 Samuel 16:7). With Him, up is down; last is first (Isaiah 55:8-9).[xxv] Through His Word, we can walk in that truth, and I'm grateful that Ralana and I did when He called.

So, what plunder came from renovating our heavier lives into a flexible, lightweight *langskip* for God? The first breakthrough came with staff and member children of many years. Children who'd grown up in that church and devout Christian homes experienced powerful encounters with Jesus and came to salvation. Next, literally *every* child who visited us—without fail—prayed to receive Jesus as Lord. By the end of two years, we saw 201 decisions for Christ!

Now, I'll say it again: Ralana and I wouldn't trade a single thing we had to sacrifice to say, "Yes!" to God. Compared to knowing and following Jesus, seeing Him transform those tiny hearts, everything else was *skúbalon*—scraps and waste. And, at the end of that two years, God called us back home. So, Ralana and I got to reunite with our girls and her family. I also saw my younger brother surrender his life to the Lord and find healing from thirty years of alcoholism! Ralana and I went *i víking* with the Lord, and He kept His promise in the Gospels to the letter:

> "Yes," Jesus replied, "and I assure you that everyone who has given up house or brothers or sisters or mother or father or children or property, for my sake and for the Good News, will receive now in return a hundred times as many houses, brothers, sisters, mothers, children, and property—along with persecution. And in the world to come that person will have eternal life. (Mark 10:29-30, NLT)

But what besides warfare did Vikings do with their *langskips*? The Icelandic sagas record not just Viking martial exploits but maritime explorations after their salvation. King Olaf Tryggvason, who came to Christ after the unknown monk's prophecy, baptized the explorer Leif Erikson and commissioned him with the Gospel. Leif reached North America five hundred years before Columbus and built its very first church on his farm in Newfoundland. His mother, Thjodhild, converted to Christianity

---

xxv   *Matthew 20:16*

and founded Greenland's first church at Brattahlid. His daughter-in-law, Gudrid Thorbjarnadottir, founded convents in Iceland after a pilgrimage to Rome. By the twelfth century, Norse gods from Norway to North America were bowing before the Galilean Storm God and the hammer of His Word (Jeremiah 23:29).[xxvi]

Christian soldier, by the inkwell of faith or unbelief, we now write our sagas. When you stand before Christ and yours is read, will it recount a lightweight life and shape-shifting obedience? Will soldiers in God's Hall hear of a berserking faith that plundered Satan's kingdom? Like the Vikings, we are but a flash in the pages of history. May our faith then be violent against hell's gates and our longboats swift for Heaven!

Tactical Takeaways

1. In this chapter, we explored Viking violence and plunder. This led to a discussion of Saul's persecution of the Church and how Christ's Gospel transformed him and the Vikings. Are there "Vikings" in your life who seem beyond God's grace? Do you pray for them? Read Luke 18:1-8 and 1 Timothy 2:1-4. Pray, listen, and talk to God about this.

2. Miracles played a pivotal role in Early Church and Viking evangelism. Do they still hold one in evangelism today? Why or why not? Has *cessationism*, the belief that certain spiritual gifts ceased with the Apostolic Age, impacted modern-day evangelism? Explain.

3. Has God ever called you to follow Him "into the deep," to a vision requiring great faith and sacrifice? How did you respond? How did the mission end? Is there a new one He's speaking into you? Is a fear of failure or love of comfort giving you pause? Ponder, pray, and journal.

---

xxvi   *Matthew 8:23-27*

BOOK IV

CHARGE OF THE KNIGHT

Hear our prayers, we beseech thee O Lord, and deign, with the right hand of your Majesty, to bless this sword with which your servant desires to be girded, so that he may be the defender of churches, of widows, of orphans, and of servants of God, against the barbarity, ferocity and cruelty of pagans and heretics; may it be the terror and fear of traitors and all those who lay snares for him. Through Christ our Lord. Amen.

—*THE PONTIFICALE ROMANUM*, A BOOK OF ROMAN CATHOLIC LITURGY

How long will you judge unjustly and show partiality to the wicked? Selah. Give justice to the weak and the fatherless; maintain the right of the afflicted and the destitute. Rescue the weak and the needy; deliver them from the hand of the wicked.

—ASAPH, PSALM 82:2-4

The tale of Europe's armored, lance-wielding warrior romanticized in the legends of King Arthur is not quite so simple or gallant at times. Nor do the concepts of chivalry, questing for sacred grails, and combating sinister evils originate from cozy cottages where "they all lived happily ever after." No, these themes, which have captured imaginations and made hearts swoon for centuries, arise from smoldering ruins where countless families lost everything, blood-soaked battlegrounds where thousands of men gave their lives, and plague-infested infirmaries where multitudes faced excruciating deaths. For millions, this was fifth-to fifteenth-century Europe, and from this seething cauldron emerged one of the world's most iconic fighting figures: the *knight*—an imposing combination of soldier, steed, and spirituality.

The medieval cavalier was not always feared for the right reasons, though, and to some no warrior image stands more distorted. But if that claim is true, where did the shining symbol of mercy and justice originate? Is there truth to the knight's tale or is it only the stuff of fables? Mount up, fellow soldier. Our quest begins in the fifth century—the real "once upon a time."

Fall of An Empire

August 24, A.D. 410. For over one hundred years, the Western Roman Empire has buckled beneath the weight of a divided realm,[1] barbarian invasions,[2] economic depression, decimating pandemics,[3] and political upheaval.[4] Now, the great city languishes under siege, and outside her walls the grim reaper awaits. Months ago, the Visigoth army of King Alaric I surrounded Rome cutting off all supply lines. Little by little, he has choked the city into submission. Reduced to cannibalism, her citizens can bear no more. A gate creaks open, the Visigoths enter, and they ravish the mother of nations. Smoke billows into the heavens. Streets stream with blood. Multiplied thousands of injured, widowed, and orphaned refugees pour into the countryside.

For Western Europe, this was a watershed moment. Mighty Rome, who'd ruled over her for five hundred years, now thrashed with a mortal wound. Every enemy pressing at her borders smelled blood in the water. By A.D. 476, Rome's last emperor was deposed, and Western Europe's fate lay in the hands of a dozen barbarian warlords vying for a piece like sharks in a feeding frenzy.

The fall of Rome's Western Empire struck Europe like an atomic bomb, ripping through all levels of society. Western Europe's central government, medicine, and education disappeared. Vital infrastructure (roads, bridges, sewers, aqueducts) deteriorated. An already troubled trade network, from North Africa to Southern France, dissolved. The Dark Ages, one of the most turbulent eras in human history, had begun.[5]

A Light in the Dark Ages

As Western Rome shattered, her eastern Christian empire, Byzantium, had been warring with Persia for almost two centuries.[6] But when Emperor Justinian I came to power, an apocalyptic series of global weather events erupted.[7] From A.D. 526-588 massive earthquakes and tsunamis rocked eastern Byzantium,[8] leveling cities, igniting fires, destroying ship fleets, and claiming up to 250,000 people in one catastrophe alone.[9] Additionally, the Medieval Warm Period (A.D. 536-550), possibly sparked by volcanic and/or meteoric activity, caused devastating droughts[10] and famine from Peru to as far as China.[11]

Still, Byzantium's nightmare continued. The deadly bubonic plague struck in 541. By 543, it swept the empire and neighboring Persia, claiming ten thousand people a day[12] and twenty-five million by century's end.[13] Just as it seemed God had forsaken Europe, however, the light began to shine. Speaking on Rome's collapse in his commentary on Ezekiel, Saint Jerome wrote:[14]

> Who would believe…that we should every day be receiving in this holy Bethlehem men and women who once were noble and abounding in every kind of wealth but are now reduced to poverty?… [T]he sight of the wanderers, coming in crowds, caused us deep pain; and we therefore abandoned…almost all study and were filled with a longing to turn the words of Scripture into action and not to say holy things but to do them….[15]

> There is not a single hour…in which we are not relieving crowds of brethren, and the quiet of the monastery has been changed into the

bustle of a guest house.... [T]he holy places, crowded as they are with penniless fugitives, naked and wounded, plainly reveal the ravages of the barbarians. We cannot see what has occurred, without tears and moans. Who would have believed that mighty Rome, with its careless security of wealth, would...need shelter, food, and clothing?[16]

With Europe collapsing and no central government, hotels or halfway houses, social security or soup kitchens, God's Church threw open her doors and Christ's arms. A monastery, a place of mere religious study, became a haven for refugees, the injured, and hungry. Jerome's words seemed almost a flashpoint. For as the Dark Ages descended on Europe, Christian charity sprang up like a brush-fire. Churches and abbeys became hostels for the pilgrim and destitute, institutions restoring learning and literacy, infirmaries caring for the diseased and elderly, and strongholds guarding the weak and defenseless. "Turning Scripture into action" became the medieval Church's clarion call, just as it had for the Early Church.

"Turning Scripture into action" became the medieval Church's clarion call, just as it had for the Early Church.

What good is it, dear brothers and sisters, if you say you have faith but don't show it by your actions? Can that kind of faith save anyone? Suppose you see a brother or sister who has no food or clothing, and you say, "Good-bye and have a good day; stay warm and eat well"—but then you don't give that person any food or clothing. What good does that do? So you see, faith by itself isn't enough. Unless it produces good deeds, it is dead and useless. (James 2:14-17, NLT)

James may have been the first person to tell Christians, "Put up or shut up!" He challenged believers that true faith produces compassionate action. John linked Christ's love to it, asking, "But if anyone has the world's goods and sees his brother in need, yet closes his heart against him, how does God's love abide in him? Little children, let us not love in word or talk but in deed and in truth (1 John 3:17-18)." Compassion doesn't just hurt for people; it helps them.

Jesus Himself set this bar. Matthew 9:36 says, "When he saw the crowds, he had compassion for them, because they were harassed and helpless, like sheep without a shepherd." Reading further, we see Christ feeding hunger and healing sickness (Matthew 10-15; esp., 14:13-21).[i] As the disciples followed in His footsteps, the Gospel exploded and the Church multiplied (Acts 6:7). And as war, famine, disease, and death charged across Europe like horsemen of the apocalypse, the medieval Church took up this same "holy war." At other times, her warfare was not so holy, but the difference always came down to turning God's words into action—not man's. As Christian soldiers, if we'll do the same, we too will shine in a dark age because Christ's compassion remains a universal language and an invincible spiritual weapon.

Charles Martel & the Battle of Tours

As Byzantium reeled from nonstop war and calamity, a new threat arose in the south. In A.D. 609, Islam (Arb., "submission") was born. Over the next twenty-three years, Muhammad's teachings were codified in the Quran, including *jihad* ("battle": holy war with the infidels);[17] *ghazwa* ("conquest," which included plunder, subjugation, and enslavement);[18] and *jizya* ("tribute": a tax on those of different faiths).[19] Following Muhammad's death (A.D. 634), Muslim armies marched on Europe with their prophet's sayings etched on their helmets.[20]

> You are the best nation which has ever been raised for the guidance of mankind.... Had the people of the Book *(Jews and Christians)* believed, it would surely have been better for them. (3:110)[21]

> O people of the Book *(Jews and Christians)*! Believe in what We have now revealed *(The Quran)*, confirming your own scriptures, before we obliterate your faces and turn them backward, or lay Our curse on you.... (4:47)[22]

> Fight and slay the Pagans wherever ye find them, and seize them, beleaguer them, and lie in wait for them in every stratagem (of war); but if they

---

i   *Matthew 15:21-39*

repent, and establish regular prayers and practice regular charity, then open the way for them. (9:5)[23]

Fight those people of the Book *(Jews and Christians)* who do not believe in Allah…until they pay jizya *(protection tax)*…The Christians say: "Messiah *(Christ)* is the son of Allah…" May Allah destroy them! How perverted they are! (9:29-30)[24]

Verse after verse drove home this eastern form of "manifest destiny" in the Muslim mind, an idea many Americans would adopt in the nineteenth century to justify atrocities with Native Americans. Dr. Patrick Franke, professor of Islamic studies at the University of Bamberg, notes:

Basically, the Muslims had a feeling of religious superiority. They were of the opinion that the Christian knights had a religion that was simply inferior to Islam. So, we find Usama ibn Munqidh beginning his chapter on the Frankish customs by comparing the Franks to animals in that they possess animal virtues such as bravery. He respected their bravery but held them to be culturally inferior….[25]

Adnan Husain, associate professor of history at Queen's University, summarizes, "Muslims believed that they were there to rule over the earth, bring about God's justice, and institute God's order."[26] And it seemed that might happen. For in less than twenty years Muslims conquered Persia, Byzantine Egypt, Syria, Mesopotamia, and Jerusalem (A.D. 633-651). As Allah's army pressed into Northern Europe, it appeared unstoppable. By 711, Spain had fallen. But, as the Muslim scimitar slashed through Southern France, burning and pillaging churches and monasteries, it encountered a Christian hammer named Charles.

This Frankish Christian and de facto king understood that seasonally fighting farmers could never defeat the Muslim army. Franks needed a professional fighting class. That meant money. So, Charles approached the Catholic Church, who gave him acres of land, which he lent to nobles for an oath of military service, creating Europe's *feudal-warrior* class. When Muslims arrived in 732, an army of thirty thousand trained, heavily armed Franks stood ready on a hill outside the city of Tours.[27] Soon, the overconfident Muslim cavalry charged into Frankish shields, spears, and swords, relying solely on fear and numbers about eighty thousand strong.[28]

Muslim cavalry fought with lances, scimitars, small shields, and wore light armor. Charles chose the ideal defense: a deeper-rowed version of the *phalanx*, the formation Sparta made famous at Thermopylae. Side-by-side, shields overlapping like a tortoise shell, each man wearing an iron helmet and seventy pounds of chain mail, the Franks could repel the Muslim attack.[29] Victory hinged on one thing: trusting Charles—not second-guessing him. "Hold, hold, hold" was the secret and, as Franks did, wave after wave of Muslim cavalry shattered against Charles' wall. The *Mozarabic Chronicle of 754* notes: "The men of the North stood motionless as a wall…like a belt of ice frozen together, and not to be dissolved, as they slew the Arab with the sword."[30] Charles' men held the line. Islam's advance into Northern Europe stopped. Western Christendom was saved. Charles earned the nickname *Martel* (Fr., "hammer") and Tours its place in history as "one of the decisive battles of the world."[31]

Frankish Faith

The Battle of Tours holds sound advice for present-day Christian combat. As demonic forces operating through lost souls pressure us at school, on the job, in politics, and in media to "break formation" with God's Word, we must stand immovable like Martel's wall. Dr. Jim Nelson Black diagnosed a core problem in American Christendom, saying:

> One of the greatest reasons for the decline of American society over the past century has been the tendency of Christians who have practical solutions to abandon the forum at the first sign of resistance. Evangelicals in particular have been quick to run and slow to stand by their beliefs….

> Our challenge today is not to run from conflict but to engage in it…. Jesus Christ did not warn us to run away, to flee to the hills, or to hide our eyes, but to go into the fields and bring forth the harvest. We are to occupy as faithful soldiers of a loving God until the Commander himself returns.[32]

That's a nice way of stating, "Christians need to grow a spine!" Too many Christ followers surrender biblical doctrine or flee the public arena the moment sparks fly. We've embraced some serpentine lies—that love means always agreeing with people, ignoring sin, and closing our mouths, which boils down to embracing a false Jesus, a fake Gospel, and a phony Holy Spirit. Paul warned the Corinthians about this:

> I am afraid that your minds will be corrupted and that you will abandon your full and pure devotion to Christ—in the same way that Eve was deceived by the snake's clever lies. For you gladly tolerate anyone who comes to you and preaches a different Jesus, not the one we preached; and you accept a spirit and a gospel completely different from the Spirit and the gospel you received from us! (2 Corinthians 11:3-4, GNT)

Note the word "tolerate." We hear it a lot these days, but it always translates into Christians shutting up and accepting evil. The biblical Jesus, however, boldly spoke truth and called people to enter His Kingdom by the "narrow gate" (Matthew 7:13-14). If He walked the earth today, He'd be accused every time He opened His mouth, just as He was then (Matthew 9:11, 34).[ii] But Christ didn't care about people's opinions. He cared for their souls and commanded our utmost allegiance:

> Do not think that I have come to bring peace to the earth. I have not come to bring peace, but a sword. For I have come to set a man against his father, and a daughter against her mother, and a daughter-in-law against her mother-in-law. And a person's enemies will be those of his own household. Whoever loves father or mother more than me is not worthy of me, and whoever loves son or daughter more than me is not worthy of me. And whoever does not take his cross and follow me is not worthy of me. Whoever finds his life will lose it, and whoever loses his life for my sake will find it. (Matthew 10:34-39)

Christ called us to love Him more than anyone. That means speaking

---

ii   *Matthew 11:19; 12:24; 26:65; John 7:20; 9:16; 19:12*

up. Love doesn't sit by as neighbors drive off cliffs or destroy society's foundations (Leviticus 19:17).[iii] Jesus engaged in compassionate yet confrontational conversations (John 4:1-26)[iv] and Paul in loving, logical debate (Acts 17:1-3, 16-34).[v]

Love doesn't sit by as neighbors drive off cliffs or destroy society's foundations (Leviticus 19:17).

As they challenged culturally entrenched sins and twisted norms, so must we. The same love that compelled Christ to challenge Pharisees on adultery and divorce should spark talks with those embracing them today (Matthew 19:1-9). The same love that constrained Paul to confront Rome's depravity and Corinth's sexual idolatry should gracefully share God's truth with the LGBT community (Romans 1:18-32).[vi] The same love beckoning babies into Jesus' lap and filling His sternest warnings should debate abortion defenders, help needy single moms, and advocate for the unborn (Proverbs 31:8).[vii] His love, biblical love—not our version—that's what Jesus commands.

Online or in line, we're commanded to "speak the truth in love" and "give an answer…with gentleness and respect (Ephesians 4:15)."[viii] Moreover, we are to "seek the welfare of the city…and pray to the Lord on its behalf (Jeremiah 29:7)." Trusting what God has said, standing our ground on Scripture, is doing just that, and it demands two things: 1.) holding to the Bible's divine inspiration and 2.) trusting its complete inerrancy. Let's break this down.

Inspiration. Though penned by men, the Bible holds to be God's Word throughout. This is the Doctrine of Inspiration, and it means that God's Spirit: a.) chose every word in the original text, and b.) though authors' personal styles are seen in Scripture, each word remains fully from God. 2 Timothy 3:16 says, "All Scripture is breathed out by God," not just the parts we like!

Inerrancy. If the Bible is God's Word, then it is the Christian standard of life and love, good and evil, sin and righteousness—our "Supreme Court." Psalm 19:7-9, NKJV says, "The law of the Lord is perfect, converting the

---

iii   *Proverbs 27:4-5*
iv   *John 5:1-14; 8:1-11*
v   *Acts 18:4-6, 19; 19:8-9*
vi   *1 Corinthians 6:9-20*
vii   *Matthew 18:6-9; Mark 10:13-16*
viii   *1 Peter 3:15*

soul; the testimony of the Lord is sure, making wise the simple; the statutes of the Lord are right, rejoicing the heart; the commandment of the Lord is pure, enlightening the eyes; the fear of the Lord is clean, enduring forever; the judgments of the Lord are true and righteous altogether." (For further study on the Bible's inspiration and inerrancy, see note 33.)[33]

Standing on God's Word is never easy. It invites conflict (2 Timothy 3:12). But, we're not here to please men (Galatians 1:10). We're here to win "one of the decisive battles of the world": to save souls from hell. To bow before the world's golden images or flee from the giants of anti-Christian bigotry is betrayal to Christ (Daniel 3).[ix] Having done all, we must "hold, hold, hold" to Scripture's sacred soil (Matthew 26:41).[x] Let's see if some praying monks can help us here.

The Monastic Warrior

The Muslim invasion transformed European warfare, prompting the invention of the feudal warrior, permanence of the mounted warrior, and future creation of the crusading martial monk—all milestone steps in the knight's evolution. Still, a crucial installment came not from a secular but spiritual source. Dr. Katherine Smith, associate professor of history at the University of Puget Sound, states:

> Beginning in the earliest Christian centuries, exegetes built up a thick carapace of interpretation around every mention of war, historical and allegorical, in the Old and New Testaments.... The Gospels and the Pauline Epistles supplied Christian writers with the concept of the "soldier of Christ," or *miles Christi*, as well as a symbolic vocabulary to describe his entirely spiritual form of warfare. By the Central Middle Ages, monastic understanding of Pauline spiritual combat had come to be mediated by a rich commentary tradition which encouraged the monk's self-identification with the *miles Christi* ideal.[34]

Paul and his New Testament fellows had introduced the concept of the "soldier of Christ" fighting sin and evil spiritual forces. In that wake,

---

ix   *1 Samuel 17*
x   *Ephesians 6:13*

early theologians from Origen to Augustine, in martially toned Bible commentaries, presented their own ideal: the praying *monk-warrior*. By the eighth century, Europe had pretty much embraced the notion. Christian monarchs like Charlemagne, Charles Martel's grandson, commissioned entire monasteries in "large-scale organized prayer networks"[35] for war campaigns because "rulers retained the view that prayers were powerful 'arms of faith,' most efficacious when deployed simultaneously by as many subjects as possible."[36]

Even as artillery units were employed to pummel foes and fortresses, Christian kings sought to spiritually blast enemies with skilled intercessors. It was not unusual for a king to look across the battlefield and see not only a cavalry form up but a band of praying monks. King Æthelfrith of Bernicia witnessed this in the Battle of Chester and ordered his men to cut them down—before they could pray! Charlemagne even threatened to cite monasteries with treason which failed to pray for his battlefield victories.[37]

Siege Warfare

While there are some concerning theological errors above, the discerning Christian soldier should not miss the point: these men recognized prayer as a potent spiritual weapon. Paul agreed, writing, "For the weapons of our warfare are not of the flesh but have divine power to destroy strongholds. We destroy arguments and every lofty opinion raised against the knowledge of God, and take every thought captive to obey Christ (2 Corinthians 10:4-5)." The apostle compared battling deeply rooted sin and deception in the human soul with besieging the great fortress-cities of his day, which featured thick walls, high towers, and well-organized defenses. These strongholds continued into the Middle Ages, could take months or years to conquer, and at times seemed impossible—just like breaking through a hardened heart.

Paul gave praying believers hope, however, noting that our weapons "are not of the flesh but have divine power." Remember that the original Greek root for "power," *dúnamis*, refers to mighty power, explosive strength, or violent force.[38] It's typically rendered as "miracle" in the New Testament. Thus, Paul is talking about spiritual weapons with miracle-working power coursing through them, weapons which produce life-changing results.

Building on this, medieval warfare's most significant siege weapon was the counterweight *trebuchét* (Old Fr., "to overthrow"). At sixty feet high, it hurled large missiles hundreds of yards, devastating defenses and personnel. Greek fire remained its most lethal rocket. Perfected by the Byzantines, it was a long-burning, top-secret mixture. Water couldn't extinguish it and, in some formulas, actually produced a hotter burn! The only thing comparable is napalm—the thick, petroleum-based incendiary invented by the U.S. and first used in World War II bombs. With this in mind, listen to Revelation 8:3-5, NIV:

> Another angel, who had a golden censer, came and stood at the altar. He was given much incense to offer, with the prayers of all God's people, on the golden altar in front of the throne. The smoke of the incense, together with the prayers of God's people, went up before God from the angel's hand. Then the angel took the censer, filled it with fire from the altar, and hurled it on the earth; and there came peals of thunder, rumblings, flashes of lightning and an earthquake.

Note first how saints' prayers were offered with incense, indicating they're holy, even worshipful. Second, the prayers arose before God's throne, meaning He hears them. Third, God doesn't just listen; the angel mixed earthly prayers with heavenly fire and hurled it back. Last, don't miss the impact: "peals of thunder, rumblings, flashes of lightning, and an earthquake." What's the lesson? Mixed with God's fire, our prayers strike the earth with supernatural force. The world is never the same when Christian soldiers pray! Let's explore this.

Heavenly Artillery. If the Sword of the Spirit is God's Word (Ephesians 6:17)[xi], I offer that prayer is "Heaven's Howitzer"—a weapon of unlimited scope designed to unleash God's fire on earth to move mountains, save cities, destroy strongholds, free captives, heal disease, and more (2 Kings 18-19).[xii]

War Engine. The most effective prayer happens in teams. A corps of organized, faith-filled believers, flowing in unity and biblical truth is

---

xi   *Hebrews 4:12*
xii   *Mark 11:23; John 14:12-14; 2 Corinthians 10:4; Ephesians 6:18-20; James 5:14-16*

like a medieval war engine or modern-day artillery unit. Its "business end" is fearsome—a place no power in hell desires to be (Exodus 17:8-13).[xiii]

Explosive Ordinance. Prayer mixed with fasting is like Greek fire or American napalm: it's highly flammable and explosive —kindling godly devotion and repentance,

Mixed with God's fire, our prayers strike the earth with supernatural force. The world is never the same when Christian soldiers pray!

igniting ministry and revival, incinerating pride and sin, and cremating satanic schemes and strongholds (Ezra 8:23; Matthew 4:1-11; 17:14-21[39]).[xiv]

The Bible's use of siege warfare imagery should compel us to pray and believe for world-impacting results. "But I can't pray like that," you reply. God answers, "Oh, yes you can!" James 5:16b-18, NLT, says, "The earnest prayer of a righteous person has great power and produces wonderful results. Elijah was as human as we are, and yet when he prayed earnestly that no rain would fall, none fell for three and a half years! Then, when he prayed again, the sky sent down rain and the earth began to yield its crops."

Without realizing, we often idolize figures like Elijah, but God assures us that he (and every other believer we see in Scripture) was just as frail and fallen as we are. So, if Elijah is just like us, our prayers can be just like his! Let's be honest: we have no excuse for prayerlessness. God is faithful and moves mightily through prayer. "Alright, I'm convinced," you say. "Where do we start?" How about with a secret of Jesus and other believers?

Psalmic Warfare

A thousand years before Christ, God's people prayed the Psalms. The Book is quoted almost two hundred times in the New Testament's 260 chapters[40] and referenced more than four hundred.[41] Most importantly, perhaps, Jesus cited the Psalms more than any other book in Scripture and drew the most from it in His final hours. Is there something here for our warfare?

At the Last Supper, Jesus said, "He who has dipped his hand in the dish with me will betray me," citing Psalm 41:9-10 (Matthew 26:23). Moments later, Judas departed. Before leaving, Jesus and the disciples sang a hymn,

---

xiii   *2 Chronicles 7:14; 20:1-29; Psalm 133; Matthew 18:19-20; Acts 1:14; 4:24-31; 12:1-19*
xiv   *Daniel 9-10; Joel 2:1-17; Jonah 3:6-10; Acts 13:1-3*

historically the *Hallel,* Psalms 113-118 (Matthew 26:30). Agonizing in Geth-semane, Jesus prayed, "Father, if it be possible, let this cup pass from me," drawing from Psalm 75:8 (Matthew 26:39). At the Cross, He quoted Psalm 22:1 and 31:5, "My God, my God, why have You forsaken Me?" "Into Your hand I commit My Spirit." Jesus' constant use of the Psalms was more than fulfilled prophecy. He waged war with them—debating Pharisees, confronting skeptics and enraged mobs, unveiling Judas' betrayal, foretelling Jerusalem's destruction, and crying out to God from Gethsemane to Golgotha. (Time fails us to cover the psalms cited by the Gospel writers.)

In Acts, the disciples carry on this "psalmic warfare," leaning on their wisdom and power. Filling Judas' apostolic office, Peter cites Psalms 41:9, 69:25, and 109:8 (Acts 1:16, 20). Preaching his first sermon, he quotes Psalms 16:8-11 and 110:1 (Acts 2:25-28, 30-31). As the Church begins, the disciples devoted themselves to "the apostles' teaching and the fellowship, to the breaking of bread and *the prayers* (Acts 2:42, italics mine)." Note the original Greek says, "THE PRAYERS"—not "to prayer" as some Bible versions render. The disciples were praying something, praying it together, and praying it regularly. What? The Psalms. When persecution broke out, they "lifted their voices" and prayed Psalm 2:1-2 (Acts 4:24-26). As the Gospel spread, psalm singing, reciting, and praying continued, and this powerful practice carried right on into the Middle Ages (1 Corinthians 14:26).[xv]

Monks observing Saint Benedict's Rule sang forty psalms a day in prayer, some one hundred plus, and others one hundred seventy. Certain monasteries began shifts of "day and night psalmody." In his Rule, Augustine urged monks to memorize psalms to pray more effectively.[42] In "pre-battle liturgical processions and prayers," monks wielded the Psalms.[43] Psalmic prayer then is an ancient art of war. Why not deploy it in yours by praying a psalm each day? Most months have thirty days; we have 150 psalms. There's five months of psalmic warfare for you, your family, and ministry.

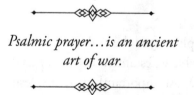

Psalmic prayer…is an ancient art of war.

If you're in a battle and need guidance, consult my martial index.

---

xv   *Ephesians 5:19; Colossians 3:16*

(Don't obsess on my titles.) Not all psalms are listed. This is just to get you started. Place a copy in your Bible or phone. Memorize a psalm. Make it this season's warfare prayer. I've emboldened my favorites.

- **Battle Prayers:** Psalm 20, **27**, 35, 46, 68, 83, 115, 144
- **Prayers for Justice:** Psalm 7, 9-10, **37**, 58, 72, 94
- **Protection Prayers:** Psalm 3, 17, 31, 43, 56, 64, **91**, 121, 140
- **Deliverance Prayers:** Psalm 18, 28, **34**, 57, 69-70, 107
- **Distress Call:** Psalm 5-6, 40, 42, **61**, 102, 130, 142-43

In studying Psalms, it becomes easy to see why Christian soldiers across history have turned to them as both a hymnbook and handbook on spiritual warfare. Dr. Smith sums it up:

> Throughout the Psalms, God is invoked in the twin roles of protector of the chosen people and destroyer of their enemies. Many passages… hearken back to the wars of the Israelites…and describe God's power and the struggles of his people in explicitly martial terms. He is the "God of armies,"[44] "mighty in battle,"[45] a just judge… The God of the Psalms is unmistakably a warrior; armed with a sword, shield, and bow, and riding in a chariot surrounded by an innumerable host, he teaches the faithful to fight and emboldens them to march fearlessly into battle against their enemies.[46] The chosen people can expect divine support on the field of battle, but only those who put their faith in God…may hope for victory in war.[47]

Psalming the Savage Beast

The Psalms and other scriptures worked their way into more than monastic battle prayers against invaders. As the Church tended a culture in crisis, she drew the Sword of the Spirit on Europe's own warriors. Seeing society's power vacuum, greedy nobles began hiring soldiers not just for personal protection but to rob farmers and rub out foes. Hand in hand, fighting men with no moral compass were all too willing to protect the homeland one day and prey on it the next. Philip Daileader, professor of history at the College of William and Mary in Virginia, explains:

Your typical medieval knight had much more in common with Tony Soprano than with Lancelot. They're thugs...violent individuals whose primary purpose is to beat people up. And the owner of a castle would unleash knights on the peasants of a neighboring territory, and they would enter the village assaulting people, taking property in an attempt to force these peasants to accept the lordship of the owner of the castle.[48]

In the Early Middle Ages, Europe's mounted warriors were little more than mounted mafia. Prior to this, however, the Church had done much to tame the Roman army. Before the legionary's belt and sword were issued, his fourth-century military oath swore him to ethical service "by God and His Christ and by the Holy Spirit."[49] In the fourth and fifth centuries, drawing from Scripture (e.g., Deuteronomy 20; Romans 13, etc.) and sources like Aristotle's *Politikos*, Saints Ambrose and Augustine set forth theories of "just war," confining warfare to national defense, maintaining peace, punishing evil, and recovering stolen land or property.[50] But when the Western Empire fell, martial mores vanished.

Now, as Europe's earthly warfare escalated, so did the Church's heavenly combat to re-tame the soldier spirit. Soldiers needed righteous counsels to govern them, honorable causes to guide them, and virtuous codes to guard their conduct. Who better to draw from than Scripture's greatest soldier: David! From the eighth to thirteenth century, psalmic quotes, derivatives, and other Bible verses flooded texts, rites, oaths, sword blades, hilts, and sheaths as the Church led the charge in what would become *chivalry*—the order of knighthood.

"Blessed be the Lord my God who teaches my hands to fight and my fingers to war," reads an engraving of Psalm 144:1 on a collection of European swords spanning six hundred years.[51] In the *Pontifical Romanum*, a liturgical book of Catholic rites containing "The Blessing of the New Soldier," a candidate knight recited this hybrid of Psalm 144:1-2 during his induction: "Blessed be the Lord my God who trains my hands for prayer and my fingers for war. He is my loving God and my fortress, my stronghold and my deliverer, my shield, in whom I take refuge, who subdues peoples under me."[52] Bestowing the knight's sword, the bishop then quoted Psalm 45:3, "Gird your sword upon your thigh powerfully," then referenced Hebrews 11:33, "And remember always that the saints conquered kingdoms through faith and not with the sword."[53] Ponder also the *Pontifical*'s "Blessing of the Sword":

> Hear our prayers, we beseech thee O Lord, and deign, with the right hand of your Majesty, to bless this sword with which your servant desires to be girded, so that he may be the defender of churches, of widows, of orphans, and of servants of God, against the barbarity, ferocity and cruelty of pagans and heretics; may it be the terror and fear of traitors and all those who lay snares for him. Through Christ our Lord. Amen.[54]

Now, compare this formula with Psalm 82:3-4's charge: "Give justice to the weak and the fatherless; maintain the right of the afflicted and the destitute. Rescue the weak and the needy; deliver them from the hand of the wicked." Place it beside Isaiah 1:17's order: "Learn to do good; seek justice, correct oppression; bring justice to the fatherless, plead the widow's cause." Finally, consider James 1:27's code: "Religion that is pure and undefiled before God the Father is this: to visit orphans and widows in their affliction, and to keep oneself unstained from the world." Watch how the twelfth-century bishop John of Salisbury wove Psalm 149:6-9 into his chivalric exhortation:

> What is the office of the duly ordained soldiery? To defend the Church, to assail infidelity, to venerate the priesthood, to protect the poor from injuries, to pacify the province, to pour out their blood for their brothers (as the formula of their oath instructs them), and, if need be, to lay down their lives. "The high praises of God are in their throats, and two-edged swords are in their hands to execute punishment on the nations and rebuke upon the peoples, and to bind their kings in chains and their nobles in links of iron."[55] But to what end? In order that they may serve either rage or vanity or avarice or their own private will? By no means…. They serve in order that they may execute…the will of God…."[56]

The twelfth-century-formed Knights Templar took the field with those same high praises. As the trumpet sounded formation, knights began singing their battle hymn: Psalm 113 (113-115 in their Bible) contained their motto, "Not unto us, O Lord, not unto us, but to Thy Name give glory... (115:1)." Noteworthy also is that almost all medieval chivalric oaths held three core virtues: justice, mercy, and faith—the same virtues the King of kings commanded His knights in Micah 6:8, NKJV—"He has shown you, O man, what is good; and what does the Lord require of you but to do justly, to love mercy, and to walk humbly with your God."

While Bible verses and values worked their way into warrior liturgy and weaponry, the Church unleashed another barrage with the tenth- and-eleventh-century movements the Peace and Truce of God. Calling them to fields across Europe, clerics confronted warriors for preying on the weak and innocent, invoked Christ's name and the witness of saintly bones and other relics, and threatened them with divine curses if they did not repent. As frightened brigands fell to their knees in sometimes very emotional displays, priests then swore them to oaths restraining violence and rechanneling martial power. Some have questioned the efficacy of these movements, but period texts show the Church took ground here, psalming heaven into some warriors and scaring the hell out of others![57] Now, let's consider some applications.

A Good Dose of Holy Fear

As evil grows in our society, Christians should freshly weigh the wisdom of medieval clerics. Much is made these days of God's mercy and grace. That's good (Jeremiah 3:22-23)![xvi] In listening to many modern believers, though, one might conclude that God's justice and wrath are not coequal attributes but those of another god altogether. A false gospel courses through many Christian circles, omitting divine consequences for sin and pride, be it through God's present-life discipline or a future hell apart from Him. Some even dare to say, "There is no hell." One must wonder what Bible they've been reading, though, since Jesus spoke of hell more than anyone in Scripture.

In parables and prose, Christ constantly warned of a hell real in its existence,[58] eternal in its scope,[59] and incomprehensible in its torment.[60] Though He sometimes mentioned hell in parables, He always explained

---

xvi   Hebrews 4:16

later that it was not fictional (Matthew 13:24-30, 36-43). Most of all, He repeatedly warned of the Day of Judgment, called everyone to turn from their sins, and believe His Gospel—to avoid hell.[61] Jesus knew the human heart, our defiance

If Jesus warned people of hell in His ministry, who are we to omit it from ours?

and depravity as fallen creatures, and that soft measures don't work with everyone (Jeremiah 17:9-10).[xvii] Some hearts are hard; some have no fear of God at all (Romans 2:4-5).[xviii] Our daily headlines confirm this. Man must be taught the fear of the Lord, which is still "the beginning of knowledge and wisdom (Job 28:28)."[xix]

In the Viking chapter, we saw how some won't believe Christ's Gospel apart from miracles. Equally, some will never see their need for God's mercy and grace until they taste His justice and wrath. This begs the question: If Jesus warned people of hell in His ministry, who are we to omit it from ours? Jesus' half-brother Jude said, "Rescue others by snatching them from the flames of judgment. Show mercy still to others, but do so with great caution, hating the sins that contaminate their lives (Jude 23, NLT)."

Note Jude's full-orbed approach to Gospel preaching: some will only come when they fear "flames of judgment": others are drawn by mercy. The New Testament teaches Christians to preach God's mercy *and* wrath and never diminishes either in evangelism. A smart fisherman keeps a well-stocked tackle box for various fish and climates; equally, the wise Christian knows how to fish for men, depending on their past experience and present nature (Mark 1:17). If they're broken, share God's mercy. If they're proud, a good dose of holy fear may be in order.

A fond memory Ralana and I share in this regard is our original stage show *Virtual Reality*. For two hours, audiences witnessed six life-and-death scenarios with heaven or hell outcomes. People came face-to-face with God's mercy and heaven's beauty while cringing at Satan's cruelty and hell's horror. In a five-year run, we saw more than five thousand decisions for Christ—two of which were my brothers David and Brad! An untold

---

xvii   *Matthew 15:18-19; John 2:25*
xviii   *Romans 3:10-18; Hebrews 3:7-13*
xix   *Psalm 34:11; 111:10; Proverbs 1:7; 9:10*

number gave their lives to Him when our video was carried into homes across America and onto mission fields in Africa, the Philippines, and beyond. Paul preached this same double-edged Gospel in Romans, asking:

> Don't you see how wonderfully kind, tolerant, and patient God is with you? Does this mean nothing to you? Can't you see that his kindness is intended to turn you from your sin? But because you are stubborn and refuse to turn from your sin, you are storing up terrible punishment for yourself. For a day of anger is coming, when God's righteous judgment will be revealed. He will judge everyone according to what they have done. He will give eternal life to those who keep on doing good, seeking after the glory and honor and immortality that God offers. But he will pour out his anger and wrath on those who live for themselves, who refuse to obey the truth and instead live lives of wickedness. (Romans 2:4-8, NLT)

Can you feel the urgency in Paul's words? A divine clock ticks down for every soul. No one knows when his/her time will be up, but the Bible assures us that only one thing comes next: eternal judgment (Hebrews 9:27).[xx] Are you ready? Have you turned from your sin-dead life to God's One and Only Son? If not, pour out your heart to Him now in prayer. Ask the Lord to forgive you of your sins. Believe that Jesus died for them and to save you from God's wrath and eternal hellfire. If you sense Him speaking to you, don't wait (2 Corinthians 6:2)! Don't take His kindness for granted, wagering you'll have time later to decide (Romans 2:4). James 4:14 warns, "You do not know what tomorrow will bring. What is your life? For you are a mist that appears for a little time and then vanishes." Stop now. Pray and ask Jesus to forgive and save you. Then, contact a Christian friend or church to tell them.

If you've already made this decision, what about those you know? Have they heard the Gospel (Mark 5:19)? Do they know you're a Christian? As Paul also said, "But how can they call to him for help if they have not believed? And how can they believe if they have not heard the message? And how can they hear if the message is not proclaimed (Romans 10:14,

---

xx   *Revelation 20:11-15*

GNT)?" Do you also presume the riches of God's kindness—by *not* telling family and friends about Jesus? Our call is to turn Scripture into action. If a knight's call centered on rescuing people from evil and suffering, how much more should we seek to rescue them from the evil one and a suffering with no end?

Chivalry's Secret Power

By the mid-thirteenth century, Scripture shaped a knight's entire world— even his sword, as Ramon Llull's *Book of the Order of Chivalry* says: "Unto a knight is given a sword, which resembles a cross in order to signify that our Lord conquered on the Cross the death to which humanity was condemned for the sin of our first father, Adam."[62] The Maltese cross of the Knights Hospitaller also held great meaning. Drawing from Plato's *Republic* and Scripture, the cross's four arms depicted the four cardinal virtues (wisdom, courage, temperance, and justice); its eight points, Christ's Beatitudes (Matthew 5:3-10). Unknown to modern millions, the fleur-de-lis of French heraldry signified the Trinity: Father, Son, and Holy Spirit.[63]

Additionally, when knights weren't singing psalms, etching them on swords, or pondering biblical imagery, chivalric poetry prompted meditation on warriors like Joshua, David, and Judah Maccabee—the three Jewish exemplars. Three pagan and Christian warriors were also mused upon: respectively, Hector of Troy, Alexander the Great, and Julius Caesar; then King Arthur, Charlemagne, and Godfrey of Bouillon. Together, they comprised the Nine Worthies of Jacques de Longuyon's fourteenth-century romance *Vows of the Peacock*. And, when we consider the Worthies' stirring tales and unique traits, it's easy to see why.

Joshua's Faith: Fiercely tested in the book named for him, God called this ex-slave and former aid to Moses to lead 1.5 million untrained Israelites to conquer a hostile land of trained armies, fortress-cities, and giant races using physical arms and some bizarre, faith-trying tactics.

David's Fervor: A poor shepherd boy turned hero and king, David's battle with the giant Goliath and rise to glory inspired knights. But the

Bible histories and Psalms reveal that David's prowess came not just from practice with a sling or sword but his love and devotion to God.

Judah's Ferocity: When Seleucid King Antiochus Epiphanes IV forbade sacrifices, forced idolatry, and murdered eighty thousand Jews in Judea, Judah revolted. His surname "Maccabee" (from *maqqaba*; Arc., "hammer") marked him a fierce foe and, likely, his weapon of choice.

Hector's Intrepidity: This mythical Trojan prince showed himself the portrait big brother when drawn into war by his younger sibling's scandalous affair with Helen of Sparta. Challenged by the unbeatable demi-god Achilles, Hector faced him and nobly died a hero.

Alexander's Ingenuity: From cutting the Gordian knot to constructing a causeway to conquer the island-fortress Tyre, Alexander the Great remains one of history's greatest generals. His resourcefulness enabled him to beat stronger enemies and seemingly impossible odds.

Caesar's Indomitability: Julius Caesar rose through Roman ranks as a priest, soldier, lawyer, officer, chief priest, praetor, governor, consul, and dictator. While ambition led to his assassination, his uncanny ability to adapt and grow challenges warriors for all time.

Arthur's Love: A fabled and romantic figure, Briton's Arthur of Camelot built his kingdom on Christian laws; the Round Table, where he and fellow knights judged as equals; and the Pentecostal Oath—their chivalric code. He stood as a beacon of Christ's love and service.

Charlemagne's Leadership: Hailed the "Father of Europe," this Frankish king united most of Western Europe and parts beyond. His visionary reign, though controversial at times, sparked an era of stability, prosperity, and renewal in the arts, education, and more.

Godfrey's Lowliness: A Frankish knight and leader in the First Crusade, after recapturing Jerusalem from Muslim rule, Godfrey accepted the kingship but refused the title and crown out of "respect for Him who had been crowned in that place with the Crown of Thorns."

In an age of knavery, each of the Nine Worthies modeled some virtue of the ideal knight. The Worthies also marked another milestone in chivalry's development by fusing religion, history, and mythology into a compelling code. But what has been our aim here, and why has chivalry endured hundreds of years and maintained such a strong sway over the soul? In the medieval chivalric works, I believe we also find four foundational truths of spiritual warfare:

1.) The Inner War. Chivalry revealed that man's greatest battle is not outward but within his own soul (mind, will, and emotions) and not with physical foes but spiritual ones (Proverbs 4:20-23).[xxi]

2.) The Power of Meditation. A central key then to spiritual transformation was/is the practice of meditation—a constant washing and immersion in goodness and truth (Joshua 1:7-9).[xxii]

3.) The Principle of Immersion. For knights, chivalry offered a world of compelling codes, rites, literature, symbols, clothing, and equipment. Knights were immersed in a system which also helped them live it (Nu. 15:37-40).[xxiii]

4.) The Power of Scripture. The secret to chivalry's power was Scripture. Even as the knight's sword slayed physical foes, priests saw that the Spirit's Sword could put to death a warrior's old, thuggish ways and carve out new, heroic paths (Isaiah 59:21).[xxiv]

Fraught with idolatry, immorality, heresy, and more, medieval Europe was not much different than the first-century Middle East. Paul taught that the Christian's greatest warfare was waged between his/her own ears (Roman 8:5-6).[xxv] In Ephesians 6:17 he ordered saints, "Take the helmet of salvation and the sword of the Spirit, which is the word of God." He admonished Christians to actively guard and guide their thought-life. Like a horse, the mind possesses great power but is prone to wander. It

---

xxi   *Proverbs 23:7; Matthew 15:19; 2 Corinthians 10:3-5; Romans 12:1-2; Ephesians 6:12*
xxii   *Psalm 1:1-3; John 8:31-32; Ephesians 5:26; Philippians 4:8; Colossians 3:16*
xxiii *Deuteronomy 6:1-9; 11:18-21; 22:12*
xxiv   *Jeremiah 23:29; Matthew 4:1-11; John 17:17; Ephesians 6:17; Hebrews 4:12*
xxv   *Romans 12:1-2; 2 Corinthians 10:4-5; Ephesians 4:20-24; Colossians 3:1-2*

must therefore be "harnessed." Meditation is a helmet for the mind and Scripture the thought-life's harness. When utilized, they unleash manifold transformation. Ancient Kingdom soldiers understood this. God told Joshua, one of the Nine Worthies:

> Only be strong and very courageous, being careful to do according to all the law that Moses my servant commanded you. Do not turn from it to the right hand or to the left, that you may have good success wherever you go. This Book of the Law shall not depart from your mouth, but you shall meditate on it day and night, so that you may be careful to do according to all that is written in it. For then you will make your way prosperous, and then you will have good success. (Joshua 1:7-8)

God not only charged Joshua to "be strong and courageous," but showed him how—by constantly meditating on His Word. Another Worthy, King David, concurred, saying:

> Blessed *is* the man who walks not in the counsel of the ungodly, nor stands in the path of sinners, nor sits in the seat of the scornful; but his delight *is* in the law of the Lord, and in His law he meditates day and night. He shall be like a tree planted by the rivers of water, that brings forth its fruit in its season, whose leaf also shall not wither; and whatever he does shall prosper. (Psalm 1:1-3, NKJV)

Paul was not one of the Nine Worthies, but may have summarized it best when he said, "Finally, brothers, whatever is true, whatever is honorable, whatever is just, whatever is pure, whatever is lovely, whatever is commendable, if there is any excellence, if there is anything worthy of praise, think about these things (Philippians 4:8)." Joshua, David, and Paul taught that a "Nine-Worthy life" starts with worthy thinking. Biblical meditation taps a power found nowhere else. Hebrews 4:12 notes, "For the word of God is living and active, sharper than any two-edged sword, piercing to the division of soul and of spirit, of joints and of marrow, and discerning the thoughts and intentions of the heart." When it comes to dealing with our souls, no weapon wields more power than God's Word.

It is a sword capable of killing our worst evils. But how do we employ it?

God's Sword & the Rhema-Strike

When it comes to dealing with our souls, no weapon wields more power than God's Word. It is a sword capable of killing our worst evils.

Years ago, I struggled with a short temper. I'd grown up with it in my home, experiencing it through physical and emotional abuse. After attending counseling to deal with the damage, though, my own short fuse remained. The Lord showed me that I needed to retrain my mind, to build a new neural pathway of belief and behavior. I asked Him to give me what I'd dubbed years earlier a "rhema-strike," a Scripture verse I could "take up" against my stronghold in meditation and prayer. *Rhema* is Greek for "word" in Ephesian 6:17's command, "Take the helmet of salvation and the sword of the Spirit, which is the word of God." Basically, *rhema* refers to an "exact answer" versus its opposite—*logos*, a "speech." When Satan attacked in Matthew 4, Jesus didn't give a speech or quote a Bible chapter. He answered each temptation with one verse—a sword stroke or "rhema-strike" (Matthew 4:4, 7, 10).

My rhema-strike was: "Whoever is slow to anger is better than the mighty, and he who rules his spirit than he who takes a city (Proverbs 16:32)." I practiced with it like a sword and pummeled my stronghold with it like Greek fire. I also employed the *Sh'ma* principle discussed in the Spartan chapter:

So love the Lord your God with all your heart, soul, and strength. Memorize his laws and tell them to your children over and over again. Talk about them all the time, whether you're at home or walking along the road or going to bed at night or getting up in the morning. Write down copies and tie them to your wrists and foreheads to help you obey them. Write these laws on the door frames of your homes and on your town gates. (Deuteronomy 6:5-9, CEV)

In this passage, God told Israel to fashion wears for their heads and hands containing Scripture. Elsewhere, He had them sew tassels on their clothes to remind them of it (Numbers 15:37-40).[xxvi] This principle of

---

xxvi *Deuteronomy 22:12*

plastering one's life with Scripture and its symbols, discussing it day and night, at home and abroad, is called "immersion." The Jews used it, so did knights, and it remains the best way to learn a new language.

Breaking strongholds is no different. Trying to break a stronghold (a "fortress of thoughts" comprised of strong yet false beliefs and feelings) is just like learning a new language. Our mind has learned to think, feel, and act one way. Now it must learn a new one. This means building a new neural pathway, and the process involves a long, steady immersion in God's Truth, which Paul called "the washing of the water of the Word (Ephesians 5:26)." James likened this process to grafting a branch onto a vine, another procedure where intricate steps must be followed to succeed (Ephesians 5:26).[xxvii]

So, what did my process look like? 1.) I wrote Proverbs 16:32 on multiple sticky notes, placing them across my home, car, and at work. I couldn't go anywhere without seeing my rhema-strike. 2.) I set a rule: every time I saw my rhema-strike, I recited it aloud and prayed it over myself. "Lord, help me be slow to anger. Make me better than the mighty. Rule over my spirit, Jesus, etc." 3.) I set phone alarms several times a day. As they went off, I recited and prayed the verse again. 4.) At lunch, I stared at the verse as I ate, letting my mind feast on it—chewing each word like a cow's cud, connecting thought with thought and other verses I knew.

The same way God's Word conquered ancient and medieval warrior hearts, it can overcome ours.

Gradually, God's Spirit began filling this dry, desert place. I started becoming more peaceful inwardly and patient outwardly (Ephesians 5:18-20). I wasn't as irritated by problems or people's behaviors or distracted from solutions. Soon, my rhema-strike had pounded my stronghold, rounded up insurgent thoughts, and executed every last one (2 Corinthians 10:3-5). As my thought-life changed, my behavior followed (Isaiah 26:3).[xxviii]

This weapon can be used against any stronghold: fear, doubt, lust, pride, greed, etc. The same way God's Word conquered ancient and medieval warrior hearts, it can overcome ours. Why not open your Bible and make

---

xxvii *James 1:21*
xxviii *Romans 12:2*

a rhema-strike or two? Start learning some for temptations and ministry opportunities. (For tips on memorization, see the Roman legionary chapter, part II, "Meditation" and the subheading "Rhema Arsenal.") If you need more peace, consider meditating on God's own set of Nine Worthies: the nine Fruit of the Spirit (Galatians 5:22-23). Here are ten other meditation themes in Scripture:

God's Mindfulness: Ps. 8:3-4   **The Sluggard's Field:** Pr. 24:30-34

God's Works: Ps. 77:5-12   **God's Mercies:** La. 3:21-26

God's Benefits: Ps. 103:1-5   **God's House:** Hag. 1:4-11

God's Judgments: Ps. 119:51-53   **God's Care:** Mt. 6:25-33

The Ant's Diligence: Pr. 6:6-11   **Christ's Sufferings:** He. 12:3

Next, pray about making some Scripture "symbols" to wear—tokens of Bible verses or values: a braided necklace, beaded bracelet, etc. Visit a craft store. Go wild! There's divine wisdom in emblems. They remind us of God's promises and prompt meditation and prayer.

Last, consider studying some of the Bible's chivalric passages like those below. Note similarities, differences, and contexts (Who's being addressed? What's happening? Where is this? Why is it being said?). Use an online or real Bible concordance to examine words like "mercy," "justice," etc. Learn original meanings and usage in Scripture. Journal your findings. Then, talk to God about it.

1 Ki. 2:2-3   **Ne. 4:14**   **Ps. 82:3-4**   **Is. 1:16c-17**

Je. 22:3   **Mi. 6:8**   **Zec. 7:9-10**   **Mt. 5:3-10**

Ja. 1:26-27   **1 Co. 16:13-14**   **1 Ti. 6:11-12**   **1 Pe. 5:8-11**

Now, let's complete our study by pondering the purpose of the military orders.

The Misunderstood Monks

No survey of the knight's evolution is complete without exploring his most controversial installment, the *martial monk*—the monastic military orders founded following the First Crusade. Launched by the Latin Church, the Crusades, in the main use of the term, were a 175-year series of eight military operations (A.D. 1096-1271) to stop Muslim expansion, reclaim stolen territory, and liberate Christians under Islamic oppression.[64] Over the years, much has been said of the Crusades by those trying to discredit Christianity. Not much has been said of the Muslim imperialism which caused them—the sack, slaughter, and subjection of Christians under *ghazwa* ("conquest"); destruction of churches, hospitals, and holy places with forced conversion or execution in *jihad* ("battle"); and taxation of Christian subjects under *jizya* ("tribute").

Islam invaded Christian Europe in A.D. 634. By 1095, two-thirds lay under its control. Thus, 461 years of Muslim domination passed before the First Crusade began. As in every war, atrocities occurred on both sides. The sum of the matter, though, is that without an Islamic *jihadist* there never would've been a crusading martial monk. The Crusades and knightly orders like the Templars were the direct result of militant Islam. Moreover, the orders were created to defend and recover Christian lands, shelter and protect pilgrims, and care for the poor and sick.

The Order of the Knights of Saint John, created for Jerusalem's defense after its Byzantine reclamation from Muslims in 1099, were not only "renowned in Europe as Christian soldiers" but "equally famous for their charities, especially for their great Hospital in Jerusalem,"[65] hence their shorter name, Knights Hospitaller. In its organizational guidelines, the hospital maintained four doctors and surgeons; provided servants for patients; regulated patient clothing, diets, and sleeping arrangements; diagnosed disease; and prescribed medicines.[66] After their expenses were met, remaining funds were given to the needy.[67]

Additionally, knights were required to not only guard but wait on each patient in a ministerial and service capacity "as if he were their lord."[68] Though scholars question the numbers, contemporary sources estimate the hospital cared for as many as one to two thousand patients at a time,[69] and it was lauded "for its inestimable works of mercy and for the practice of charity, which it demonstrated on an extraordinary scale."[70] By the mid-thirteenth century, the care provided by the Knights' Hospital had spurred the formation of numerous European institutions to treat the ill, particularly in the West where only few had existed.

Similarly, the German Order of the Teutonic Knights was founded in a hospital, under the headship of the Hospitallers, and established hospitals. The Order of Saint Lazarus of Jerusalem offered specialized care for lepers. The Knights of the Cross of the Red Star supplied general medical practice. Finally, the Brotherhood of the Knights of Saint Thomas cared for the sick and injured, buried Crusader knights, and fundraised to ransom knights captured by Muslims.[71]

But despite the Crusader's retaking of Jerusalem, Muslim attacks on Christian pilgrims continued. In response, Hospitallers provided escorts. Thousands of travelers arriving and departing daily, however, made manpower scarce. Hugues de Payens, Godfrey de Saint-Omer, and seven other knights soon offered their swords. Legend holds that neither Hugues nor Godfrey could afford separate horses in their beginning. So, they rode together, inspiring the two-knights-on-one-horse seal of the Poor Fellow Soldiers of Christ and the Temple of Solomon, a.k.a., the Knights Templar. Founded in 1119, they were the first solely focused martial order.

By the mid-twelfth century, with Islamic militancy rising, the Templar's charge grew to guarding pilgrims and strategic positions across eastern Crusader states. To facilitate operations, they constructed and fortified many castles. To safeguard pilgrims' funds, they created credit-note banking. Using their system of houses, merchants could deposit funds at one house for a note, spend it, or cash it at another. By the 1200s, the Templars were an established lending institution underwriting kings' budgets, cathedral construction, and other Christian endeavors.[72]

The Poor Fellows weren't so poor anymore, and when King Philip IV grew indebted to them in the fourteenth century he destroyed them with Pope Clement V's help. Philip charged Templars falsely, tortured them into confession, then burned them at the stake. Pope Clement dissolved the order, and so came their end—but not the other orders guarding pilgrims, protecting holy sites, fighting pagans, policing cities, and providing shelter and other assistance.

How often do we hear this, though, in modern Crusade narratives? Why do some recite tracts of evils yet ignore volumes of good? Every historic movement and organization has seen hypocrites, but counterfeits never preclude the genuine article. They presuppose it! Judas cannot exist without Jesus.

Moreover, emphasizing atrocities or phonies is often nothing more than a deflection. As Dr. Frank Harber notes:

> Focusing on the atrocities of so-called Christians for some is really a smoke screen to avoid the real issue. Christianity has far more positive achievements than negative influences. Christianity has been instrumental in the formation of countless hospitals, schools, colleges, orphanages, relief agencies, and charity agencies. No other organization in history can compare to achievements of the Christian Church.[73]

Humbly, I suggest that the greatest crusade of the Middle Ages was not a war of religion but to rebuild ransacked Europe. Furthermore, the greatest soldiers of that period did not wield man's sword against their foes but God's Sword against society's deepest needs. Theologians like Augustine and Durand crafted just-war theory and codified chivalry, restraining martial violence, restoring order, and rechanneling warrior energy. Alcuin of York, Theodore of Tarsus, Hadrian, and Gratian were only a few clerics and canonists reestablishing schools, renovating learning systems, and creating university models. But for monks like Venerable Bede, scores of classical works would be lost. Without Templar and Teutonic Knights, millions would have been enslaved or slaughtered. Millions more would have suffered and died without hostels and hospitals established by priests like Jerome and orders like the Hospitallers. That is the real story of the medieval and modern Church—not the hypocrisy of the few.

The greatest crusade of the Middle Ages was not a war of religion but to rebuild ransacked Europe.

Modern-day "orders of knights" exist everywhere, helping widows and the elderly, serving the poor and sick, visiting the lonely, assisting with food, clothing, bills, and unplanned pregnancies. They mow lawns and do handyman jobs; build houses, orphanages, and hospitals; mobilize medical and restoration teams in disaster; provide free dentistry and other care domestically and abroad. Chivalry is not dead. It beats in the heart of God and every true Christ follower. But the world will believe it's dead if His soldiers do nothing as she bleeds. It's time for a few more knights to heed the King's call and turn scripture into action.

Tactical Takeaways

1. As Dark Age Europe fell into chaos, the Church modeled Christ's compassion in many beautiful ways. Review the section "A Light in the Dark Ages" and list some.

2. A.) In "Charles Martel & the Battle of Tours," Charles built a warrior class to stop an invasion. Our talk turned to the culture war for the modern West. Jim Black said, *"One of the greatest reasons for the decline of American society...has been the tendency of Christians...to abandon the forum at the first sign of resistance. Evangelicals...have been quick to run and slow to stand by their beliefs...."* Why have so many believers fled the battlefields of government, education, etc.? How has this impacted America? Gauge your own response: have you prayed more, shared the Gospel, become active in local missions, your child's school, government and politics, used social media to share Christ's truth, etc.?

   B.) Read John 4:1-26; 8:1-11 and Acts 17:1-3, 16-34; 19:8-9. How did Jesus and Paul handle conflict? How should we? (Read Jeremiah 29:7; Daniel 3:16-18; Luke 19:13; Ephesians 4:15; 1 Peter 3:15.)

3. Lawlessness was rampant in the Dark Ages, and warriors played a central role. How did the Church respond? How can she help battle lawlessness in our day? (Review "Psalming the Savage Beast" and "Chivalry's Secret Power" to refresh.)

4. Has God laid someone on your heart who needs a compassionate soldier to battle for them—a single mom, a sick person, an elderly shut-in, or a family in need?

BOOK V

OATH OF THE GLADIATOR

We took an oath to obey Eumolpus; to endure burning, bondage, flogging, death by the sword, or anything else that Eumolpus ordered. We pledged our bodies and souls to our master most solemnly, like regular gladiators. When the oath was over, we posed like slaves and saluted our master…. We offered a prayer to Heaven for a prosperous and happy issue and started on our journey.

—Petronius, referencing the Oath of Gladiators, Satyricon 117

We are pressed on every side by troubles, but we are not crushed and broken. We are perplexed, but we don't give up and quit. We are hunted down, but God never abandons us. We get knocked down, but we get up again and keep going. Through suffering, these bodies constantly share in the death of Jesus, so that the life of Jesus may also be seen in our bodies. Yes, we live under constant danger of death because we serve Jesus, so that the life of Jesus will be obvious in our dying bodies. So we live in the face of death, but it has resulted in eternal life for you.

—Paul, 2 Corinthians 4:8-12, 1996 NLT

For almost seven hundred years they captivated Roman society, battling in some of the most gruesome spectacles of the ancient world. Their ranks swelled with men from almost every background—native and foreigner, lawbreaker and law-abiding, civilian and soldier, slave and free. On land and water, by foot and horseback, in bare breast and full armor, they fought for glory, freedom, and their very lives. Occupying a seat among the most bizarre warrior cultures of history, their Latin name meant the "swordsmen." We know them as the *gladiators*.

The bloody saga of the Roman gladiator began in 264 B.C. Rather than observe the typical custom, sacrificing a few slaves on the gravesite of their dearly departed, Marcus and Decimus Junius Brutus cut a new path. Clearing away the stinky pens of the cattle market, these two grieving sons forced six unarmored serfs to fight to the death, quite ironically, to keep their deceased father's memory alive.[1] In a little more than a century, however, this gladiatorial *munus* or "duty" to the dead became a game for the living—a state-sanctioned blood sport reinforcing Roman attributes like *virtus*: prowess in taking life and poise in facing death.[2]

By the second century A.D., the fifty thousand–seat wonder now known as the Colosseum served as the ultimate stage for this "theater of terror," pitting man against man or man against beast.[3] Here came the cry of battle and clash of iron, the promise of glory and plea for mercy. During its one hundred–day inauguration (A.D. 80), "over nine thousand animals were killed and, according to some, five thousand…in a single day," along with two thousand people.[4] Dr. Cameron Hawkins, assistant professor of religion and classics at the University of Rochester, has estimated some five thousand gladiators died yearly during Rome's Imperial Period (27 B.C.-A.D. 476), calculating to more than 2.5 million perishing in the arenas.[5] This figure does not even factor those slain during the Republic Period (509 B.C.-27 B.C.) or the pregame executions of countless Christians, criminals, and prisoners of war sentenced to die by flame, beast, or sword. Welcome to the stone-cold, bloodstained world of the gladiator!

Owner & Slave

For its first two hundred years, gladiator culture consisted mainly of criminals, captives, rebels, and slaves. By personal background or prior profession then, many were experienced killers and some quite proficient. Gladiator training only augmented an existing skill set and steeled an already thick skin. Only a handful of gladiators were freeborn.[6] Fewer came from upper social echelons. Despite their accepted place in Roman culture, however, which commanded popular respect, gladiators embodied the dregs of society, "the lowest of the low...commodities to be dumped when economic factors made them unacceptably expensive."[7]

The gladiator world revolved around a triad of powerful figures: the *lanista*, the *doctor*, and the *editor*. The journey began with a *lanista* who purchased the would-be gladiator from the slave market according to Roman law. Next, kneeling before the altar of a warrior-cult god like Mars (Rome's god of war), the slave recited the *auctoramentum gladiatorium*, the "gladiators' wage."[8] Roman statesman and satirist Petronius noted that a gladiator pledged "body and soul" to his lanista and "to endure burning, bondage, flogging," and "death by the sword."[9] After his vow, the *fighter-slave* arose to salute his new master. Any personal rights were now forfeit; all prior aspirations or claims upon him—null and void. The fighter-slave belonged solely to his lanista-lord as an instrument for his service and the glory of the empire, and this truth was promptly seared into his flesh by a red-hot branding iron marking him forever as a member of the *familia gladiatorium*, the "family of gladiators."

These truths make fine soil to begin our lesson, for, like gladiators, most of us were worldly "nobodies" before we met Jesus. Greater still, some of us had gone as low as possible. Sin had shipwrecked our lives, placed us on death's doorstep, and men had written us off. Only God's mercy prevented our death. Paul sums up our state well:

> For consider your calling, brothers: not many of you were wise according to worldly standards, not many were powerful, not many were of noble birth. But God chose what is foolish in the world to shame the wise; God chose what is weak in the world to shame the strong; God chose what is low and despised in the world, even things that are not, to bring to nothing things that are, so that no human being might boast in the presence of God. And because of him you are in Christ Jesus, who became to us wisdom from

God, righteousness and sanctification and redemption, so that, as it is written, "Let the one who boasts, boast in the Lord." (1 Corinthians 1:26-31)

Scripture teaches that, before we met Jesus, all of us were professional sinners, and some of us quite proficient (Romans 3:10-23). Captives of impurity and iniquity, hopeless rebels against God's ways and laws, we were His "enemies"—"by nature children of wrath (Romans 5:10)."[i] "Of the flesh," "sold under sin," "slaves of sin," "dead in sin," and "bound for destruction," our focus was self; our boast; our shame; our god: our sinful appetite (Romans 6:17).[ii]

Yet in His mercy, while we were still sinful dregs, the Heavenly Lanista—the Lord Jesus, bought us off the slave market of sin and death in accordance with God's Law. Christ ransomed us from that hellishly doomed way of life by dying for us on the Cross (John 3:16).[iii] Now, by God's grace, through faith in Him, and the irrevocable seal of His Spirit, we've become part of a forgiven family and a house of elite spiritual warriors (John 10:28-29).[iv]

What too many Christians have forgotten, though, is that Jesus purchased us. We are not our own. Like Roman slaves, any personal rights, prior aspirations, or claims upon our own lives became null and void when we surrendered to our Master Christ. By His blood, we belong to Him. 1 Corinthians 6:19-20, NLT, asks: "Don't you realize that your body is the temple of the Holy Spirit, who lives in you and was given to you by God? You do not belong to yourself, for God bought you with a high price. So you must honor God with your body." Romans 6:22 adds that we have been "set free from sin and have become slaves of God." Now, we are to present our bodily "members as slaves to righteousness (Romans 6:19)."

The Gladiator & Suffering

All of this means we have become instruments for our Lanista's service and glory. Part of that means sharing in His sufferings. "God has given

---

i   *Ephesians 2:3*
ii   *Romans 20; 7:14; Ephesians 2:1-3; Philippians 3:18-19*
iii   *Romans 5:8; 8:2*
iv   *2 Corinthians 1:22; Ephesians 1:13-14; 2:8-9, 19; 4:30; 6:10-18; 2 Timothy 2:3*

you the privilege not only to believe in Christ but also to suffer for him (Philippians 1:29, GW)," Paul said. Suffering for Christ's sake, that God's will may be done on earth, stands inseparable to the Christian warfare, and there's no better example here than Paul (Matthew 6:10).

Suffering for Christ's sake, that God's will may be done on earth, stands inseparable to the Christian warfare...

When false apostles dared to question his loyalty and credentials, he came out swinging—with a different kind of resumé.

> Are they Hebrews? So am I. Are they Israelites? So am I. Are they offspring of Abraham? So am I. Are they servants of Christ? I am a better one... with far greater labors, far more imprisonments, with countless beatings, and often near death.

> Five times I received at the hands of the Jews the forty lashes less one. Three times I was beaten with rods. Once I was stoned. Three times I was shipwrecked; a night and a day I was adrift at sea; on frequent journeys, in danger from rivers, danger from robbers, danger from my own people, danger from Gentiles, danger in the city, danger in the wilderness, danger at sea, danger from false brothers; in toil and hardship, through many a sleepless night, in hunger and thirst, often without food, in cold and exposure. And, apart from other things, there is the daily pressure on me of my anxiety for all the churches. (2 Corinthians 11:23-28)

Consider what Paul endured and recall the gladiator oath: burning, bondage, scourging, sword.... Paul suffered deeply, yet like a nightmare to Satan he just kept coming! Listen to his gladiator-like grit in the 1996 *New Living Translation* of 2 Corinthians 4:8-12:

> We are pressed on every side by troubles, but we are not crushed and broken. We are perplexed, but we don't give up and quit. We are hunted down, but God never abandons us. We get knocked down, but we get up again and keep going.

Through suffering, these bodies constantly share in the death of Jesus, so that the life of Jesus may also be seen in our bodies. Yes, we live under constant danger of death because we serve Jesus, so that the life of Jesus will be obvious in our dying bodies. So we live in the face of death, but it has resulted in eternal life for you.[10]

Paul's words read like an oath for spiritual gladiators, displaying an indomitable spirit, unflinching devotion, and Kingdom-minded perspective. Compare this with the weak commitment we often see among Christians today. When pressed by troubles, we break quickly. When perplexed, we quit regularly. When Satan hunts us, we think God has abandoned us. When knocked down, we stay down instead of getting up. We lose many battles because we lack the fortitude of the Early Church—their tenacious "never quit, never say die" spirit—and our constant retreat from suffering is costing the Kingdom much in the modern age.

I can't count how many times I've been knocked down over the years. But, just when I thought of giving up, this passage began playing like an anthem in my head. See, one of the greatest lessons I've learned is: the battle does not go to the smartest or strongest, but the most stubborn—the one who refuses to quit, who keeps getting up, who "having done all" simply chooses to "stand" (Ecclesiastes 9:11).[v] In the arena of warfare, endurance is just as much a weapon as the Word itself because when we choose to get up or stand firm, we're choosing to trust God's Word—His promises (Psalm 91:4).[vi] We're saying, "Let God be true and every man a liar (Romans 3:4)."

Endurance is just as much a weapon as the Word itself because when we choose to get up or stand firm, we're choosing to trust God's Word...

And here's a truth to go with that: Satan and his minions don't have God's indwelling Spirit (John 14:16-17). We do! Every Christian possesses unlimited fortitude, but few tap from this bottomless well when trial comes. "I can do all things through Christ who strengthens me," Paul

---

v   *Ephesians 6:13*
vi   *Luke 18:1; Romans 5:3-5; 2 Co. 1:20; Ephesians 6:18*

said (Philippians 4:13). We etch these words in gold calligraphy on some overpriced floral portrait in a Christian bookstore—without a thought that Paul wrote them from rusty bonds in a dank dungeon. Satan cannot claim this promise. Neither can he declare, "Greater is He who is in me than he who is in the world." And, because he cannot, his strength will inevitably fail (1 John 4:4). That means if we choose to trust God, if we keep getting up, the devil loses.

Still, we all grow weary. That's when we must recall that, unlike gladiators, suffering for Christ is never in vain. As Paul points out, by "living in the face of death," we bring life to others—God's truth, love, liberty, and salvation. It's high time then we start seeing suffering as the honor Jesus said it is and stop retreating from it. In Christ's suffering, Paul saw the breadth and depth of God's love, and that truth enabled him to bear up under suffering like Atlas (Ephesians 3:18-19). Equally, Acts 5:41, NLT, reveals that the apostles

Suffering was the gladiator's soul and glory, and it remains the heart of the Christian's calling and warfare.

left the presence of the Jewish High Council "rejoicing that God had counted them worthy to suffer disgrace for the name of Jesus." That's a different perspective and, if we wish to be useful to God, we must embrace it. Suffering was the gladiator's soul and glory, and it remains the heart of the Christian's calling and warfare.

Instructor & Beast Fighter

Returning to the gladiatorial trinity, working under the lanista's watchful eye was every gladiator's bane and best friend: the *doctor*—the weapons instructor. A doctor had studied the fighting arts, training till weapons were extensions of himself. He'd seen the gore of the arena, taken the wounds of combat, and given the death blow numerous times. A well-seasoned champion, he held class daily in the *ludus gladiatorium* or "school of gladiators."

Here, through a gauntlet of drills and adversaries, the doctor imparted his veteran knowledge, identified strengths and weaknesses, and honed the survival and killer instincts. Slaves were hammered into fighters; trainees into highly specialized combatants. If a gladiator wished to survive, he listened to the doctor because he understood the stakes, which were often *sine missione*—only one warrior emerging from a no-holds-barred death match. The doctor also understood the opponent, which wasn't always human.

The *bestiarius* was a "beast fighter." To prepare for these deadly encounters, the doctor trained him in the ways of his animal opponents. Bears and bulls, pythons and panthers, a *bestiarius* studied them all for he never knew which foe he might face or how many. Likewise, to help Christians prepare for our combat with Satan, the Holy Spirit, the Doctor of God's gladiators, employs a fascinating teaching tool in Scripture. Assigning animalistic traits to something non-animal is called *zoomorphism*. In the Bible, God compares Satan to three of nature's fiercest beasts to expose his three most common schemes. These zoomorph lessons hold great wisdom, and Christians who master them become ferocious Kingdom beast fighters!

Zoomorph Lesson #1: The Lying Serpent

> But I am afraid that as the serpent deceived Eve by his cunning, your thoughts will be led astray from a sincere and pure devotion to Christ. For if someone comes and proclaims another Jesus than the one we proclaimed, or if you receive a different spirit from the one you received, or if you accept a different gospel from the one you accepted, you put up with it readily enough.
>
> —2 Corinthians 11:3-4

Writing to the zealous but gullible Corinthian church, Paul warned them against "spiritual snake-bite." Smooth-talking, fake apostles had slithered into their midst. And, just as Satan had questioned God's character in Eden to discredit Him and inject Eve's mind with lies, false apostles now challenged Paul's credentials in Corinth to poison believers with false doctrines—like asserting there was no resurrection of the dead (Genesis 3:1-5).[vii] Not unlike some modern-day Christians in their rush to "spiri-

---

vii   *1 Corinthians 15:12*

tuality" and "relevance," the Corinthians took the bait. How could they overcome this attack? Let's consider another parallel.

The Independent, a British online news source, reported that "up to two million people a year are bitten by poisonous snakes. One hundred thousand die and three times that are permanently affected." In Nigeria, "one-in-ten hospital beds are occupied by snakebite victims," and "most of the bites are from the carpet viper," whose venom destroys the blood's clotting ability, causing victims to bleed to death in minutes, inducing tissue death and organ failure. Lest Westerners think themselves far from this threat, rattlesnake venom contains these same toxins.[11]

But John Landon, professor of chemical pathology at Saint Bartholomew's Hospital in London, made an astonishing discovery: among all animals, the blood of a lamb produces the most potent antivenom. Antivenom is made by injecting an animal with snake venom, triggering antibody production.[12] Antibodies are then harvested to create antivenom. The lamb's antivenom is so strong that it's also been employed against two of Australia's deadliest arachnids, the redback and funnel-web spiders, and other poisonous creatures all over the world.[13]

The point here is that Jesus referred to Satan as the "Father of Lies (John 8:44)," and, like snake venom, Satan's lies contain lethal "toxins": doubt, discouragement, unbelief, and fear, which kill hope and destroy faith (John 10:10).[viii] Paul also points out that a key way Satan's lies enter our minds is through false teachers—those who cannot straightly cut the Word of Truth because of ignorance or intentionally distort it for selfish ends (2 Corinthians 4:2).[ix] When anyone (Christian or not) believes just one of Satan's lies, destruction follows. Relationships, health, spiritual vision, ministry…the resulting damage can be vast.

Scripture, however, calls Jesus the "Lamb of God (John 1:29, 36)," and we can inoculate ourselves with His "antivenom" by routine injections of His Word—regular reading, meditation, and memorization (Joshua 1:8).[x] After all, our ability to recognize a fake depends on our fluency with the real article. This is true for bankers, artists, curators, etc., and Christians are

---

viii   *1 Corinthians 13:13; 2 Timothy 2:18*
ix   *11:13-14; 2 Timothy 2:15; 2 Peter 3:16-17*
x   *Psalm 1:1-3; Acts 17:11*

The Lamb of God's Word immunizes His beast fighters to the Serpent's venomous lies...

no different. We cannot rely on feelings to recognize God's voice or simply take people at their word. We must "search the Scriptures" daily so that we know what God has said and what He has not (Acts 17:11). We need to know the Bible so well we can quote it, cite the reference, and break a verse down like a soldier fieldstripping a rifle.

Jesus said, "If you abide in my word, you are truly my disciples, and you will know the truth, and the truth will set you free (John 8:31-32)." If we know God's Truth, we can reject Satan's Lie. The Lamb of God's Word immunizes His beast fighters to the Serpent's venomous lies and sharpens our eyes to spiritual con artists trying to "quick-change" false teaching for biblical truth. When was your last vaccination?

Zoomorph Lesson #2: The Prowling Lion

> Humble yourselves, therefore, under the mighty hand of God so that at the proper time he may exalt you, casting all your anxieties on him, because he cares for you. Be sober-minded; be watchful. Your adversary the devil prowls around like a roaring lion, seeking someone to devour. Resist him, firm in your faith, knowing that the same kinds of suffering are being experienced by your brotherhood throughout the world.
>
> —1 Peter 5:6-9

Peter compared Satan's ruthless tactics with a lion looking for easy prey. But what defines "easy"? For insight, consider one of history's most terrifying tales of the king of the jungle. In 1898, the British Army commissioned Lieutenant-Colonel John Henry Patterson to build a railway bridge over Kenya's Tsavo River, which means "slaughter."[14] Upon arrival, Patterson faced this very thing. Two male lions more than nine feet long began stealing into camp, dragging sleeping men from their tents, then mauling and devouring them. Many locals believed that the "Ghost" and the "Darkness," as they dubbed the lions, were demon possessed for sometimes they ate their prey, but other times seemed to kill for fun.

As months passed, even with bonfires and thick thorn hedges surrounding camp, the attacks increased. Men vanished, work stopped, and workers fled. Patterson doubled his efforts, taking vigil in the treetops and setting traps below. Soon, from his high vantage point, Patterson sighted the first lion we'll refer to as the "Ghost," wounding him in the hind leg. The Ghost vanished but returned that evening stalking Patterson. This time he landed a kill-shot in the banshee's heart. The Ghost would never haunt Tsavo again. The Darkness remained at large.

Days later from a high scaffold, Patterson's rifle flashed again. The Darkness bolted into the night, but light had pierced him. Eleven days later, two more bullets found their mark. Still, the shadowy stalker escaped. The next morning, as dawn broke through the brush, three more shots cut the predator's paws from beneath him. Still refusing to die, the Darkness clawed his way toward Patterson, who now leveled a third rifle. With three more shots, silence fell on the savannah. Twelve days, three rifles, and nine bullets ended the reign of the Darkness,[15] but not before he and the Ghost claimed 135 men.[16] What can we learn?

Tsavo's trouble boiled down to one thing: neglectful, napping men. Bonfires and hedges were no substitute for a hunter holding vigil on high. Equally, attending the best church and believing the soundest doctrine will never replace a Christian's personal time in the tower of prayer. Habakkuk 2:1, NLT, says, "I will climb up to my watchtower and stand at my guardpost. There I will wait to see what the Lord says and how he will answer my complaint." Just as a tower of wood placed Patterson above the brush to spot and shoot the lions, the tower of prayer positions the Christian above worldly distractions to dis-

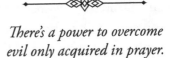

There's a power to overcome evil only acquired in prayer.

cern and defeat the devil. There's a power to overcome evil only acquired in prayer. Peter learned this the hard way.

On the night of His betrayal, Jesus warned His disciples that hell's lion was prowling when He said, "Simon, Simon, Satan demanded to have you [all], that he might sift you like wheat (Luke 22:31)."[17] He then foretold Peter's three denials, which went unheeded (Luke 22:34). As the scene moved to Gethsemane and Satan drew near, Jesus prodded Peter. "Stay here and keep watch," He said as He knelt a stone's throw away to do the same (Mark 14:34). One hour later, was Peter in the tower? No. "Simon, are you asleep? Could you not watch one hour? Watch and pray so that you may not enter into temptation...(Mark 14:37-38)." We know how the story ends: three prompts to pray; three naps instead; three denials of Christ (Mark 14:41, 72). Coincidence?

Jesus indicated Peter's denials were not chance when He said, "Watch and pray *so that* you may not enter into temptation" (italics mine). The Greek conjunction *hina* ("so that") closes the case. Jesus tied victory over temptation directly with prayer. Still, what was Satan's lion-like "devouring" in 1 Peter 5:8? What was Peter warning Christians to watch against? 1 Peter 5:7 tells us: "Casting all your anxieties on him, because he cares for you." Anxiety was ravaging first-century saints, and in two thousand years not much has changed. Anxiety remains the rifest mental disorder in the U.S. today, afflicting 40 million adults age 18 and older (18.1 percent of the population)[18] and 284 million people worldwide.[19]

But the beast Anxiety prowls with a dark companion. In 2017 "an estimated 17.3 million adults in the United States had at least one major depressive episode," representing "7.1 percent of all U.S. adults."[20] Also, "an estimated 264 million people in the world experienced depression."[21] "Depression is the leading cause of disability worldwide," according to the World Health Organization, and almost 1 million people suffering from a mental disorder end their lives every year.[22] Finally, the Anxiety and Depression Association of America notes: "It's not uncommon for someone with an anxiety disorder to also suffer from depression or vice versa. Nearly one-half of those diagnosed with depression are also diagnosed with an anxiety disorder."[23] Nothing gnaws more at the soul than these spectral predators. Anxiety and Depression are the Ghost and the Darkness of our age, devouring millions of souls daily.

Can the watchtower of prayer help us overcome them? Scripture shouts, "Yes!" Paul, writing from a dungeon, says, "Do not be anxious about anything, but in everything by prayer and supplication with thanksgiving let your requests be made known to God. And the peace of God, which surpasses all understanding, will guard your hearts and minds in Christ Jesus (Philippians 4:6-7)." First, Paul describes anxiety's soul-shredding force in the Greek *merimnaó* ("be anxious"), meaning "to go to pieces… pulled apart in different directions."[24] Anxiety and depression clamp down on our souls with canines of doubt and fear, then tear us apart.

To overcome, Peter and Paul beckon us to "throw" all anxiety and heaviness at Christ's feet in prayer, promising a great exchange: our chaos for His peace. If this seems like nonsense, recognize that the *Journal of Clinical Nursing* has stated, "Prayer can reduce levels of depression and anxiety in patients, according to research. Researchers gathered data from twenty-six studies that identified the active involvement of patients in private or personal prayer…. Findings show that praying, measured by frequency, is usually associated with lower levels of depression and anxiety" and "most of the studies showing positive associations were in areas with strong Christian traditions and involved samples with strong religious beliefs."[25]

Moreover, "researchers from Baylor University found that people who pray to a loving and protective God are less likely to experience anxiety-related disorders—worry, fear, self-consciousness, social anxiety and obsessive-compulsive behavior—compared to people who pray but don't really expect to receive any comfort or protection from God."[26] Further still, "another recent study by Columbia University found that participating in regular meditation or other spiritual practice actually thickens parts of the brain's cortex, and this could be the reason those activities tend to guard against depression—especially in those at risk for the disease."[27]

Lastly, noting "prayer is a special form of meditation," the *Indian Journal of Psychiatry* reports:

Different types of meditation have been shown to…produce a clinically significant reduction in resting as well as ambulatory blood pressure, to reduce heart rate, to result in cardiorespiratory synchronization, to alter levels of melatonin and serotonin, to suppress corticostriatal glutamatergic neurotransmission, to boost the immune response, to decrease the levels of reactive oxygen species as measured by ultraweak photon emission, to reduce stress and promote positive mood states, to reduce anxiety and pain and enhance self-esteem and to have favorable influence on overall and spiritual quality of life in late-stage disease. Interestingly, spiritual meditation has been found to be superior to secular meditation and relaxation in terms of decrease in anxiety and improvement in positive mood, spiritual health, spiritual experiences, and tolerance to pain.[28]

Science has confirmed what God said eons ago: Prayer is a towering support and rifle-like weapon to deliver our souls from the lions of anxiety and depression (Isaiah 26:3; Philippians 4:6-7).

Zoomorph Lesson #3: The Accusing Dragon

> And the great dragon was thrown down, that ancient serpent, who is called the devil and Satan, the deceiver of the whole world—he was thrown down to the earth, and his angels were thrown down with him. And I heard a loud voice in heaven, saying, "Now the salvation and the power and the kingdom of our God and the authority of his Christ have come, for the accuser of our brothers has been thrown down, who accuses them day and night before our God. And they have conquered him by the blood of the Lamb and by the word of their testimony, for they loved not their lives even unto death.
>
> —Revelation 12:9-11

Our last zoomorph comes from Scripture's final book. These verses and the surrounding context of Revelation twelve and thirteen reveal that Satan's dragon-like attack is a downright dirty one. The threat of his serpentine attack dwells in his venomous lies and biblically unimmunized Christians; his lion-ish attack in his constant prowling for anxious, prayerless souls. But what danger is the dragon?

The term rendered "devil" throughout the New Testament offers a good clue. It's the Greek compound *diábolos*, whose root means "to hurl or cast through" with words or objects, especially to bring charges against someone with malice. A *diábolos* is a false accuser, one seeking to harm others by slander or libel.[29] The term "accuser" refers to a legal prosecutor, whose allegations may be true or false.[30] Like the mythical dragon then, Satan uses his "fiery breath" to wage war, showering us with accusation, slander, and propaganda. He seeks to incinerate our self-image and scorch our public one; to ignite anger, jealousy, and fear; to sway opinion and sabotage relationships, offices, and opportunities; and, overall, to smolder our faith in God and people, leaving us emotionally cauterized (Re. 12:10, 16).[xi]

Prayer is a towering support and rifle-like weapon to deliver our souls from the lions of anxiety and depression.

Yes, the great dragon loves to slander and accuse and ever spies for human puppets to assist him. In Job 1 and 2, he slanders Job before God's Throne, charging his faith as fake. He then manipulates Job's "friends" to repeatedly accuse him, alleging his predicament is God's payback for some unconfessed sin. In Zechariah 3:1, the saint's prosecutor stands again before Heaven's Bench accusing the high priest Joshua. In 1 Kings 21:10, two of Satan's spiritual offspring, "sons of Belial," bear false witness against the innocent Naboth so King Ahab can stone him and steal his vineyard. Finally, in 1 Timothy 3:11, Paul warns of female *diábolous*, "she-devils," idle women walking about the Church as slanderers (see also 1 Timothy 5:13). Let's underscore this with an illustration.

There are no studies or historic accounts of dragons to help unveil this scheme, but some powerful media can aid us. In *The Hobbit*, J.R.R. Tolkien introduces the hate-spewing "Smaug," a great dragon who boasts, "My armour is like tenfold shields, my teeth are swords, my claws spears...and my breath death!"[31] Breath of death indeed! Like the flames he exhales, Smaug also hurls accusations with every flick of his tongue.

In Tolkien's tale and the movie *The Hobbit: The Desolation of Smaug*, the wicked worm's first words to Bilbo Baggins are, "Well, thief...." When the wee hero politely engages him, Smaug spits back, "You have nice manners—for a thief and a liar." As conversation continues, Smaug's rancor deepens. His words cut the hobbit's heart, moving from accusing him to his dwarf friend, Thorin Oakenshield. "You are being used, thief in the shadows. You were only ever a means to an end. The coward Oakenshield has weighed the value of your life and found it worth nothing!" Bilbo shakes his head, struggling to clear his mind. But it's not until Bard the Bowman's black arrow pierces the gap in Smaug's armor that his slander

---

xi   *Revelation 13:4-6, 11*

stops.[32] Similarly, only the Bible's "Black Arrow" can silence the Accusing Dragon's tongue.

God's Black Arrow bears two lethal blades: Christ's blood and the Word of Testimony. Only Christ's blood can purge and forgive sin—before anyone comes to Him for salvation and long after (Leviticus 17:11).[xii] But, we must be honest: Satan's accusations aren't always baseless; sometimes we *have* sinned and need to repent.

How will God respond when we do? David assures us, "For you, O Lord, are good and forgiving, abounding in steadfast love to all who call upon you (Psalm 86:5)." God is ready to forgive when we come to Him, waiting with bathwater and clean clothes—not a disappointed scowl or demeaning reprimand. John echoes David's comfort, promising: "If we confess our sins, he is faithful and just to forgive us of our sins and to cleanse us from all unrighteousness (1 John 1:9)." Confessing our sin to God—calling it what He calls it, then asking for forgiveness and help to turn from it—extinguishes Satan's fiery charges (Psalm 38:18).[xiii]

But how is Satan's accusation actually overcome? God *extinguishes* it, as Jeremiah 31:34b says, "I will forgive their iniquity, and I will remember their sin no more." In other words, unlike the devil and hateful people, God forgives and forgets. He never brings up what He's forgiven. The devil (the Lord of the Flies) and his human puppets, from politicians and tabloid media to hateful relatives and coworkers, dig through our trash to accuse us—not God. At the Cross, Jesus said, "It is finished (John 19:30)." He meant it!

Concerning the Black Arrow's second blade, the Word of Testimony, it's crucial to know *what* the testimony is and *who* testifies. John didn't leave that to guesswork.

And *the Spirit is the one who testifies*, because the Spirit is the truth. If we receive the testimony of men, the testimony of God is greater, for *this is the testimony of God* that He has borne concerning His Son...*that God gave us eternal life, and this life is in his Son. Whoever has the Son has life;*

---

xii   *Hebrews 9:22-28*
xiii   *Proverbs 28:13*

whoever does not have the Son of God does not have life. (1 John 5:6b, 9, 11b-12, italics mine)

So, what is the testimony? "God gave us eternal life, and this life is in His Son." In other words, forgiveness and salvation are found only in Jesus (John 14:6).[xiv] John further clarifies: "whoever has the Son has life." In other words, we don't *hope* we have life. If we have Christ, we do! We're saved. No devilish charge can stick to us. God has purged us of all sin—past, present, and future—because we have trusted in Christ's sacrificial blood.

Finally, who testifies? "The Spirit," John answers (1 John 5:6). Paul confirms this, saying, "The Spirit himself bears witness with our spirit that we are children of God (Romans 8:16)." In Galatians 4:6 he adds, "And because you are sons, God has sent the Spirit of his Son into our hearts, crying, 'Abba! Father!'" No testimony outweighs God's: any objection to the Blood of the Lamb or the Word of Testimony, any challenge to our forgiveness and salvation in Christ—by the Accuser of the Brethren or anyone else—is overruled. Case dismissed!

No testimony outweighs God's: any objection to the Blood of the Lamb or the Word of Testimony...is overruled...

In three profound zoomorphs, our Doctor-Trainer exposes Satan's three main schemes: a lying serpent, a prowling lion, and an accusing dragon. With these and so many other eye-opening scriptures, it's hard to believe that 40 percent of professing Christians "strongly agreed that Satan is not a living being." Another 19 percent "said they agree somewhat with that perspective." Last, 8 percent "were not sure what they believe about the existence of Satan."[33] What an indictment of our biblical illiteracy and unreadiness to face him! Cover to cover, Scripture testifies that Satan is a conscious, willful, and formidable foe. It discloses his...

1.) Former Estate: He was a holy angel of great rank who fell to pride and was cast out of Heaven. [xv]

---

xiv   *Acts 4:12*
xv   *Isaiah 14:3-21; Ezekiel 28:11-19; Luke 10:18; 1 Timothy 3:6.*

2.) Modus Operandi: He accuses, ambushes, attacks, deceives, disguises, hinders, hunts, schemes, slanders, and more!^{xvi}

3.) Vast Organization: He heads a huge syndicate of evil spirits around the world actively warring against God and mankind.^{xvii}

Furthermore, the Lord labels this infernal beast with a series of war names—like the Adversary (1 Chronicles 21:1),[34] the Enemy (Matthew 13:39), the Slanderer (Matthew 4:1),[35] the Accuser of the Brethren (Revelation 12:10), the Oppressor (Isaiah 14:4), the Evil One (Matthew 13:19), the Corruptor (Isaiah 54:16), the Tempter (Matthew 4:3), the Father of Lies (John 8:44), the Deceiver of the Whole World (Revelation 12:9), a Murderer from the Beginning (John 8:44), and the Destroyer (Revelation 9:11). Then, speaking of Satan's place in the cosmic hierarchy, the Lord dubs him the Prince of Demons (Matthew 9:34), Prince of the Power of the Air (Ephesians 2:2), Belial ("Lord of the Forest" - 2 Corinthians 6:15), Beelzebub ("Lord of the Flies" - Matthew 10:25), the Ruler of this World (John 14:30), and the God of this Age (2 Corinthians 4:3-4).

Now, if the FBI told you their most wanted criminal—a pathological liar, expert con artist, serial predator, mass murderer, and international terrorist—was after you and your family, would you make some life adjustments to prepare? Scripture profiles Heaven's Most Wanted Enemy. What are you doing to equip your family as spiritual beast fighters?

Giver & Receiver

In our equipping thus far, we've met two of three gladiatorial figureheads: the owner (*lanista*) and the trainer (*doctor*). We'll now greet our third: the *editor*, the giver of the games—the producer and financier. Originally a private citizen, the editor staged gladiatorial games as a gift to honor a deceased relative. Next, people of influence seeking favor, like senators in election time, began giving games. Finally, as the Roman State adopted games for its own ends, the office of editor almost invariably fell to the

---

xvi   Genesis 3:1; 1 Chronicles 21:1; Job 1-2; Zechariah 3:1-2; Matthew 4:3; Luke 4:13; 1 Corinthians 7:5; 2 Corinthians 2:11; 11:3-4, 13-14; Ephesians 6:11-13, 16; James 4:7; 1 Thessalonians 2:18; 1 Peter 5:8-9; Revelation 12:9-11

xvii Daniel 10:12-13, 20; Matthew 9:34; 10:25; 12:24-29; Luke 10:17-20; John 10:10; 14:30; 2 Corinthians 4:3-4; 6:15; Ephesians 2:1-3; 6:11-13; Revelation 12

emperor whose powers manifested in three ways: the *pompa*, *probatio*, and *pollice verso*.

Like its English derivative "pomp," the *pompa* was a grand pregame procession. Packed with musicians, gladiators and their assistants, statues of war gods like Hercules and Mars, and the editor riding in a chariot and arrayed in majestic apparel, it was a sight to behold.[36] As the pompa circled the arena and passed under the editor's seating box, he dismounted to meet with lanistas and complete his first duty: the matchmaking.[37] Lots were cast for each contest with the editor making the final call. His oversight guaranteed gladiators of comparable skill faced off, ensuring exciting matchups. As each match was made, the herald announced it and onto the fight card it went.[38, 39] With the card complete, the editor moved on to the *probatio*.

In the *probatio armorum* ("inspection of arms"), the editor examined every piece of armament—shields, spears, swords, helmets, etc.[40] Blades sliced through vegetables, proving their edges. Wooden clubs pounded armor, testing its integrity.[41] Nothing escaped the editor's all-scrutinizing eye, and "most members of the crowd watched…with great attentiveness," historian Alan Baker notes. Audiences appreciated this part of the pregame, as it ensured matches would be decided by skill, not malfunctioning weapons.[42]

With pregame duties fulfilled, the editor signaled the games to begin. As each match climaxed, his final power manifested as one gladiator inevitably stood over a knelt opponent, who raised an index finger in submission and a plea for mercy. Resting his sword on his foe's neck, the victor turned toward the editor's box. Standing, the editor raised his arm so all could see the *pollice verso* or "turned thumb"—down meaning mercy; up, death's sword point.[43] Before, during, and after then—inspecting each weapon, selecting every foe, watching every battle, and deciding every outcome—stood the editor, the final figure of the gladiator trinity.

Not unlike the gladiatorial world, guided by a powerful triad, Scripture teaches that a Triune God—Father, Son, and Holy Spirit—oversees our every battle and superintends each detail. Nowhere is this truth better seen than Job. But before going there, we need to meet one more gladiator: the *andabaté*. No gladiator faced a greater test than him. This fully armored fighter wielded two swords, making him more lethal than others. What made him truly unique, though, was his helmet, which had no eye holes.[44] He fought blind! Needless to say, he leaned heavily on his training to survive. If there ever was a spiritual *andabaté*, Job was it.

Job: The Andabaté

The Book of Job opens in Heaven's throne room. All the "sons of God," an Old Testament term for holy angels, are reporting.[45] Satan appears. A talk with God ensues and ends with God granting Satan permission to attack Job: "Everything he has is in your power, but you must not lay a hand on him (1:12, GW)!"[46] Satan leaves, blindsides Job, kills all ten of his children, all but four servants, and his entire estate in one day—a staggering loss.

But what happens next is even more staggering: Chapter 1 ends not with Job shouting at the Editor's box but kneeling before it in worship. "Naked I came from my mother's womb, and naked shall I return. The Lord gave, and the Lord has taken away; blessed be the name of the Lord (v. 21)." Job's pinpoint theology wastes any notion that Satan ever acts beyond the superintendence of God. Satan reports to the Lord, asks to attack, receives strict parameters, and obeys. From the beginning, God allows or disallows, gives and takes away in between, and it is God whom Job worships at day's end.

When we would wail from a fetal position or scream profanity at Heaven, Job worships. How? Because even though he's fighting as blind as an andabaté, not knowing why he's being attacked, he knows who sits in the Editor's box. Job understands his match was laid out beforehand—time, place, weapons, opponent, and outcome. Satan drew first blood, but Job already held the high ground: the unassailable position of God's sovereignty, the foundation of spiritual warfare. Job recognized that God must sign off on whatever happens in His universe, and Job tenaciously holds that ground as all hell breaks loose again in chapter 2.

As that curtain rises, the angels are back at God's throne with Satan. God rubs Satan's nose in his failure to turn Job, and the devil basically calls, "Double or nothing! Let me touch him this time. When I'm done, he'll cuss you up one side and down the other!" "Do whatever you want, but spare his life (v. 6)," God replies, and round 2 begins. Satan strikes

Job with burning, oozing boils from head to toe (2:7-8). His flesh hardens and crawls with maggots (7:5). Tissue dies and falls from his body. He's afflicted so badly that his three friends weep at his unrecognizable form (2:12; 30:30). His bones burn in pain (30:17, 30). He's riddled with nightmares (7:13-14). He cries to God with no response (19:7; 30:19-20). The public despises him, his family forsakes him, and his three "friends" blame him for the calamity.[xviii] Finally, as the accusing dragon moves in for the kill, Job's wife, in a moment of weakness, becomes Satan's mouthpiece: "Do you still hold fast your integrity? Curse God and die (2:9)."

One can almost hear Satan chuckling, "Go ahead now. Curse God good and long, Job. Show that heavenly goody-goody that your faith is just as fake as I said." Satan waits. God watches. How will the battered rancher respond? Then, it comes…loving, focused, and penetrating: "You speak as one of the foolish women," Job replies to his wife. "Shall we receive good from God, and shall we not receive evil (2:10)?"[47]

Job's poise astonishes me. Languishing under incalculable grief and pain, he still finds the grace to handle his wife's heart in meltdown and apostasy. She attacks him. He aims at the issue, contrasting her behavior with an unbeliever's to nudge her back to faith. He doesn't shout, "You foolish woman!" He says, "You're talking *like* one." In other words, "I know you're hurting, but this is not you. You're acting like an unbeliever—not the woman I married. You've fumbled your identity. Let me help you find it again." Well done, Job!

Next, after reminding her of who she is, Job asks the ultimate question: "Shall we receive good from God, and shall we not receive evil?" In other words, "Do we only praise God in the good times—when we like what He's doing? Are we real followers or fair-weather friends?" As friends accuse and his wife taunts, Job's reply rings out like a gladiator's cry in the Colosseum, "Though He slay me, I will hope in him, yet I will argue my ways to his face (13:15)."

Trusting God's sovereign hand and praising him in personal tragedy is the Christian's greatest battle—the peak of warfare. Because of sin, our existence is fraught with evil, injustice, pain, and mystery. In the fog of

---

xviii   *Job 4-5; 8; 11; 15; 18; 20; 22; 25; 19:13-19; 30:1, 9-14.*

cosmic warfare, there are times we all want to turn to the Editor's box and question, and it is unbiblical nonsense to tell grief-stricken people, from our own safe circumstances or some lofty pulpit, to not ask, "Why, God?" A two-word summary of the Book of Job is just that. But there is a right and wrong way to wrestle with the Almighty.

The God Who Wrestles

Part of being created in God's image encompasses man's unique place to reason and wrestle with Him.[48] We see God's gladiators doing this throughout Scripture: Abraham over Sodom and Gomorrah (Genesis 18:22-33); Moses for Israel on Mount Sinai (Exodus 33:12-17); David regarding the wicked in the Psalms (Psalm 6; 13; 35); Paul and his thorn in the flesh (2 Corinthians 12:7-10). It's also the great lesson of Jacob's encounter with the Angel of the Lord, the Preincarnate Christ (Genesis 32:22-32). God could've snapped His little heel-grabber like a twig, yet tussled with him all night and blessed him in the most bizarre way: bestowing a permanent limp, along with a new name—Israel, "God wrestles (v. 28)."[xix]

More than any other book in Scripture, Job wrestles with life's greatest dilemmas—the problems of evil and suffering and God's sovereignty over them. Devoting forty-two chapters, 1,070 verses, and 18,098 words to the matter, its length alone reveals that the Lord never dodges hard questions like some slick politician or downplays life's pain with religious platitudes. Where many saints flee, Job charges into the controversy, feeling the emotions, cutting the legs beneath false theology, and demanding real answers.

As suffering lingers and his "miserable comforters" droll on, Job grows indignant, longing to plead his case with God (16:2). "Oh, that I had one to hear me! Here is my signature! Let the Almighty answer me!" he shouts (31:35a). To his shock, Heaven's Chief Justice grants his petition, and in a four-chapter whirlwind showers Job with some seventy-seven questions (38-41). "Where were you when I laid the earth's foundations? Who gave the sea its boundaries? Ever command the morning to appear? Where does light come from? Can you guide the stars in their courses? How would you feed all the beasts of the field and birds of the air? What

---

xix   *Hosea 12:1-6.*

about humbling the proud? Have you ever made a dinosaur?"

At first glance, God's reply seems like the rant of an irate parent. In just minutes, though, He's schooled Job with a Creator's crash course spanning fields of scientific study—geology, cos-

Trusting God's sovereign hand and praising him in personal tragedy is the Christian's greatest battle—the peak of warfare.

mology, oceanography, physics, meteorology, astronomy, zoology, biology, anthropology, paleontology, and beyond—leading Job to the conclusion that he's caught up in something much larger than himself. A far greater purpose is being worked out. Job replies to God:

> I know that you can do all things, and that no purpose of yours can be thwarted. "Who is this that hides counsel without knowledge?" Therefore I have uttered what I did not understand, things too wonderful for me, which I did not know. "Hear, and I will speak; I will question you, and you make it known to me." I had heard of you by the hearing of the ear, but now my eye sees you; therefore I despise myself, and repent in dust and ashes. (Job 42:2-6)

Job's recap of his encounter offers great comfort for suffering spiritual gladiators. First, his personal mountains of anger, pride, grief, and pain instantly melt before God's majesty (Psalm 97:5). The words of a great hymn come to mind: "Turn your eyes upon Jesus; look full in His wonderful face, and the things of earth will grow strangely dim, in the light of His glory and grace."[49] Surprising to some, Job's consolation proves not to be a theological "what" or philosophical "why" but a relational "who" as he says, "I had heard of you by the hearing of the ear, *but now my eye sees you*" (v. 5, italics mine). When this world's sorrows and Satan's cruelty overwhelm us, we want to know God's purpose. But Job's lesson is that what we truly need is His presence. Hear me: This is not some stupid cliché. It's liberating truth (John 8:31-32)! It's seeing the Lord, intimately relating with Him, and experiencing His presence, that satisfies Job's longing and changes his outlook—not an explanation from God, which

It's seeing the Lord...that satisfies Job's longing...not an explanation from God...or a theological discourse...

Job thought he deserved, or a theological discourse, which his friends thought he needed (Psalm 16:11; 17:15).

Isaiah reacted similarly. "In the year that King Uzziah died I saw the Lord sitting upon a throne, high and lifted up; and the train of His robe filled the temple," he says (Isaiah 6:1). He sees the amazing six-winged seraphim standing in God's presence, calling, "Holy, holy, holy is the Lord of hosts; the whole earth is full of His glory (v. 3)." As God speaks, His voice shakes the foundations, the house fills with smoke, and the prophet cries, "Woe is me! For I am lost; for I am a man of unclean lips, and I dwell in the midst of a people of unclean lips; for my eyes have seen the King, the Lord of hosts (v.5)!"

Peter also falls apart at Christ's revelation. In Luke 5, he's arguing with a Nazarene carpenter-turned-Rabbi about fishing one moment. But when a miraculous catch appears in his nets, the proud fisherman falls to his knees exclaiming, "Depart from me, for I am a sinful man, O Lord (v.8)."

So, we're discussing more than the belief that God is almighty, one whose ways and power are past finding out, and more than the knowledge that He is holy—without sin or a shadow of turning (Romans 11:33)[xx] What makes the biblical God so breathtaking, versus all other contenders, is His earnest desire to relate to us when He has no need to do so. When we catch a glimpse of Immanuel, "God with Us"—the Grand Editor stepping down from His heavenly box; the Great Lanista walking into our humanity; the Divine Doctor wrestling with us in our infirmity—this is the victory that overcomes the world (Isaiah 7:14).[xxi] It's His love, His humility, His willingness to leave His glory and become the lily in our valley that removes death's sting, satisfies our deepest longings, and makes the unbearable bearable (Psalm 22:26).[xxii]

There's something else in Job's recap, though, that makes me weak in the knees. Most versions render Job's quoting of God in 42:4a as, "Hear, and I will speak," or "Listen now, and I will speak." The original Hebrew

---

xx   *James 1:17*
xxi   *Matthew 1:23; 1 John 5:4-5*
xxii   *107:8-9; Song 2:1; Romans 8:18; 2 Corinthians 2:14*

reads, *"Shema, na, weanoki adabber."* The interjection *"na,"* whose primary usage is a "particle of entreaty" as in "I beg you" or "I beseech you," is what's so telling—how loving this conversation was versus God flinging open a bedroom door and thundering at Job like an angry parent.[50] As seen above, many Bibles render *"na"* as "now" or omit it entirely, but I believe the New King James words it best, saying: "Listen, please, and let me speak...."

Now, when we think of God appearing in a whirlwind or elsewhere in the Old Testament, don't we typically picture the "Mount Sinai thing"— God's voice shaking the earth, smoke and fire billowing, à la, "I am Oz, the great and powerful"? Maybe I'm alone, but before this study I never really thought of the Old Testament God saying, "Please." Yet here, in a tragedy beyond words (Job's children dead, estate wiped out, health shattered, almost an entire staff killed, wife and friends forsaking him), God appears to Job not thundering as his Lord but pleading as Father and Friend. Think about it: God is using Job's life in what will one day be the textbook example of patience in suffering—the go-to model for saints (Romans 15:4).[xxiii] To say, "This is important," would be one of the greatest understatements in history. For God so loved a people yet unborn, who will one day face all kinds of hell in this world, that He allows Satan to ransack another son's life to equip them. What a type and shadow!

In the midst of His great purpose, however, God still has time to appear and wrestle with His hurting son—to not only instruct, but help Job not miss His heart. How He opens the conversation is huge, and it's this same God who would later teach Solomon, "A soft answer turns away wrath, but a harsh word stirs up anger (Proverbs 15:1)." I assert: what transformed Job's tragedy was not just God's majesty, but His kindness. God's majesty instantly outweighed Job's problems, but His kindness melted mountains of anger and pain, salved Job's sorrow, and led him to repentance, transforming what Job previously heard of Him.

That must mean something because God said there was no one on earth like Job at this time (Job 1:8).[xxiv] When we find ourselves like Job then, before some tragic ash heap, maybe the best prayer is: "Lord, I've heard

---

xxiii   James 5:11
xxiv   Romans 2:4

about you in the past, but I've never been in this place before. Please, give me eyes to see and a heart to trust You here."

Fighting For Dad

It's hard to trust God within the battle, to keep praising Him in our pain. One of the most painful aspects of my salvation was a family who misunderstood, mocked, and attacked my faith. My old-school, farm-raised father thought I'd "joined a cult," as he said. My older half-brothers and their friends dubbed me "holy-roller" and "Billy Graham, Jr." And, in a stupor, Mom went off the rails, cursing me. As she screamed and tore at my jacket, the Lord stood with me and I told her, "Mother, I can't go back to being the man I was. That man is dead. 'It is no longer I who live but Christ who lives in me (Galatians 2:20).' I'm going to spend the rest of my life serving Him, and nothing in hell will stop me!" A year later, with a new atheist husband, she disowned me.

Fast-forward to present day. I can't tell you how grateful I am for the grace God gave me to hold fast to my integrity, persevere in prayer, and keep sharing His Word with my family because I've had the honor of leading some to Christ, along with old friends, classmates, and more. You previously heard about the salvation decisions of my brothers David and Brad. At the writing of this chapter it's December, and I'll always treasure this month because it marks not only Christ's coming into our world but my father's coming to Him.

On a cold, wet Thursday evening, November 30, 2006, I was resting at home. My father, in the ICU at a local hospital, had cycled from nursing home to hospital to long-term acute care facility and back for several months. Suddenly, the Lord told me, "Get your Bible, and go read your dad the Christmas story." I didn't hesitate. I grabbed my Bible, coat, and told Ralana what I'd heard. "I'll be praying," she said as I left for the hospital, praying the whole way.

Dad turned over as I entered the room. I held up my Bible. "Could I read you a story?" I asked. "Been a long time since someone read me a story, son," he said grinning and waving me over. I pulled a chair next to his bed and read the Nativity stories from Matthew and Luke. With Dad turned fully toward me, I could see him weighing every word. Finishing

Luke's account, I said, "Dad, we've had many conversations about the Lord over the years, talked of what it means to surrender your life to Jesus and trust Him for salvation. In all that time, you've never made a decision. Don't you want to know that, when you pass from this life and stand before God, you'll spend eternity with Him?"

"Well, son," he replied, "I've always believed that, if you live a good life and try to do the right thing, it'll all work out." My heart sank. I could not count how many times I'd heard this, how many conversations we'd had about Jesus, or how often I'd sought the Lord on Dad's behalf. Inwardly, I pled, "Lord, please give me something! Dad will never see, unless you open his eyes." Then, God spoke to my heart and gave me the question to unlock my father's: "If all of that is true, if a man can just erase everything he's ever done wrong and get to God all by himself, then why did Jesus come into the world?" I asked.

Dad's eyes dropped and darted back and forth. His bushy brow furrowed. You could see the gears turning, gears which had barely budged, it seemed, despite years of dialogue and prayer. Suddenly, he looked up at me with those steel-blue eyes, nodding quietly. God's question had cut through Dad's religious confusion like sunrays through fog. Seeing it on his face, I asked, "Are you ready to pray?" He nodded again. "Alright, I'll pray first. Then, I'll lead you in prayer to receive the Lord," I said. "No, son. You pray. Then, I'm gonna pray," he whispered.

An angel must've been holding me in that chair because I wanted to bounce all over that room like Daffy Duck, "Woo-hoo! Woo-hoo! Woo-hoooooo!" I bowed my head and prayed, thanked God for His mercy, patience, and amazing grace. "Amen," I said. Then, I heard one of the most beautiful sounds in my life: my daddy rolled onto his back, looked up to heaven, and spoke in the sweetest, hillbilly grammar he could muster. "Lord, sure do need ya..." He paused searching for words, then opened his hands toward Heaven and said, "And ask ya ta come into our lives. Help us, Lord," he whispered. "Be with us...[another pause]. Amen."

I wept at my dad's humble prayer and adorable grammar. That old, bar-bouncing, bronc-riding, Korean War leatherneck had just said, "Yes," to Jesus with all his being, and God's peace fell on that room like a warm blanket. We basked in His glory for I don't know how long. Over the next few days, Dad's face beamed like never before. One week later, December 7, Pearl Harbor Day, he went to his eternal home. At his funeral, I shared how Dewey Duncan Brannan met his Lord. It took fifteen years of spiritual gladiator combat—unrelenting love, prayer, and service; weathering mockery, rejection, and pain to reach that moment. But the choice to endure, to keep getting up, "resulted in eternal life" for him (2 Corinthians 4:8-12).

In the throes of his blind andabaté match with Satan, Job endured far more. But, in the end, he received twice what he had before because he clung to his gladiator-like oath. "Though He slay me, I will hope in him (Job 13:15a)." These words resemble those uttered before the Emperor Claudius before a gladiator battle in A.D. 52: "Hail, Emperor! Those about to die salute you!"[51] See, the question Job answers for every Christian fighting in the spiritual arena is not, "Can we endure?" but "Will we?" When the lying serpent, prowling lion, and accusing dragon hissed, "Curse God and die," the gladiator from Uz replied, "Hail, Jesus! Those about to die salute you." Burning, bondage, scourging, or sword, may our answer be the same.

Tactical Takeaways

1. Endurance was the most powerful theme in our study. We noted how the battle often goes "to the one who refuses to quit," and that endurance itself is a weapon because "when we choose to stand firm, we're choosing to trust God's Word." Read 2 Corinthians 4:8-12 and Ephesians 6:13. Recall a prior battle. How did endurance play a role? Are you in a fight now requiring this virtue?

2. The *bestiarius* (beast-fighting gladiator) helped expose three satanic schemes. Read the verses below. Identify the scheme and God's answer. (References have been abbreviated.)

Scheme #1: The Lying Serpent (2 Co. 11:3-4)
God's Answer (Jos. 1:8; Ps. 1:1-3; Jn. 8:31-32; Eph. 6:14):

_____

Scheme #2: The Prowling Lion (1 Pe. 5:6-9)
God's Answer (Hab. 2:1; Mk. 14:37-38; Php. 4:6-7; 1 Pe. 4:7):

_____

Scheme #3: The Accusing Dragon (Re. 12:9-11)
God's Answers (Pr. 28:13; 1 Jn. 1:9; 5:6; Re. 12:11):

_____ & _____

3. The *andabaté* (blind gladiator) and *editor* (game-giver and overseer) helped reveal the battle to trust in God's sovereignty and love. Read Genesis 45:4-8, Job 1:21-22; 13:15, and Romans 8:28-39. Reflect and journal on the importance of seeing our battles through these lenses. Then, pray and ask our Grand Editor to help you trust Him like the gladiator from Uz.

Book VI

MARK OF THE LEGIONARY, PART I

We find that the Romans owed the conquest of the world to no other cause than continual military training, exact observance of discipline in their camps and unwearied cultivation of the other arts of war…. A handful of men, inured to war, proceed to certain victory, while on the contrary numerous armies of raw and undisciplined troops are but multitudes of men dragged to slaughter.

—VEGETIUS, *EPITOMA REI MILITARIS*, BOOK I

In conclusion, be strong in the Lord [be empowered through your union with Him]; draw your strength from Him [that strength which His boundless might provides]. Put on God's whole armor [the armor of a heavy-armed soldier which God supplies], that you may be able successfully to stand up against [all] the strategies *and* the deceits of the devil.

—THE APOSTLE PAUL, EPHESIANS 6:10-11, AMPC

From her republic's mythical founding to the mighty fall of her Western Empire (753 B.C.-A.D. 476), the story of Rome encapsulates more than a thousand years of culture and conquest. No ancient empire holds more sway over the modern world than "the mother of nations," and at the heart of her global domination stood one of history's most ferocious fighting machines: the Roman Legion.[1] By A.D. 117, the Legion had conquered foes from Africa to England, expanding imperial borders to over two million square miles and the rule of the Caesars to one quarter of the global population.[2] But the power of the *legionarius*, the Roman soldier, laid not in the typical advantages of warfare. In the beginning, all of Rome's great foes outclassed her in wealth, strength, size, skill, knowledge, or numbers.[3] How then did she become the superpower of her day? The answer comes from a Roman of high office in the late fourth century A.D.

With the army deteriorating and barbarians invading Rome's borders, Flavius Vegetius Renatus pored over the manuscripts of military sages to rediscover the secrets of her conquest. His resulting treatise, *Epitoma Rei Militaris* (La., "Concerning the Military"), went on to become the military bible of medieval Europe and an annotated field companion of General George Washington.[4] Drawing from the wisdom of Cato the Elder, Augustus, Trajan, and others, Vegetius diagnosed the Legion's systemic disease, which began two centuries earlier. Let's explore that fateful series of events as we unpack our lessons from the Legion.

Decimating the Legion

When Marcus Aurelius ascended the throne (A.D. 161), all seemed right in Rome. Coffers brimmed with a surplus of 2,700 million sesterces, and the Legion stood unmatched in her corner of the world.[5] As the army sacked the Parthian Empire city of Seleucia (modern-day central Iraq), however, a deadly disease sacked her soldiers. Soon the Antonine Plague,[6] riding on the back of the Legion, invaded other parts of Asia Minor, Egypt, Greece, and Rome herself in 165.[7]

As the plague, which most scholars now believe to be smallpox, hacked its way through Rome's close-quartered legions and tightly packed bazaars, her Germanic foes spied an opening. Providentially, their spread-out social structures had hindered the virus' spread. So, with superior numbers, the

Marcomanni tribe and a horde of allies attacked Rome's northern frontier (c. A.D. 166). With no alternative, Aurelius slashed legionary qualifications. Soon, farmers, slaves, vigilantes, and more filled the ranks as Rome wrestled with invasion and pandemic.

Fifteen years later, the Antonine Plague completed her devastating siege. Historian Raoul McLaughlin tallies Rome's losses at an astonishing 30 to 40 percent of her frontier army; 30 percent of her revenue; 25 percent of the urban population; 14 percent of her overall citizenry;[8] and the life of Marcus Aurelius.[9] In the end, Aurelius' recruitment solution stopped the invasion, but a dangerous precedent had been set and Rome's economy shattered.[10] As the army stretched to repel continuous German intrusion in the west and Persian invasion in the east, Rome plunged into crisis again when the Legion assassinated Emperor Severus Alexander in A.D. 235.[11]

On and off over the next fifty years, the mother of nations warred with herself—legion against legion, cycling like a serial killer through twenty-six emperors and annihilating her veteran ranks.[12] If all this was not enough, tragedy struck again with the Cyprian Plague in A.D. 249. The end result: in about 120 years, Rome's Iron Legion had been gutted. Relentless plague and war; a ransacked economy; catastrophic veteran casualties; and mass recruiting of foreign, criminal, and mercenary elements destroyed the foundations of a world-conquering force. Sacred bonds, values, and strategic training became diluted then disappeared. By the fourth century, the Legion was a shadow of its former self. Vegetius concluded, "The name of the legion remains indeed to this day in our armies, but its strength and substance are gone...."[13]

Like Coach Vince Lombardi then, who, after a heartbreaking championship loss, approached the 1964 Green Bay Packers' training camp with his famous "gentleman, this is a football" speech, Vegetius took nothing for granted. Discipline, drilling, arms, organization...he covered all the basics in his manual. Similarly, as false teaching invades Christendom, cuddly stories replace sound biblical exegesis, and spiritual disciplines go widely neglected, an analysis for much of Christ's army could be: "The Name of Jesus remains in our armies, but His strength and substance are gone." With our Lord's grace, though, genuine repentance, soul-searching, and study, perhaps we can turn back the plague afflicting our legion and prevent a spiritual calamity.

The Mark & the Oath

Endeavoring to reset the Roman army, Vegetius extolled many fundamentals in his work. Two of the most basic elements were the military mark on a soldier's hand and the military oath. Vegetius said:

> The military mark, which is indelible, is first imprinted on the hands of the new levies, and as their names are inserted in the roll of the legions they take the usual oath, called the military oath. They swear by God, by Christ and by the Holy Ghost; and by the Majesty of the Emperor who, after God, should be the chief object of the love and veneration of mankind…. The soldiers, therefore, swear they will obey the Emperor willingly and implicitly in all his commands, that they will never desert and will always be ready to sacrifice their lives for the Roman Empire.[14]

The military mark and oath were prerequisites to becoming a soldier and offer two striking illustrations for lessons the Church must review in this hour. Interestingly, Christ also set two conditions to becoming His soldier, saying, "The kingdom of God is at hand; repent and believe in the Gospel (Mark 1:15b-c)." Wherever the New Testament presents Christ's Gospel, the tenets of repentance and faith are present.[15] The absence of either—or addition of anything else—constitutes a false gospel, one which cannot save (2 Corinthians 11:3-4).[i]

To begin, while Christians don't take an oath, we do make a confession—marked by repentance and faith. As Paul said, "If you confess with your mouth that Jesus is Lord and believe in your heart that God raised him from the dead, you will be saved (Romans 10:9)." Notice how repentance—a changed attitude toward sin, self, and the fallen world—is token with Jesus' lordship. John the Baptist tied repentance to a new life when he commanded, "Prove by the way you live that you have repented of your sins and turned to God (Matthew 3:8, NLT)." Paul echoed him,

---

i   *Galatians 1:8-9*

preaching that all "must repent of their sins and turn to God—and prove they have changed by the good things they do (Acts 26:20, NLT)." Jesus tied everything together when He asked, "Why do you call Me, 'Lord, Lord!' and not do what I tell you (Luke 6:46)?"

The idea...that one can sincerely claim Jesus as "Lord," yet cling to life on his/her own terms is a devilish lie.

The idea then that one can sincerely claim Jesus as "Lord," yet cling to life on his/her own terms is a devilish lie. Like Marcus Aurelius, who lowered recruiting requirements to fill legionary ranks, many modern preachers water down Christ's Gospel to fill church seats. They toss out repentance and the Spirit's work in breaking the human heart over sin for a milk-toast message often referred to as "cheap grace." Cheap grace is the wrong terminology, though, because God's grace is not in it. It's *another* gospel, as Paul said.

The result of this "feel-good movement" has been a huge influx of people into local churches who believe God's grace is simply a license to go on living the exact same way, people who "claim they know God but deny Him by the way they live (Titus 1:16a, NLT)." This is nothing new, though. It had become an issue before the New Testament's completion, and Jude, Jesus' half-brother, waged spiritual war on it and urged Christians to join the fight:

> Dear friends, although I was very eager to write to you concerning the salvation we share, I felt it was necessary for me to write, to urge you to continue to contend for the faith that was delivered to the saints once and for all. For certain individuals slipped in secretly, about whom it was written some time ago that they are condemned. They are ungodly people who turn the grace of our God into a license for sin and deny our only Master and Lord, Jesus Christ. (Jude 3-4, EHV)

Note Paul and Jude's connection: turning God's grace into a license to practice sin is tantamount to denying Jesus as Lord (1 John 3:8-10; 5:18). We can't have our sinful cake and eat it too. Paul attacked this same phony "believism" in the church at Rome, asking:

What shall we say, then? Shall we go on sinning so that grace may increase? By no means! We are those who have died to sin; how can we live in it any longer? Or don't you know that all of us who were baptized into Christ Jesus were baptized into his death? We were therefore buried with him through baptism into death in order that, just as Christ was raised from the dead through the glory of the Father, we too may live a new life. (Romans 6:1-4, NIV)

Paul taught that God's grace purchased the believer a new life, not a permission slip to get comfy in an old one. Genuine grace, he argued, teaches believers to turn from sin:

For the grace of God has appeared that offers salvation to all people. It teaches us to say "No" to ungodliness and worldly passions, and to live self-controlled, upright and godly lives in this present age, while we wait for the blessed hope—the appearing of the glory of our great God and Savior, Jesus Christ, who gave himself for us to redeem us from all wickedness and to purify for himself a people that are his very own, eager to do what is good. (Titus 2:11-14, NIV)

Repentance, turning our back on the ways of the world and our old sinful life, is the first part of the Christian confession. It's what Paul meant when he said, " I have been crucified with Christ and I no longer live, but Christ lives in me (Galatians 2:20a, NIV)." If we have been truly crucified with Christ, our attitude toward God, sin, and all else will change. A new desire emerges to make God the "chief object of our love and veneration," to live for Him—not ourselves (Matthew 22:37-38).[ii]

The second part of Galatians 2:20 and verse 21 describe the Gospel's second tenet. "The life I now live in the body, I live by faith in the Son of God, who loved me and gave himself for me. I do not set aside the grace of God, for if righteousness could be gained through the law, Christ died for nothing (NIV)!" Faith—complete trust in Christ's death, burial, and resurrection to make us right with God and give us eternal life—goes hand

---

ii   2 Corinthians 5:15; Galatians 6:14; Philippians 2:13

in hand with repentance. From the day we meet Jesus to our final day on earth, faith looks solely to Him for redemption for "salvation belongs to the Lord (Psalm 3:8a)."[iii] Equally, Ephesians 2:8-9 declares, "For by grace you have been saved through faith. And this is not your own doing; it is the gift of God, not a result of works, so that no one may boast."

Paul taught that God's grace purchased the believer a new life, not a permission slip to get comfy in an old one.

The verb "saved" in the original Greek here means to "heal, preserve, rescue; to deliver out of danger and into safety."[16] Set in the perfect tense, it also indicates a complete action with ongoing effect. In other words: "You have been saved—now and forever." By its original language, numerous verses, and vivid illustrations, Scripture teaches when anyone places trust in Jesus for redemption, salvation's work is done! This brings us to our second illustration.

As noted earlier, the military mark, tattooed onto the legionary's hand, set him apart forever. At any time or place, the mark identified him, basically stating, "This one is the property of Rome and a servant of the Emperor." Similarly, the Bible teaches that when anyone trusts in Jesus for salvation, God's Spirit indwells that person—permanently. Jesus said, "And I will ask the Father, and he will give you another Helper, to be with you forever, even the Spirit of truth, whom the world cannot receive, because it neither sees Him nor knows Him. You know Him, for he dwells with you and will be in you (John 14:16-17, NIV)."

Paul later compared the Holy Spirit's indwelling of the believer to an official mark or seal, like those used by kings, military leaders, and others of his day, saying, "And you also were included in Christ when you heard the message of truth, the gospel of your salvation. When you believed, you were marked in him with a seal, the promised Holy Spirit, who is a deposit guaranteeing our inheritance until the redemption of those who are God's possession—to the praise of his glory (Ephesians 1:13-14, NIV)." *Helps Word-Studies notes that the phrase "marked with a seal" means* to place a seal or mark upon an object with a signet ring or stamp to validate it,

---

iii   *Jonah 2:9b*

Our salvation stands secure because God's nature is immovable and His mark, the Holy Spirit, irremovable!

specify ownership, and ensure its security. *Helps* adds, "Sealing in the ancient world served as a 'legal signature' which guaranteed the promise (contents) of what was sealed. Sealing was sometimes done in antiquity by the use of religious tattoos—again signifying 'belonging to.'"[17]

We see this ancient practice in Esther 3:12 and 8:10, as the Persian King Ahasuerus seals official decrees with his signet ring. Context here and in Daniel 6:8, 12, and 15 reveal that, once the king affixes his seal, an edict is irrevocable. This ancient custom powerfully symbolizes the Holy Spirit's sealing of the believer for the day of redemption (Ephesians 4:30). The person who's trusted in Jesus for salvation never stands in danger of losing it, not because he has earned God's good grace or found the strength to keep himself there, but because God swore by His own Name and never changes nor lies (Genesis 22:16-18).[iv] The King of kings' salvation decree stands as irrevocable law, and the mark of the Christian, the indwelling Holy Spirit, testifies at all times: "This one is the property of Heaven, a servant of the True Emperor: Jesus (Romans 8:15-16)!"[v]

This core Gospel truth cannot be overemphasized. For even as Satan deceives thousands with a fake gospel omitting man's repentance, he torments masses with another overlooking God's faithfulness. God's faithfulness remains the Christian's confidence. The legionary's sandal-boots (*caligae*) featured an intricate hobnail grid pattern across the bottom, offering the foot additional support and wonderful traction. On the battlefield's miry soil, where shield walls crashed and soldiers scuffled, Romans never feared slipping. Like football cleats, their boots dug into the earth, ensuring their footing. That's the believer's confidence in Christ. Our salvation stands secure because God's nature is immovable and His mark, the Holy Spirit, irremovable!

Marked upon enlistment, sealed by God's Spirit, and enrolled in the Lamb's Book of Life, we confidently trust in the Emperor who swore by

---

iv   *Numbers 23:19; Malachi 3:6; Hebrews 6:13-19; 13:8; James 1:17*
v   *Galatians 4:6*

His own Name to save us (Luke 10:20).[vi] It's one thing to commit our lives to serving Jesus, though, and another to bolster that service with iron-core virtue. That will be the focus of our next lesson.

A Revival of Discipline

The *Via Romana* ("Roman Way") comprised a litany of virtues which Romans strived to embody. It originated from an oral tradition of beliefs and bonds dating back to Rome's founding.[18] Historian R. H. Barrow cites several prized virtues such as *gravitas* (seriousness), *industria* (hard work), *constantia* (steadfastness), *firmitas* (determination), *virtus* (manliness), and *disciplina* (discipline—"the training which provides steadiness of character").[19] For soldiers, the greatest of these, according to Vegetius, was *disciplina*, as he said:

> Victory in war does not depend entirely upon numbers or mere courage; only skill and discipline will insure it. We find that the Romans owed the conquest of the world to no other cause than continual military training, exact observance of discipline in their camps, and unwearied cultivation of the other arts of war.[20]

At its height, the Legion was an engine of military art and innovation. Tactics and technology were continually refined. Daily drilling and draconian punishments hardened soldier bodies and minds like iron. Conquest became a science and legionaries ruthless, proficient killers. In a dream, the prophet Daniel saw four beasts representing four great empires of history: Babylon, Persia, Greece, and Rome (Daniel 7). His vision of the fourth beast, which occurred about four hundred years before its fulfillment (c. 553 B.C.), is hair-raisingly accurate: "Then in my vision that night, I saw a fourth beast—terrifying, dreadful, and very strong. It devoured and crushed its victims with huge iron teeth and trampled their remains beneath its feet. It was different from any of the other beasts...(v. 7, NLT)." From elite training to battlefield precision, sturdy iron arms to

---

vi   *Revelation 21:27*

city-destroying siege craft, by 146 B.C., this was the Roman Legion, each soldier one razor-sharp tooth in the mouth of a monstrous war machine.

The first-century Jewish historian Josephus confirmed Vegetius' theory, saying:

> If you study very carefully the organization of the Roman army, you will realize that they possess their great empire as a reward of valor, not as a gift of fortune. For the Romans, the wielding of arms does not begin with the outbreak of war, nor do they sit idly by in peacetime and move their hands only during times of need. Quite the opposite! As if born for the sole purpose of wielding arms, they never take a break from training, never wait for a situation requiring arms.

> Their practice sessions are no less strenuous than real battles. Each soldier trains every day with all his energy as if in war. And therefore they bear the stress of battle with the greatest ease. No confusion causes them to break from their accustomed formation, no fear causes them to shrink back, no exertion tires them. Certain victory always attends them since their opponents are never equal to them. And so it would not be wrong to call their practice sessions bloodless battles and their battles bloody practice sessions.[21]

According to ancient historians, the secret to the Roman Legion was discipline. While other nations relied on money, muscle, and martial prowess, Rome relied on old-fashioned, hard-core discipline, and it made her undefeatable. In fact, *disciplina* was not just a legionary virtue but a cult goddess. While Christians believe there is only one God, the fruit of the Legion's religious dedication to discipline remains incontestable. Discipline always reaps a bountiful harvest (Proverbs 6:23).[vii] Equally, as discipline built strong legionary backs, her opposite sent shivers up their spines.

Neglegentia (negligence) in the barracks spelled disaster on the battlefield, and Vegetius espoused this when he wrote, "A handful of men, inured to war, proceed to certain victory, while on the contrary numerous armies of raw and undisciplined troops are but multitudes of men dragged to

---

vii   *1 Corinthians 9:24-27; Hebrews 12:3-11*

slaughter."[22] Discipline carved the Roman path to conquest. But, in the quiet of peacetime and afterglow of many victories, negligence infected the Legion and spread through her ranks like gangrene. Soldiers exchanged a chiseled, disciplined deity for a soft, negligent idol and paid for it in blood. Vegetius explained:

> The security established by long peace has altered their dispositions, drawn them off from military to civil pursuits and infused into them a love of idleness and ease. Hence a relaxation of military discipline insensibly ensued, then a neglect of it, and it sunk at last into entire oblivion.... After the defeat of many consuls and the loss of many officers and armies, they were convinced that the revival of discipline was the only road to victory and thereby recovered their superiority. The necessity, therefore, of discipline cannot be too often inculcated...."[23]

As barbarian nations invaded the Roman empire, Vegetius called for a revival of discipline in the Legion. I submit that the state of the Church demands the same. God's army desperately needs a revival of spiritual discipline—a move of repentance refocusing us on our relationship with Christ and the practices which cultivate it. The Bible's most pivotal passage on spiritual warfare, Ephesians 6:10-20, summarizes this truth. Verse 10 begins with: "Finally, be strong in the Lord and in the strength of His might." The original Greek rendered "be strong," means to "fill with power."[24] The English word "dynamite" comes from its root, which refers to miraculous power, explosive strength, and violent force.[25]

"Be strong" is a present-tense verb set in the imperative mood, adding urgency. *"Do this now."* Set in the passive voice, it also indicates this power comes from outside ourselves.[26] In all of this, Paul says, "Remain in a place where you are filled with power." He then names that place: "in the Lord" or, more practically, "in union or association with the Lord." In other words, power for victory comes from a close walk with God—an active, vibrant relationship with Him. The *Amplified Bible, Classic Edition* sums up Paul's idea, saying, "In conclusion, be strong in the Lord [be empowered through your union with Him]; draw your strength from Him [that strength which His boundless might provides]."

In verse 11, Paul builds on his axiom, ordering, "Put on the whole armor of God, that you may be able to stand against the schemes of the devil." Set also in the imperative mood, "put on" means "to clothe or be clothed with."[27] So, Paul ties nurturing our relationship with God with a soldier dressing for war, begging the question, "What fool charges into combat undressed?" This is where our spiritual walk proves vital. To not pull aside with God, before our day begins, equates with a soldier taking the field naked!

Many believers approach life this way; they forget they're at war. Daily time with God sits dead last on their list. They may get to Him; they may not. It makes no difference. In their mind, they don't "live and move and have their being in Him (Acts 17:28)." He's not the "vine" Jesus spoke of, the source one must draw life from (John 15:4-5). Their lifestyle reveals that God is simply their life vest—something kept in a cabinet and strapped on *after* disaster has struck.

And, because seeking God remains last in their priorities, they wonder why they have no strength to resist temptation and the abundant life remains elusive. But James said: "Submit yourselves therefore to God. Resist the devil, and he will flee from you (4:7)." In other words, "*Start* with God. Get that right. Then, turn to the devil and watch him run!" The first must be in place or the second never follows. "Seek first the Kingdom of God and his righteousness, and all these things will be added to you (Matthew 6:33)," Jesus promised. Fellow soldier, if you've not been pulling aside to pray, meditate in God's Word, and fellowship with His Church—placing time with Him at the top of your priorities, repent. About face now into a disciplined spiritual life because victorious spiritual combat begins not with warring against the devil but walking with God!

Victorious spiritual combat begins not with warring against the devil but walking with God!

The Walk of Discipline

Just as Rome's great military thinkers held discipline as the key to conquest, God's warfare sages knew the secret to spiritual victory lay in an intimate, disciplined walk with Him, and they carefully tended that sacred fire. Take a moment to consider some of their testimonies.

Noah: With his generation drowning in evil and racing toward judgment, Noah needed strength, wisdom, and stability as he built the ark. Where did he find it? Genesis 6:9b-c says, "Noah was a righteous man, blameless in his generation. Noah walked with God."

Abraham: Leaving all he'd known for a land he'd never seen, Abraham faced famine, feuds, battle, barrenness, and more. But everywhere he went he built an altar and called on the Lord (Genesis 12:8).[viii] Late in life, he said, "The Lord, before whom I have walked, will send His angel with you and prosper your way…(Genesis 17:1)."[ix]

Moses: When God called Moses to face Pharaoh and rescue Israel from slavery, he was a stuttering mess. By the end, he'd become Israel's greatest prophet (Deuteronomy 34:10). Exodus 33:11a shares his secret: "The Lord used to speak to Moses face-to-face, as a man speaks to his friend." Moses was a friend of God. Out of that came signs, wonders, and all his great exploits.

Joshua: "Be strong and courageous," God said, as he ordered Joshua to lead 1.5 million ex-slaves to take a land of trained armies, fortress-cities, and giant races (Joshua 1:7). But He also told Joshua where to find strength and courage: "Keep this Book of the Law always on your lips; meditate on it day and night…. Then you will be prosperous and successful (1:8, NIV)."

David: How does a mere shepherd become a giant-killer and king? David answers, "He who dwells in the secret place of the Most High shall abide under the shadow of the Almighty (Psalm 91:1, NKJV)." The psalm teaches that God's presence clothes, protects, and empowers the one who dwells in His "secret place." (See also Psalm 18 & 27)

---

viii   *Genesis 13:4, 18; 22:9*
ix   *Genesis 24:40a*

Isaiah: Perhaps the chief of the Messianic prophets, Isaiah shared deep insights of God's ways, judgments, and the coming Christ. He knew the power of a strong relationship with God, writing, "Those who wait on the Lord shall renew their strength; they shall mount up with wings like eagles, they shall run and not be weary; they shall walk and not faint (Isaiah 40:31, NKJV)."

Micah: A contemporary of Isaiah, Micah prophesied judgment upon the wealthy of his day preying on the poor. Calling rebellious Israel to repent of her sin and false religion, he said, "He has shown you, O man, what is good and what does the LORD REQUIRE OF YOU BUT TO DO JUSTLY, TO LOVE MERCY, AND TO WALK HUMBLY WITH YOUR GOD (MICAH 6:8, NKJV)?"

Jesus: Throughout His ministry, He rose before dawn, left crowds, found quiet spots, and prayed all night (Matthew 14:23).[x] Jesus stayed connected with His Father and urged us to do the same, saying, "I am the vine; you are the branches. He who abides in Me, and I in him, bears much fruit; for without Me you can do nothing (John 15:5, NKJV)."

All of Scripture's greatest soldiers led a disciplined walk with God. Through that, they turned the world upside down (Acts 17:6). Satan understands this. So, his schemes always aim to destroy this vital connection. What assassin in his right mind would attack a well-armed soldier when he could simply cut off his supply? If Satan can get between us and our walk with God, he wins because we can't do one thing apart from Him. Lewis Sperry Chafer, the first president of Dallas Theological Seminary, communicated this precept when he said:

> The attack against the children of God is not in the sphere of "flesh and blood," but in the sphere of their heavenly association with Christ. That is, the believer may not be drawn away into immorality, but he may utterly fail in prayer, in testimony, and in spiritual victory. Such failure, it should

---

x   *Mark 1:35; Luke 5:16; 6:12*

be seen, is as much defeat and dishonor in the sight of God as those sins which are freely condemned by the world.[28]

The Christian's walk with God will always be a two-sided coin: a relationship and a discipline. It's not all passion and romance. Our spiritual walk demands sacrifice and commitment, just like a healthy marriage. That's why we refer to practices in our walk like prayer, meditation, and fellowship as spiritual *disciplines*. Setting aside time, doing them faithfully, and pouring our whole self into them never comes easy. Discipleship goes against the grain of our fleshly nature, Satan's kingdom, and the sway of this fallen world because it drives us deeper into God's heart (Luke 14:25-33).[xi] But, it's the only key to growing in vibrant relationship with Him. Thus, it remains the engine of the Christian life and warfare. A spiritual walk ushering transformation into our lives and the world around us will never emerge from a microwave Christianity.

A spiritual walk ushering transformation into our lives and the world around us will never emerge from a microwave Christianity.

In *Celebration of Discipline*, Richard Foster affirms this, noting:

> Superficiality is the curse of the age. The doctrine of instant satisfaction is a primary spiritual problem. The desperate need today is not for a greater number of intelligent people, or gifted people, but for deep people. The classical Disciplines of the spiritual life call us to move beyond surface living into the depths. They invite us to explore the inner caverns of the spiritual realm. They urge us to be the answer to a hollow world.[29]

From his first sentence, Foster attacks the plague of western Christendom: negligence—the laziness that leads to a weak, anemic spirituality. We live in a day where two-minute, toilet-read devotionals promise life-changing results. Depth is downplayed, doctrine dismissed, and "discipline" a four-letter word. Yet thousands professing Christ confess to little or no

---

xi   *Galatians 5:16-26; Ephesians 6:10-20; 1 John 2:15-17*

church attendance;[30] no vital connection with their faith;[31] rejecting a biblical worldview of God, Christ, creation, sin, morality, and scriptural authority;[32] and believing that evangelism is wrong.[33] Unsurprisingly, these same people are adrift with the world and in bondage to the enemy.

We must face the truth: when it comes to our spiritual walk, many of us remain our own worst enemy. God is merely an acquaintance; someone

We need a return to spiritual depth, and that will only come with a revival of spiritual discipline!

we bump into—not the close friend He was to our fathers in the Faith. By living such a shallow, self-reliant, and unscriptural faith, we only ensure defeat when Satan attacks, and failure when ministry moments arise. As Vegetius warned, we are multitudes of raw and undisciplined troops being dragged to slaughter. We need a return to spiritual depth, and that will only come with a revival of spiritual discipline!

The Legionary Archetype: The Heavily Armed Soldier
Discipline could be seen in every aspect of legionary equipping. Historian R.G. Grant reveals that no soldier hit the field better outfitted:

> A legionary on the march not only had to bear the weight of his armor, shield, and weapons, which could be as much as 44 lbs., but also had to carry a bulky pack of equipment—ranging from entrenching tools to cooking pots and pans. This could add 33 lbs. or more to his total load.... The standard weapons of an infantryman in the Imperial period were two *pila* (javelins), used to either halt a charge or to soften up the enemy before the Roman forces attacked, and a short sword for fighting at close quarters once battle was joined. Many...also carried a short dagger.[34]

Josephus unveiled the contents of the legionary's "bulky pack," saying, "The equipment...includes a saw, a basket, a pick and an axe, not to mention a strap, a bill-hook, a chain, and three days' rations, so that an infantryman is almost as heavily laden as a pack mule."[35] Vegetius added to that list: pitchforks, spades, shovels, wheelbarrows, and noted both hatchets and axes.[36] Pack mule indeed! But what are we driving at here?

In the reading of history, one thing becomes clear: the Roman warrior ideal was *armatura gravis* ("heavily armed"), a *heavy infantryman* ready for any scenario. God envisioned the same for His soldiers. Describing the believer's equipping, the Bible unveils a "bulky pack" containing all we'll ever need. Consider seven verses from the New King James Version relating this truth.

John 10:10—The thief does not come except to steal, and to kill, and to destroy. I have come that they may have life, and that they may have *it* more abundantly.

2 Corinthians 9:8—And God *is* able to make all grace abound toward you, that you, always having all sufficiency in all *things,* may have an abundance for every good work.

Ephesians 1:3—Blessed *be* the God and Father of our Lord Jesus Christ, who has blessed us with every spiritual blessing in the heavenly *places* in Christ.

Philippians 4:19—And my God shall supply all your need according to His riches in glory by Christ Jesus.

Philemon 1:6—That the sharing of your faith may become effective by the acknowledgment of every good thing which is in you in Christ Jesus.

2 Peter 1:3—As His divine power has given to us all things that *pertain* to life and godliness, through the knowledge of Him who called us by glory and virtue.

Psalm 68:19—Blessed be the Lord, who daily loads us with benefits, the God of our salvation! Selah.

Does God's equipping fall short in any area? By no means. In these and other verses, we find a divine outfitting enabling us to become heavily armed soldiers. Life abundant, life and godliness, all grace, all sufficiency, every good thing.... That's a bulky pack! Josephus said that Rome loaded legionaries down like pack mules. David employed the same metaphor in Psalm 68:19, saying, "Blessed be the Lord, who daily *loads* us with benefits," which can also be rendered "bears our burden."[37] God loves removing our burdens *and* loading us down with blessings. Christ's sacrifice made provision for both.

But, if Jesus secured these blessings, why do so many soldiers walk in defeat? Is He a liar? No. As Christians, we must grasp the difference between Christ acquiring these benefits and us *appropriating* them. The failure to connect these dots leaves many Christians disillusioned.

Jesus is the Prince of Peace. In our spiritual inheritance, He offers us a peace the world cannot match (Isaiah 9:6).[xii] But Isaiah and Paul reveal it's in the disciplines of meditation and prayer His peace is appropriated. Isaiah notes: "You keep him in perfect peace whose mind is stayed on you, because he trusts in you (Isaiah 26:3)." Paul says, "Do not be anxious about anything, but in everything by prayer and supplication with thanksgiving let your requests be made known to God. And the peace of God, which surpasses all understanding, will guard your hearts and your minds in Christ Jesus (Philippians 4:6-7)."

Jesus purchased God's peace and "uploaded" it to heaven, but we must "download" it daily, which only happens *in* meditating, praying, petitioning—*engaging God in relationship*. Do you want peace? An exchange must take place, but God will not force the meeting. We must go to Him. "Come to me, all who labor and are heavy laden, and I will give you rest. Take my yoke upon you, and learn from me, for I am gentle and lowly in heart, and you will find rest for your souls. For my yoke is easy, and my burden is light (Matthew 11:28-30)." God desires to make these daily exchanges, bearing away our burdens and loading us down like pack mules with His benefits (Psalm 68:19).[xiii] The New Testament word for "prayer," in fact, means to "exchange wishes."[38]

Notice God's contingencies in Scripture and their relationship with the disciplines:

---

xii   *John 14:27*
xiii   *Psalm 103:1-5; 1 Peter 5:7*

Need rest?	Come to Me (Mt. 11:28-30).
Need renewal?	Wait on Me (Is. 40:31).
Need fruitfulness?	Connect with Me (John 15:5).
Need peace?	Pray to Me (Php. 4:6-7).
Need freedom?	Praise Me (Ac. 16:25-26)
Need success?	Meditate on Me (Jos. 1:8).
Need victory?	Armor yourself in me (Eph. 6:10-11).

God beckons us to walk daily with Him through the spiritual disciplines, down the sacred paths where these exchanges occur in communion with Him. Clearly, the more intimately we walk with Him, the more effectively we'll war with the enemy. The disciplines lead us into a lifestyle of fellowship with God where we become "heavily armed"—our souls wrapped in biblical truth; hearts armored with His righteousness; thought-life covered with the hope of salvation; steps stabilized by the Gospel's sure-footing; lives shielded with hell-extinguishing faith; and hands weaponized with His Word (Ephesians 6:10-18).

The disciplines lead us into a lifestyle of fellowship with God where we become "heavily armed"...

Vegetius said, "The Romans owed the conquest of the world to no other cause than…exact observance of discipline in their camps, and unwearied cultivation of the other arts of war." In this chapter, we explored legionary discipline and that of great soldiers of the Faith. In the next, we will cultivate our arts of war.

Tactical Takeaways

1. Plague, war, veteran fatalities, and more destroyed legionary foundations. Soon, sacred bonds, ideals, and elite training vanished. Vegetius
said, "The name of the legion remains... in our armies, but its strength
and substance are gone." Do you agree that "as false teaching invades
Christendom, cuddly stories replace sound exegesis, and spiritual
disciplines are widely neglected, an analysis for much of Christ's army
could be: 'The Name of Jesus remains in our armies, but His strength
and substance are gone?'" Why or why not?

2. In "The Mark & the Oath," we discussed the false doctrine called
"cheap grace," which discards the Gospel tenet of repentance. Read
the following verses. Then, discuss whether you believe this to be a
serious issue in the Church. Offer reasons to support your position.
(Matthew 3:8)[xiv]

3. In the second half of "The Mark & the Oath," we saw the value of
grasping the security of our salvation, which Satan constantly attacks.
As noted, God offers us many assurances in original language, metaphor, and more. Place a check mark after reviewing each one below.

_____ **Faith & Grace.** Salvation is *only* by God's grace and received *only*
by faith in Jesus and His work. Skim a few verses and note Scripture's
clear teaching.[xv]

_____ **Saved.** "Saved" (Gk., *sōzō*) in verses like Ephesians 2:5 and 8 means
to heal, preserve, deliver out of danger and into safety. It's set in the perfect
tense, meaning a complete action with ongoing effect. In other words,
"we were, are, and will be saved!" Jesus uses the same tense to describe his
redemption in John 19:30, saying, *"It is finished."*

_____ **Sealed.** Sealing in the ancient world was typically done by a king's

---

xiv   *Acts 26:20; Titus 1:16; 2:11-14; Jude 3-4*
xv   *Genesis 15:6; Acts 13:39; 15:10-11; Romans 5:1-2, 9; 10:9-10; 11:6; Galatians 2:20-21; Ephesians
2:5, 8-9; Titus 3:4-7*

signet ring. It authenticated an item and ensured royal protection. God uses this to symbolize the believer's security in Christ.[xvi]

_____ **Guarded.** In Acts 23:12-35 the Jews plan to assassinate Paul, but a Roman tribune calls for a battalion to escort him safely to the governor. Peter uses this custom to affirm that we who've trusted in Jesus will arrive safely one day to God: 1 Peter 1:3-5.

_____ **Kept.** Also in this passage, Peter contrasts an earthly inheritance, which decays and will perish, with the believer's heavenly inheritance (hence, salvation and future) in Christ, which is supernaturally kept. Compare with Matthew 6:19-21.

_____ **Engraved.** Foreshadowing the Cross, God compares His relationship with His chosen with that of a mother nursing her child (Isaiah 49:15-16). He asks if a woman can forget her suckling babe, admits it can happen because of evil human nature, but promises He cannot because we're "engraved" (Heb., *chaqaq*—"to cut") on His palms. Thus, God asserts the only way we could be lost is if Christ's nail scars could be removed!

_____ **Adopted.** Paul uses adoption five times to describe Christian security.[xvii] Jews had no such custom but could disown and ostracize children. Under Roman law, biological children could be disowned. Adopted ones could not because they were chosen by parents then assigned rights by the state, including a new identity, expulsion of any debts, bonds, etc., and a right to the estate.

4. The key to Roman conquest was found in practicing *disciplina* ("discipline") and rejecting *neglegentia* ("negligence"). Vegetius said, "A handful of men, inured to war, proceed to certain victory, while on the contrary numerous armies of raw and undisciplined troops are but multitudes of men dragged to slaughter." What kind of role does spiritual discipline play in spiritual warfare? Discuss and defend your position.

---

xvi   *Esther 3:12; 8:10; Daniel 6:8, 12, 15; Ephesians 1:13-14; 4:30*
xvii   *Romans 8:15-16, 23-24; 9:3-4; Galatians 4:4-6; Ephesians 1:4-6*

Book VII

MARK OF THE LEGIONARY, PART II

No state can either be happy or secure that is remiss and negligent in the discipline of its troops. For it is not profusion of riches or excess of luxury that can influence our enemies to court or respect us. This can only be effected by the terror of our arms.... For the consequences of engaging an enemy, without skill or courage, is that part of the army is left on the field of battle, and those who remain receive such an impression from their defeat that they dare not afterwards look the enemy in the face.

—Vegetius, *Epitoma Rei Militaris, Book I*

Don't you realize that in a race everyone runs, but only one person gets the prize? So run to win! All athletes are disciplined in their training. They do it to win a prize that will fade away, but we do it for an eternal prize. So I run with purpose in every step. I am not just shadowboxing. I discipline my body like an athlete, training it to do what it should. Otherwise, I fear that after preaching to others I myself might be disqualified.

—The Apostle Paul, 1 Corinthians 9:24-27, 1996 NLT

Among their many purposes, the Bible's spiritual disciplines are ancient paths to walk with God and equip believers for spiritual combat (Jeremiah 6:16).[i] Some disciplines are practiced privately, others communally with Christ's Body, but all have expressions in both settings. Like bodily exercise's many health benefits, spiritual disciplines also have profound physical and spiritual impacts. Thus, a healthy way to view them is as God's "daily exercises for the soul." Paul seeded this idea to Timothy, writing, "Train yourself for godliness. For while bodily training is of some value, godliness is of value in every way, as it holds promise for the present life and also for the life to come (1 Timothy 4:7b-8)." The Greek word for "train" (*gumnazō*), from whence we derive "gym," "gymnasium," and "gymnastics," means:

> To exert intensely, like a pro-athlete; [it] presumes full discipline, necessary to be in "top working condition" (full agility, skill, endurance). This is gained only from *constant*, rigorous training (exercise). [It] conveys acquiring *proficiency through practice*—regular exercise with graduated resistance (the physical element is also included with the spiritual of being in "God's gymnasium").[1]

Using this same allegory, Paul prodded Corinthian Christians to turn from their selfish and divisive ways toward a spiritually athletic and fleshly combative type of faith, asking:

> Don't you realize that in a race everyone runs, but only one person gets the prize?

> So run to win! All athletes are disciplined in their training. They do it to win a prize that will fade away, but we do it for an eternal prize. So I run with purpose in every step. I am not just shadowboxing. I discipline my body like an athlete, training it to do what it should. Otherwise, I fear that after preaching to others I myself might be disqualified. (1 Corinthians 9:24-27, NLT)

---

i   *Ephesians 6:10-20*

We could think of the spiritual disciplines then as "God's Workout Program." Exercising with them yields a "ripped" devotional life—builds spiritual muscle, steels our core, and drives us forward in the Kingdom. Like physical exercise, each discipline works specific "spiritual muscles" and has variations to keep things fresh. Many books on the disciplines have greatly contributed to Christian discipleship. But a confusing point is that each author comes with his own list. Admittedly, I'm no exception. The greater issue I see, though, lies in discipline lists too long to even remember. Twelve seems to be a common length, which surprises me because God usually limits Himself to shorter lists—five ministry offices (Ephesians 4:11-12), six pieces of armor (Ephesians 6:14-17), nine spiritual gifts (1 Corinthians 12:8-10), etc.

Authors have also divided the disciplines between actual practice (e.g., meditation, prayer, fellowship, etc.) and guiding precept (solitude, secrecy, simplicity, etc.). For example, Jesus departed into a solitary place to pray (Mark 1:35). Prayer was the practice; solitude was just the precept enhancing prayer's focus. Jesus said to give alms and pray secretly—not for public praise (Matthew 6:1-6). Prayer and alms were the "what" to do; secrecy was simply "how" to do them. Throughout Scripture, confession of sin is part of a healthy prayer life—never its own discipline (Ezra 10:1).ii And, while we see prayer without fasting in Scripture, we never see fasting without prayer. Even where prayer isn't cited with fasting, the text implies it (See Esther 4). Like confession then, fasting is an *extension* of prayer (Ezra 8:21-23; 9:5-15).iii

Bible reading, study, memorization, musing on God in a sermon or His creation— all are meditation.

With that said, for our purposes, we'll focus on the four core disciplines: meditation, prayer, worship, and fellowship. When soundly practiced, they armor the believer's life. With each discipline, we'll get a brief overview, then explore ideas to supplement your walk. From this point on and to

---

ii   *Nehemiah 1:6; Psalm 32:5-6; Daniel 9:4-5, 20; James 5:16*

iii   *Nehemiah 1:4; 9; Daniel 9-10; Joel 2:12-17; Jonah 3:6-10; Matthew 17:21²; Acts 13:3; 14:23; 1 Corinthians 7:5*

save some space, biblical references within the *applications* following each spiritual discipline will be abbreviated.

Meditation

Expressions: *Reading, Reflection, Study, & Memorization*

Overview: Meditation is the mainspring of the spiritual disciplines as it sets our thoughts on God and His Kingdom. It's more than musing on His words or works, though. As Scripture reveals, its ultimate aim is union with God's will, which instantly connects it with prayer and other disciplines (Psalm 1:1-3).[iv]

No book exalts meditation more than Psalms. Its first chapter extols the "blessed man" who meditates day and night on God's Law and, thus, leads a fruitful life. Its longest chapter (119), references meditation some 144 times and focuses on Scripture using about 52 verbs like: behold, cling, delight, fix, hide, long, observe, seek, think, and trust. But what does this mean?

Bible reading, study, memorization, musing on God in a sermon or His creation—all are meditation. So, "day and night" meditation isn't just for elites, but something all believers can do (Joshua 1:8).[v] Here are some applications to strengthen your walk via meditation.

Daily Reading (Is. 34:16a). "Seek and read from the book of the Lord," Isaiah says. Bible reading makes great meditation, and reading plans exist all over the web. If you're new, try one chapter a day. Seven months have thirty-one days; there are thirty-one proverbs. Longer plan? Try Psalms. Most have only eight verses. Read one a day. For short New Testament readings, a typical Pauline letter (Galatians, Ephesians, etc.) has four chapters. In fact, three-fifths of the New Testament (all the minor epistles) can be read in sixty-two days.

Daily reading is easy! We just need a plan, and Scripture blesses us whenever we read because its words contain power (De. 8:3; 32:46-47).[vi] If you don't know where to start, download the plan Ralana and I created for free at **thesoldiercode.com**.

---

iv   *Psalm 77:11-13; 119:15-17, 97-104; Joshua 1:8; James 1:22; Romans 12:2*
v   *Psalm 1:2*
vi   *Hebrews 4:12*

Scripture Reflection (Pr. 4:20-22). Musing on Scripture is salve for the soul. Gentle background music only enhances it, and options are endless (Christian arrangements, classical *adagios*, movie soundtracks, etc.). Choose a passage and turn on the tunes. Recite it aloud slowly. Savor each word. Let the passage wash over and still your soul. If God points something out, prayerfully respond. If you're new, don't fear. I'll share some ideas to get you started:

- **Divine Romance:** So. 2:10-13; Lovland: Secret Garden, *Adagio* 2046
- **Grace:** Ps. 103:8-14; Beethoven: Sonata "Pathetique," *2nd Mvt.*
- **My Shepherd:** Ps. 23; Rachmaninoff: Piano Concerto No. 2, *2nd Mvt.*
- **God's Love:** 1 Co. 13; Rodrigo & Williams: Concerto de Aranjuez, *Adagio*
- **Mercy:** La. 3:21-26; Marcello: Oboe Concerto in D Minor, *Adagio*

Rhema Arsenal (Mt. 4:4, 7, 10). When Satan attacked in Matthew 4, Jesus had a Scripture arsenal ready, quoting Deuteronomy 8:3; 6:16, and 6:13. In the Gospels, He said, "It is written," twenty-one times and quoted Scripture in sixteen of them. So, Jesus memorized Scripture and commands us to also (De. 11:18).[vii] Memorizing may seem difficult, but we do it with songs, stats, poems, etc. We just need a way, and I have one: S.I.M.—Summarize, Integrate, and Mutter.

Summarize: First, summarize the memory verse(s) in one or two words; give it a "file name." Let's say we're memorizing Philippians 4:13, "I can do all things through Him who strengthens me." "Strength" is a good, one-word file name.

Integrate: Next, we integrate a visual aid, making a memory verse card to carry with us and review. You can make cards by hand or computer, out of index or pre-made cards. But be neat. Here's a pattern to mimic:

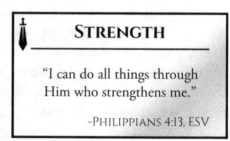

STRENGTH

"I can do all things through Him who strengthens me."

-PHILIPPIANS 4:13, ESV

---

vii   *Psalm 119:11; Proverbs 4:21; 7:3; Colossians 3:16*

Mutter: Finally, to memorize, we mutter everything aloud repeatedly. First, say the file name: "strength"; second, the verse: "I can do..."; third, the reference: "Philippians 4:13." To etch the verse into your memory, use this

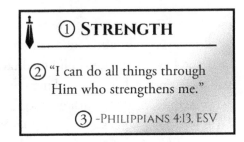

① **STRENGTH**

② "I can do all things through Him who strengthens me."

③ -PHILIPPIANS 4:13, ESV

tool each time you practice. Try it now aloud. Use the file name, the verse, then the reference.

Now that we're ready to memorize, here are some verse ideas with simple file names focusing on essential doctrines, values, and disciplines. Their aim is to give you a basic foundation. Feel free to choose your own verses and file names as God leads you.

Creation: Ge. 1:1	**Devotion:** Mt. 6:33	**Church:** Mt. 16:18
Sin: Ro. 3:23	**Love:** Jn. 13:34-35	**Forgiveness:** 1 Jn. 1:9
Salvation: Jn. 3:16	**Scripture:** 2 Ti. 3:16	**Giving:** 2 Co. 9:7
Grace: Eph. 2:8-9	**Prayer:** Php. 4:6-7	**Strength:** Php. 4:13

Summary: In the Spartan chapter, I shared how Ralana and I met about one year after I became a Christian. Within a month of our meeting, though, she asked me to disciple her. Why? "Duncan knew the Word of God better than most people I knew who'd been Christians their whole lives—people raised in Christian homes, who grew up in church, and went to Sunday school. I saw a stability in Duncan's faith that was lacking in my own, which was more like a roller coaster—up one day and down the next," she says.

The stability Ralana saw was me dwelling in God's Word and it dwelling in me (Joshua 1:8).[VIII] Soon, she was studying the Bible like never before, memorizing Scripture, and studying it for answers on life, relationships,

---

viii   Psalm 1:2; 119:9,11; Colossians 3:16

and more. She experienced a revival and began ministering to friends and family, sharing her faith, and making an impact everywhere.

If you haven't already, build meditation into your spiritual walk. Start reading Scripture daily and add memorization to your life. I promise: you'll never be the same! We must get God's Word into our hearts for these evil days. It's the cavalier's compass (Deuteronomy 32:46-47), the warrior's weapon (Ephesians 6:17), the seeker's searchlight (Psalm 119:105), and the sojourner's sustenance (Deuteronomy 8:3). Without meditation in God's Word, we're unequipped for life, defenseless before Satan, and lost in this world. Now, let's ponder this thing called prayer.

Prayer
Expressions: *Supplication, Fasting, Intercession, & Thanksgiving*
Overview: Prayer originated after mankind's Fall, as "people began to call upon the name of the Lord (Genesis 4:26)." While men have created lists of different kinds of prayer, Paul simplified it to four, saying, "I urge that supplications, prayers, intercessions, and thanksgivings be made for all people, for kings and all who are in high positions...(1 Timothy 2:1-2)." Supplication asks God for specific needs. Prayer, which means "to exchange wishes,"[3] seeks to exchange man's need for God's provision (sin for forgiveness, anxiety for peace, sickness for healing, etc.). Intercession pleads for His mercy and miraculous intervention in tough situations. Thanksgiving praises God in all circumstances (1 Thessalonians 5:18), remembering that He makes "all things work together for good, for those who are called according to his purpose (Romans 8:28)."

Best of all, Scripture reveals prayer as an expression of personal relationship with God as believers: 1.) address Him as Father (Mt. 6:9; Eph. 3:14) and exercise the freedom to 2.) pray anywhere (Mt. 11:25-26)[ix], 3.) at any time (Ps. 5:3; 119:164)[x], 4.) for any length (Mt. 6:9-13)[xi], 5.) in any posture (Ge. 24:26)[xii]; and 6.) silently, aloud, or in writing (1 Sa. 1:12-13).[xiii] From

---

ix   *Mark 1:35; Luke 3:21; John 11:41; 1 Timothy 2:8*
x   *Lamentations 2:19; Acts 3:1*
xi   *Luke 6:12*
xii   *Numbers 20:6; 1 Kings 8:54; 2 Kings 20:2; Mark 11:25*
xiii   *John 17; Ephesians 1:15-23*

this light, Paul's command to "pray without ceasing" is inspiring—not burdensome (1 Th. 5:17)! Here are three ways to grow your prayer life:

Scriptural Prayer (1 Jn. 5:14). "This is the confidence that we have toward him, that if we ask anything according to his will he hears us," John says. There's no better way to pray God's will than to pray His Word. Praying Scripture "pours gasoline" on prayer, lighting our inner darkness, igniting godly passion, and refocusing us on God's priorities. Studying prayer in Scripture can reshape our prayer life, whether exploring the prayers of Old Testament saints

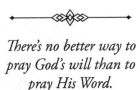

There's no better way to pray God's will than to pray His Word.

like Ezra (Ezr. 9:5-15), Nehemiah (Ne. 1), Solomon (1 Ki. 8:22-53), or Daniel (9:4-19) or surveying the New Testament prayers of Jesus (Mt. 6:9-13; 11:25-26; 26:39-42; 27:46)[xiv] or Paul's for the churches (Eph. 1:15-23; 3:14-21).[xv] The simple fact is: people in Scripture prayed Scripture.

Agreeing Prayer (Mt. 18:19-20). "Again I say to you, if two of you agree on earth about anything they ask, it will be done for them by my Father in heaven. For where two or three are gathered in my name, there am I among them," Jesus promised. Jesus knew that group prayer isn't always possible. Finding one or two to agree with us, though, is and God loves it when we pray like this. The Old Testament also shines light here. Ecclesiastes 4:12, NLT, says, "A person standing alone can be attacked and defeated, but two can stand back-to-back and conquer. Three are even better, for a triple-braided cord is not easily broken." If you've never had a regular prayer partner, believe me, you don't know what you're missing!

Prayer & Fasting (Ezra 8:23). Prayer with fasting is "prayer on steroids." It wields great power because it kills our pride and self-reliance, making us trust God more (Ezr. 8:23).[xvi] Jesus also expects it of us, saying in Matthew 6:16, "*When* you fast…" not, "*If* you fast." Isaiah 58 holds the Bible's largest discourse on fasting—an entire chapter devoted to it. When starting a fast, it's a good chapter to review as a spiritual "gut check." Prayer and fasting's main purposes are: repentance and freedom from sin,

---

xiv   *Luke 23:46; John 11:41-42; 12:27-28; 17*
xv   *Philippians 1:3-11; Colossians 1:3-12; 1 Thessalonians 1:2-10*
xvi   *Psalm 69:10*

sanctification for God's purposes, breakthrough in spiritual warfare, and divine intervention for impossible situations. Here are some references to help you study it a bit more.[xvii]

Prayer Journaling (Ps. 45:1). The Bible records 222 total prayers of God's people. 72 of these are in the Psalms, and 50 are David's.[5] God's Spirit led David and the other writers to do this to give us models and show how He works through prayer (2 Chr. 7:14).[xviii] A great lesson here is the honesty and emotion in David's confessions. In Psalms 13 and 35, for example, David's anger at his foes and frustration with God are very apparent. We see his restlessness and potential for violence. Equally tangible are his humiliation and brokenness in Psalms 38 and 51. One can almost feel his quill trembling and tears wetting the page as he writes, "I confess my iniquity; I am sorry for my sin (38:18)."

In all of this, we feel God's yearning for connection with us. We see that humility and faith move His hand, not eloquence and long speeches (Mt. 6:7-8).[xix] We also find that He never abandons broken souls or sincere seekers, but draws near to cleanse, heal, and help (Ps. 25:8-9).[xx] As we record our prayers then, we should mimic the biblical writers, seeking God's heart, pouring out our own, yielding to His instructions, and trusting His promises.

Summary: One of my greatest joys and bulwarks of faith is a weekly prayer time with my friend David Grover. David is to me what Epaphroditus was to Paul: my brother, co-laborer, fellow soldier, and personal minister (Philippians 2:25). He loves the title "armor-bearer," and, if I am any sort of "Jonathan," then that's certainly what he is to me (1 Samuel 14). Dave and I pray together for one hour, four to five times a week. We battle for our families, friends, Christian brothers and sisters, the Church, our city, and beyond as God leads. There's simply no way to count the miracles, blessings, and "earthquakes" we've seen in answer to our prayers (1 Samuel 14:15). Some healings I mentioned in the Viking chapter, in fact,

---

xvii   *Ezra 8-10; Nehemiah 1-2:7; 9; Daniel 9-10; Joel 2:1-17; Jonah 3:6-10; Matthew⁴:1-11; 6:5-18; 17:21;4 Acts 13:2-3; 14:23; 1 Corinthians 7:5*
xviii   *Psalm 65:2; Romans 15:4*
xix   *Hebrews 11:6*
xx   *Psalm 27:9-10; 34:4-18; 138:6*

like emphysema and Lou Gehrig's disease, came in the wake of our prayer time at a church where we both ministered.

If your prayer life has grown cold or ineffectual, ask a friend to join you. Don't fret if you can't pray an hour because of kids or other commitments. Do what you *can*! Adjust start times, end times, etc. Let God's Spirit lead, and let His grace bathe this holy time (2 Timothy 2:1). It may become one of the greatest strongholds of God's Presence and power in your life.

Worship

Expressions: *Proclamation, Singing, Dancing, Kneeling, Making Music, etc.*
Overview: Like prayer, worship begins after the Fall with altars and sacrifices (Genesis 4:3-4).[xxi] Yet the worship God sought was not in outward ritual but inward relationship, a truth seen between Abel's best, accepted offering and Cain's stingy, rejected one (Genesis 4:3-4). David further noted, "You do not desire a sacrifice, or I would offer one.... The sacrifice you desire is a broken spirit. You will not reject a broken and repentant heart, O God (Psalm 51:16-17, NLT)." Ending the debate, Jesus said that those who worship God "must worship in spirit and truth (John 4:24).'"

Worship also has many outward expressions. The Psalms speak of kneeling, dancing, lifting hands, playing instruments, singing, shouting, and all-out celebration (Psalm 33:1-3).[xxii] Paul taught the Early Church that a key to Spirit-filled living is "singing psalms, hymns, and spiritual songs," and, of course, worship is chief in the activity of heaven (Ephesians 5:18-19).[xxiii] Still, worship's highest expression remains the "sacrifice of thanksgiving"—praise in time of trouble (Ps. 50:23).[xxiv] God's heart leaps when, from trial's ashes, His people cling to His sovereignty and love and proclaim His faithfulness like Job (1:13-21), David (Psalm 57:6-8), and Habakkuk (3:17-19).

This is where worship becomes more than music. Because God inhabits (Heb., yashab),dwells within the praises of His people, praise is a "weapon of our warfare" with thermonuclear capability (Psalm 22:3; 2 Corinthians

---

xxi   *Genesis 8:20; 12:8*
xxii   *Psalm 95; 134:2; 149:3; 150*
xxiii   *Colossians 3:16; Revelation 4-5*
xxiv   *Psalm 56:11-12; 69:29-30; 107:17-22; Hebrews 13:15*

Many battles are won and lost at the worship altar, where we choose to trust and praise God or doubt Him and withhold it.

10:4). Many battles are won and lost at the worship altar, where we choose to trust and praise God or doubt Him and withhold it. Oh, that we would get a vision of the power unleashed when we praise God! Let's explore a few tools and ways to do this.

Corporate Worship (Ps. 35:18). Though David was a biblical author and worship leader, Psalms unveils his struggles with despair, anger, and fear and offers great insight to overcome these destructive forces. In Psalm 35, his anguish takes centerstage as he compares his enemies' attacks with bloodthirsty lions (vv. 16-17), which calls to mind 1 Peter 5:7-8 where Satan, working with anxiety, "prowls like a roaring lion seeking someone to devour." So, it's not just emotions or people tearing at David but, arguably, unseen demonic powers also.

As the trial wears on, David pleads, "How long, O Lord, will you look on? Rescue me from their destruction, my precious life from the lions (v. 17)!" He follows with God's solution, which isn't isolation, a vacation, or shopping spree. "I will thank you in the great congregation; in the mighty throng I will praise you (v. 18)." Going against our fleshly tendency to rebel and Satan's scheme to isolate, David chooses to not just praise God, but praise Him *with* His people.

Next, he calls the corporate worship gathering the "great congregation" and "mighty throng." In the original text of Psalm 35:18, "great" (Heb., *rab*) is set in synonymous parallel with "mighty" (*atsum*). In the Mosaic tradition, the Hebrew *gadol* ("great") is often set before *atsum* ("mighty") in a turn of phrase referring to nations "great in size" and "mighty in strength (Nu. 14:12)."[xxv] *Rab* is used similarly to denote large numbers of people or long periods of time some 182 instances from Genesis 6:5 to Psalm 35:18. The point is: David's not speaking redundantly. He's saying Israel's corporate worship is like an army—"great in size and mighty in strength!" David and the psalmists knew that God blesses our private worship, but saw a special blessing when His people assemble (Ps. 42:4).[xxvi]

xxv   Deuteronomy 4:38; 9:1; 11:23; 26:5; Joshua 23:9
xxvi   Psalm 55:14; 84; 122:1; 133

Jehoshaphat affirmed this truth. Heading into battle against an axis of evil, this Judean king set the worship team ahead of the army—to *lead* them into battle. Earthly generals would shout, "Are you mad?!" Yet "as they began to sing and praise, the Lord set an ambush against the men of Ammon, Moab, and Mount Seir…so that they were routed (2 Chr. 20:22)."

Will God manifest this same power, though, when only a few can gather for worship? Paul and Silas shout, "Yes!" At midnight, in chains and maximum-security detention, with whipped bodies and every prisoner listening, they prayed and sang hymns to God (Ac. 16:25-34). The result? God's Spirit fell on the Philippian jail in an earthquake, blowing every door open, bursting every bond, and bringing the jailer and his family to Christ. Jesus said the gates of hell would not prevail against the Church (Mt.16:18). No wonder: Praise is God's battering ram!

The Hymns (Mt. 26:30). Did you know the Bible is packed with hymns? The Psalms, of course, contain many.[xxvii] On the night of Jesus' betrayal, the apostles sang what Jewish tradition calls the Lesser and Great *Hallel* ("Praise"), Psalms 113-118 and 136. Paul and Silas may have been singing these hymns when the earthquake struck the jail. The original Greek reads, "Around midnight, Paul and Silas were praying and *hymning* to God (Ac. 16:25)." Psalm 114:7, coincidentally, cries, "Tremble, O earth, at the presence of the Lord…." Would this not have been His perfect entrance cue?

Paul and Silas may also have sung the hymn Paul included in Philippians 2:6-11, the Christ hymn, telling of Jesus' humiliation on the Cross and later exaltation. Imagine that prison rattling as they reached the words "every knee should bow" and "every tongue confess that Jesus Christ is Lord." Would it not make perfect sense why the jailer came in and fell to his knees asking, "Sirs, what must I do to be saved (Ac. 16:29-30)?" They just sang it!

Biblical history reveals that our ancient brothers and sisters didn't just turn to Scripture as we know it when trouble came, but a tradition of great "psalms, hymns, and spiritual songs" thousands of years old, many of which God's Spirit led biblical writers to include in His Word (Eph. 5:19).[xxviii] These beautiful stanzas, which praise God's character and deeds, are just as powerful put to music as when preached because they're God-breathed

---

xxvii *Psalm 8, 19, 24, 29, 33, 46-48, 76, 104, 113-118, 135-136, 145-150*
xxviii *Colossians 3:16; 2 Timothy 3:16; 1 Peter 1:21*

(2 Ti. 3:16).[xxix] They comprised a vast arsenal of the Early Church and saints of old, weapons which felled many foes and strongholds, weapons which newer generations must freshly unearth in this age of war—not just penning their own lyrics. Here are a handful of references you've probably read a dozen times, yet never known they were hymns.[xxx] What if you put some of these or other verses to a tune?

I'll add here that the classic hymns of the Church, though not God-breathed, have proven formidable arms down through the ages. Like lions, embattled believers have roared out hymns like "How Great Thou Art," "Amazing Grace," "A Mighty Fortress Is Our God," and "It Is Well With My Soul" in desperate hours. These songs were our forefathers' lifeblood, and must not be forgotten by modern generations.

Equally, older generations should pray for younger ones and trust God's Spirit as He leads them in worship. It's tragic when old and young in the Church war with one another, deriding the worship experience of the other. This is divisive and demonic. It must stop (Mt. 12:25)![xxxi] There is room for both "old and new wineskins," to borrow Christ's analogy (Mt. 9:16-17). Those clinging to one over the other should remember Scripture is God-breathed—not their musical preference, and stop passing judgment on fellow servants (Ro. 14:4).

Personal Playlists (Ps. 113-118). Let's wrap this section with one more idea. Above, I mentioned the *Hallel*, a group of psalms sung by Old Testament Jews and New Testament Christians. It was like a "playlist." They grew up learning these and other hymns and songs (which Paul referenced and wove into the epistles), and could call on them for worship and warfare at a moment's notice (Eph. 5:19).[xxxii] To say these came in handy as ancient Israel faced invasion or the Early Church endured persecution would be an understatement!

The Early Church thrived on well-crafted hymns praising God's attributes and deeds, along with compact creeds containing essential doctrine. These

xxix   *1 Peter 1:21*
xxx   *Amos 4:13; 5:8-9; 9:5-6; John 1:1-5; 1 Corinthians 8:6; Ephesians 1:3-14; Philippians 2:6-11; Colossians 1:15-20; 1 Timothy 3:16; Titus 3:4-7*
xxxi   *1 Corinthians 1:10; 3:1; 11:18; Galatians 5:20*
xxxii *Colossians 3:16*

heirlooms of faith helped immunize young believers against the heresy and evils of the Roman world. Christians knew them by heart, sang them at gatherings, and drew strength from them daily (1 Co. 14:26).

Summary: As our society grows darker, with the vilest forms of politics, propaganda, and entertainment surging like sewage through media and personal electronics, Christian soldiers need a spiritual "minuteman" equipping. We must keep, on smart tablets and heart tablets, a playlist of praise songs to constantly lead us into God's Presence and help us call on Him when warfare comes. It takes only minutes to download worship music and make playlists in our smart devices as preemptive weapons and fortifications, and they can change the atmosphere and our whole outlook in seconds.

In the gladiator chapter, I shared how my mom disowned me after my conversion. Sadly, within a few years, she had also rejected my three brothers and the rest of the family. To this day, we pray for her and her husband, Jerry, a hostile atheist, and have extended the olive branch many times. Earlier this year, though, her oldest brother, my Uncle Bill, suddenly passed. So, reluctantly and prayerfully, I drove to her home to share the news, knowing Jerry would intercept a phone call or letter with the same venom shown before. Mother had forgone her previous husband's funeral (my father), a friend's funeral, and missed almost all of the adult lives and youthful years of children and grandchildren. Jerry answered the door like a dungeon master, spewing profanities and showing zero care or cooperation to let me speak with her. Ignoring his curses, I called out to her. She came to the door, was visibly touched by the news, but still closed it with stunning quickness.

When Uncle Bill's funeral details were released, I prayed about how to get her the information and resolved that sending a certified letter was the way. In that letter, the family once again offered the olive branch, assuring her and Jerry they'd be warmly welcomed. No answer. Maybe you're surprised at how graciously I handled this. But it was God—not me, and when the family patted me on the back for how I'd responded to Jerry, I pointed to God and how much my armor-bearer and I had been praying.

Meltdown came a few weeks later, though, when I received word the mailman had violated the postal code by giving Jerry the letter—not Mom.

Our postmaster even acknowledged the violation but refused to refund the money for the unrendered service. All I could see in that moment, however, was that prayed-over, thoughtfully crafted, and hoped-for letter being torn up and thrown in a trash can—despite all my requests that it get to Mom. Did it get there? I can't say. I can only tell you this was the camel's straw. I wept. I was done.

Most of all, I got really mad at God and had a "Job-like" exchange with Him. I wanted answers. Most of all, I wanted a reckoning—not just for me but our entire family and all the pain and loss over the years—because our prayers, fasts, olive branches, and whatnots seemed like a big waste of time. It felt like God had ignored us.

So, I crashed—hard. I didn't want to hear from or speak to anyone. I was long past the spiritual "pep talk." As I noted in the samurai chapter, the enemy "knocked my heart out." Ralana saw the disappointment and hurt, but wisely stepped back and gave me space to mourn and process. Meanwhile, she reached out to family and friends to pray. Then, she picked up her trusty weapon.

I'd been in the bedroom trying to rest, which was as elusive as peace at that moment, and came out to the sound of worship and her—weeping in prayer. The sight broke me, but when she began to worship I felt God enter the room. I listened for a bit, but confess that when I heard the lyrics, *"He is with you! He is for you!"* my heart replied, "Really? Where?!"

The Holy Spirit kept working on me as the music played, and Ralana kept worshiping, arms up and singing her heart out. I sensed the Lord beckoning me to my knees, to talk and reason with Him (Isaiah 1:18). My flesh did not want to kneel, but I did. As soon as my knees hit the carpet, I broke. As David said, I poured out my complaint and told God my trouble (Psalm 142:2). Shortly, I was one big, bawling mess. That's when it happened: the song ended, the Spirit fell, and Ralana thundered! The Lion of Judah roared through her, and I know that every demon within a mile trembled at the holy power pouring out of her.

She wept, shouted God's praise, and declared His faithfulness. She prayed everything I could not in that moment, and beat the daylights out of despair, unbelief, and any unclean spirit in that room. Heaven poured down like fire on us, and she was the conduit. God's Spirit rushed upon her, flooded from her like a bursting dam, and drove darkness out like a torrent tearing through a forest. When I could not pick up the Spirit's Sword, she brought down His Hammer. "'Is not My Word like fire,' declares the Lord, 'and like a hammer that shatters a rock (Jeremiah 23:29)?'" It's not just a verse. It's a weapon, and my worshiping wife swung it! Satan's attack was broken, my heart healed, and—though breakthrough still tarries—we're waiting for it. We know "it will surely come" and "will not delay (Habakkuk 2:3)."

I urge you to pray, invest some time and creativity, and build a worship arsenal. It could blow hell right out of the room—like a thunder strike from Thor's hammer—when you need it. Now, let's look at our final discipline.

Fellowship

Expressions: *The Local Church, Small Groups, Discipleship, Ministry Retreats, etc.*

Overview: Many Bible verses reveal God's call to fellowship, man's hardwired need for it, and its divine pattern in Scripture. But with offenses, wounds, and unforgiveness affecting so many today, fellowship may be the most foregone of all spiritual disciplines. As noted in the samurai chapter, Barna Research from 1993 to 2020 showed American weekly church attendance dropped from 45 percent to 29 percent.[6] Many factors play into these numbers, but at the heart of the matter lies the age-old question: "Do we really trust God?" If we're honest about this issue, not giving a pat "Christianese" answer, the response for many is, "No." Why do I say this? Let's return to Eden.

In the beginning, after forming Adam from the dust, "The Lord God said, 'It is not good that the man should be alone; I will make him a helper fit for him (Genesis 2:18).'" That help came from another human, Eve, and the institution of marriage (2:22-25). But God didn't stop there. Next came His institution of family and, later, spiritual community and the common gathering.

Following God's fellowship pattern into the Mosaic Covenant, we find Him directing the Jews to keep His seventh-day Sabbath, allowing man and beast to reassemble from fields and markets and rest from their labors

(Genesis 2:1-3).[xxxiii] With this, He also instituted the weekly assembly, saying, "The seventh day is a Sabbath of solemn rest, a holy *convocation*... (Leviticus 23:3a). "Convocation" (Heb., *miqra*) means "assembly" and "reading," and comes from the word *qara* ("called out").[7] On the sabbath then, God not only called Jews out of their labors, but their homes and worlds, to assemble with others for the reading of Scripture (Nehemiah 8:1-8). Finally, He added seven yearly feasts, each one also marked by sabbaths and assemblies (Leviticus 23:4)[xxxiv], mandated their observance, and required pilgrimage for three of them to a specific place (Exodus 23:14, 17).[xxxv] In all this, we see His purpose of fellowship—each gathering affirming, "It is not good that man should be alone."

King Solomon gave us the "why" when he said:

> Two people are better off than one, for they can help each other succeed. If one person falls, the other can reach out and help. But someone who falls alone is in real trouble. Likewise, two people lying close together can keep each other warm. But how can one be warm alone? A person standing alone can be attacked and defeated, but two can stand back-to-back and conquer. Three are even better, for a triple-braided cord is not easily broken. (Ecclesiastes 4:9-12, NLT)

Notice Solomon didn't limit this connection to two. If he had, we might think marriage was God's end-all, be-all solution. But the Lord showed him, "Three are even better," pointing toward spiritual community. Jesus reiterated this in Matthew 18:19-20, speaking of two or three gathering in His Name and the power of prayerful agreement. In these and other scriptures lay the foundation for small groups, Bible studies, and more. The pinnacle of God's fellowship pattern, however, manifested in bringing His people together in a common place of worship. We see this as the Hebrews assembled at the entrance to the *mishkan* ("tabernacle") (Exodus 25:1)[xxxvi] and the city gates (Nehemiah 8:1); as David and the prophets gathered at

---

xxxiii *Exodus 20:8-11; 23:12; Leviticus 23:3*
xxxiv *Leviticus 7-8, 21, 24, 27, 35-36*
xxxv *Exodus 34:23-24; Deuteronomy 16:16*
xxxvi *1 Chronicles 21:29*

the *bayith* ("house") of the Lord (Judges 19:18)[xxxvii]; and at the dedication of a permanent fellowship structure—the *hekal* ("temple") (1 Kings 18:1).[xxxviii] We're even confronted with this as we study history and find, around the third century B.C., the Jewish "synagogue"—from the Greek *sunagógé*, which means "a bringing together."[8]

As previously noted, David and other writers recognized distinct blessings when God's people collectively assembled (Psalm 42:4).[xxxix] The sons of Korah, the authors of Psalm 84, wrote, "Blessed are those who dwell in your house; they are ever praising you. Blessed are those whose strength is in you, whose hearts are set on pilgrimage. As they pass through the Valley of Baka, they make it a place of springs; the autumn rains also cover it with pools. They go from strength to strength, till each appears before God in Zion (vv. 4-7, NIV)." Note the pronouns "they" and "those." God's emphasis is outward—toward others, not an inward "me" and "my." This mindset contrasts with the selfish, Corinthian-type attitude we often see today. Too many believers focus on what they want out of the local church: music style, message length, congregational size, etc., rather than what they might contribute. They're consumers—too consumed with themselves to hear God calling them to a higher purpose.

Second, look at the outcome of the pilgrims' fellowship journey as they reach the Valley of Baka, which means to bewail, sob, or weep bitterly.[9] Sooner or later, through financial hardship, personal illness, or loss, we all reach this valley. When we arrive, what allows us to "stand up beneath the weight" of the temptation is being on pilgrimage with spiritual family— because, as Psalm 84 demonstrates, they "pass through" (1 Co. 10:13). They don't build a home there, falling into lifestyles of bitterness or self-pity. Why? Because God blesses the fellowship of believers! They look after one another, draw strength from one another, lift each other up as Solomon noted, and press forward. Moreover, as they pool their faith in the bonds of fellowship and the common assembly, God transforms the valley of weeping into a wellspring of victory and testimony.

This kind of miracle does not happen for rebels who do their own thing.

---

xxxvii *Malachi 3:10*
xxxviii *Malachi 3:1*
xxxix *Psalm 55:14; 84; 122:1; 133*

Proverbs 18:1 says, "Whoever isolates himself seeks his own desire; he breaks out against all sound judgment," while Psalm 68:5-6, NIV, declares, "A father to the fatherless, a defender of widows, is God in his holy dwelling. God sets the lonely in families, he leads out the prisoners with singing; but the rebellious live in a sun-scorched land." In other words, God leads people into fellowship and spiritual family—not away from them. Carnal man has a nasty habit of forgetting family and forsaking fellowship. In Psalm 27:10, David said, "For my father and my mother may have forsaken me, but the Lord will take me in." Hm. How does the Lord take in the forsaken? What's the primary way He champions orphans and widows? He leads them to institutions He made to meet those needs—family and fellowship, which brings us to the latter part of our discussion.

Coming to the New Testament, Jesus unveils something new: "And I tell you, you are Peter, and on this rock I will build my church, and the gates of hell shall not prevail against it (Matthew 16:18)." He shares three truths: 1.) Jesus names His new thing the *ekklesia* ("church")—*ek* meaning "out from and to," *kaleo* being "to call"—the "called out" ones.[10] This corresponds with the Old Testament *miqra* from earlier, the called-out assembly and reading. 2.) He claims this institution, saying, "*My* church." In other words, "This is My purpose, My blueprint, My operation." It's not some lump of religious clay for man to remodel in his image. Those who do will answer to Him. 3.) Jesus declares that the gates of Hades will never overcome nor withstand *this* institution. Religious counterfeits cannot make this claim.

Next, as Jesus' plan unfolds and the Church launches in Acts, we see His called-out family crashing hell's gates, just as predicted. Repeatedly, He confirms the Gospel through signs and wonders (Acts 2:43)[XL], guides the apostles to create Church government (Acts 6:1-7)[XLI], fleshes out spiritual gifts and ministry offices to equip the saints (1 Corinthians 12)[XLII], tends and feeds His sheep through the apostles' teaching (John 21:16-17)[XLIII], and

---

xl   *Acts 5:12; 6:8; 8:6, 13; 14:3; 15:12*
xli   *Acts 14:23-16:4; 1 Timothy 3; Titus 1*
xlii *Ephesians 4:11-16*
xliii *Ac. 15:35; 18:11; 20:20; 28:31*

deals with division, persecution, famine, heresy, and a myriad of other moral and spiritual issues threatening His infant Church (Acts 6).[xliv]

Most significantly, as the Gospel spreads, God's pattern never changes: A.) The Gospel is preached in a city. B.) People are saved. C.) An apostle stays for a while to disciple. D.) Elders and deacons are appointed to govern. E.) The apostle leaves. F.) Life continues on for the new believers, centering around the local church.

Even as the apostles hit the mission field, Paul and Barnabas, who'd founded churches across the Mediterranean, were "set apart," "appointed to go up," and "sent on their way by the church" at Antioch—their local church (Acts 13:1-4).[xlv] Later, we also read that "it seemed good to the apostles and the elders, with the whole church [at Jerusalem], to choose men from among them and send them...(15:22)." Finally, as Barnabas takes John and Mark, Paul takes Silas, and the Holy Spirit leads them back into the field, what is their business? "Strengthening the churches (15:41)!"

Nowhere in Acts or the epistles do we see Jesus endorsing a model beside His Church. He never once blesses spiritual knockoffs following their own model, nor do we see apostles running around like mavericks with no accountability. In some biblical blend, apostles are always sent *by* a local church, *to* a local church, and to *found* or *strengthen* a local church.

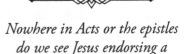

Nowhere in Acts or the epistles do we see Jesus endorsing a model beside His Church.

The local church remains THE New Testament thing and, no different than the Old Testament, every believer should be rooted in spiritual family (Psalm 92:12-13).

From the Church's beginning in Acts 2:42-47, we see this holy and determined call to fellowship with the local body of believers, which Luke beautifully captures:

And they devoted themselves to the apostles' teaching and the fellowship, to the breaking of bread and the prayers. And awe came upon every soul, and many wonders and signs were being done through the apostles. And all who believed were together and had all things in common. And they

xliv Acts 8:1-3; 11:27-30; 15; 1 Corinthians 1-16; Galatians 1-6
xlv Acts 15:2-3

were selling their possessions and belongings and distributing the proceeds to all, as any had need. And day by day, attending the temple together and breaking bread in their homes, they received their food with glad and generous hearts, praising God and having favor with all the people. And the Lord added to their number day by day those who were being saved.

Look at the devotion and awe, the signs and wonders, the favor and generosity they walked in—how God blessed them. "And, and, and...." The blessings just keep coming. Notice also the word "devoted." This is God's fellowship heart, a heart many today have lost. This Greek verb *proskarteréo* is another compound: *pros* meaning "to, towards, or with" and *karteréo*—steadfast or prevailing strength and endurance; hence, "staying in a fixed direction."[11] With strength and endurance, the Church prevailed over persecution, division, and darkness. They gathered, gave, prayed, preached, and strove for the Gospel. Nothing could stop them, though the devil tried with ten Roman persecutions across their first three hundred years!

No different than our day, though, as the New Testament wound down, so did some believers' devotion to the fellowship. God hadn't even finished the Book, and some were already going their own way. To these and all who would follow in their footsteps, the writer of Hebrews said, "We should not stop gathering together with other believers, as some of you are doing. Instead, we must continue to encourage each other even more as we see the day of the Lord coming (10:25, GW)." Western Christendom has reached a critical hour. Many have formed the habit of no longer physically gathering with the local church. The Lord of Fellowship is calling for repentance that He may bring His called-out ones together again. This was His design from the beginning, and it must remain ours. Here are three questions to consider as you cultivate the discipline of fellowship.

Local Church (Ps. 92:12-13): Question #1—"Are you planted in a local church or doing life on your own?" These verses say, "The righteous flourish like the palm tree and grow like a cedar in Lebanon. They are planted in the house of the Lord; they flourish in the courts of our God." We'll never reach full potential outside of God's House, and individual families can't face hell alone. We need God's army! (Ps. 52:8-9)[xlvi]

Small Groups (Mt. 18:19-20): Question #2—"Do you have one or two believers you walk with in regular, intimate fellowship?" Examples abound: Moses had Joshua; David, Jonathan; Daniel, Hananiah, Mishael, and Azariah; Jesus had Peter, James, and John; Paul had

Sometimes we need expert care or strategic-level equipping... like professional counseling to heal emotional wounds or break strongholds of addiction, false religion, fear, etc.

Barnabas, then Silas, and Barnabas took Mark. If it helps, think in military terms. At the most basic levels, there's the company, below that the platoon, then the squad. The local church is your company, its men's or women's ministry your platoon, and a small group your squad. Who's your squad—your personal ministers, armor-bearers, and fellow soldiers you can call 24/7? (Pr. 17:17)[xlvii]

Specialized Ministry & Training (Eph. 4:11-12): Question #3—"Do you need specialized ministry or training to fulfill your calling?" God has given each of us a unique purpose in Christ (Ex. 9:16).[xlviii] To equip us, He gave the Church apostles, prophets, evangelists, pastors, and teachers, and the local assembly as a primary training ground. Sometimes we need expert care or strategic-level equipping which can't be found there, like professional counseling to heal emotional wounds or break strongholds of addiction, false religion, fear, etc. It could also mean college, seminary, parachurch ministry, or beyond. If this resonates, take time to pray, fast, talk with trusted counsel, and plot a course.

On this note, **The Quest Life** is a ministry I helped my dear friend Richard Henderson found years ago. It offers a dynamic series of retreats on biblical manhood and womanhood, vision and calling, worship, and marriage, and the testimonies of transformed lives abound! Check it out at **thequestlife.com**. If this book has helped you, but you desire to go deeper, additional training and tools expanding on these concepts are available at **thesoldiercode.com**.

---

xlvi   *Psalm 68:5-6; 122:1; Matthew 16:18; Hebrews 10:24-25*
xlvii   *Proverbs 27:5-6, 17; Ecclesiastes 4:9-12; Daniel 3; Acts 4:1-22; 13:1-4; 16:16-40; Philippians 2:25*
xlviii *Job 42:2; Proverbs 19:21; Acts 20:24; Ephesians 2:10; Philippians 2:13*

Summary: As we've seen, though vital to our spiritual health and calling, the discipline of fellowship is frequently neglected. And, while personal offenses and wounds are often valid and hurtful, the sins of others never excuse forsaking church altogether. Psalm 119:165, says, "Great peace have those who love Your law; nothing can make them stumble." In other words, "Those who love God's Word enjoy a peace which overcomes offenses." We might stumble. But we do not stay down!

My friend, have you allowed an offense to make you stumble and break fellowship with Christ's Body? If you need to process further here, read back through the section "Way of the Ronin" in the samurai chapter and work through its steps. Whatever you do, though, reengage with a local church. Allow Father to graft you back into a spiritual family and phalanx.

Finally, allow this fresh look at the spiritual disciplines to be a catalyst for your faith—not a source of condemnation (Romans 8:1). The disciplines are not a legalistic scale to compare our walk with others, but ways to commune with a holy God. They're expressions of relationship between our Father and His children, the Son and His Bride; bonds of love and grace, not law and guilt. When we see them from this view, we're not bound to keep them, but free to enjoy them—the way two lovers enjoy intimacy. We don't hear His voice calling, "Where are you?" but whispering, "Rise up, my darling! Come away with me, my fair one (Song 2:10)!"

As the disciplines drive us deeper into relationship with God, we'll also find that "lover" and "fighter" are not exclusive ideas but two sides of the same coin. On every page, Scripture reveals the greatest God lovers are always His greatest soldiers. King Solomon's words to the Shulamite underscore this well: "You are beautiful as Tirzah, my love, lovely as Jerusalem, awesome as an army with banners (Song 6:4)." Speaking of banners, let's finish with our King's.

The Man of Triumph & His Spoils

Many Roman generals ascended the imperial throne and continued leading the army long after. Constantine the Great (A.D. 306-337) stands as one of the most memorable, not only for stopping 250 years of Christian persecution (A.D. 64-313) but for his fabled vision. The Christian bishop and historian Eusebius of Caesarea recorded Constantine's account of how he and his army saw a fiery cross in the midday sky and the phrase "by this conquer," embellished over the years into the more familiar "by this sign, you will conquer." That evening, Jesus allegedly visited Constantine in a dream, telling him to create a military standard of the Cross to protect the Legion and lead them to victory.[12]

Constantine's tale is almost certainly apocryphal and raises theological flags. I note it here only to bridge to a time in biblical history where the Lord led Moses to lift up an ensign to save His people. Numbers 21 marks one of ten occasions in the Exodus where the children of Israel rebelled. In judgment, the Lord sent "fiery serpents (v. 6)," dubbed so because of their hemotoxin, which produces an excruciating burning sensation and massive hemorrhaging. Now identified as the saw-scaled viper and "considered by many scientists to be 'the world's most dangerous snake,'" many Israelites died from its bite.[13] When Moses interceded for his snake-bitten countrymen, God replied, "Make a fiery serpent and place it on a pole, and everyone who is bitten, when he looks to it, shall live (v. 8)."

Almost 1,500 years later, Jesus took up this sign to speak of His coming crucifixion, saying, "Even as Moses lifted up the serpent in the wilderness, so must the Son of Man be lifted up; that whoever believes in Him will have eternal life (John 3:14-15)." The *Life Application Bible* Commentary explains that "to be lifted up in Jesus' time—according to the usage in John (see 8:28; 12:32-34)—was a euphemism for death on the cross (the victim was literally lifted up above the earth); it also spoke of his subsequent glorification."[14] Days from His Cross, Jesus declared, "Now judgment is upon this world; now the ruler of this world will be cast out. And I, if I am lifted up from the earth, will draw all men to Myself (John 12:31-32)."

In all of this, Heaven's General announced that "by this sign"—His Cross—He would conquer the serpent Satan, his army, sin, and death forever (Genesis 3:14-15).[xlix] The Cross is the standard of Christ's army, and salvation the center of our warfare. All else is secondary (Matthew 28:19). [l, 15]

The Cross is the standard of Christ's army, and salvation the center of our warfare.

---

xlix   *1 Corinthians 15:56-57; Revelation 12:9*
l   *Luke 15; 19:10; John 3:16-17; 2 Corinthians 5:17-21*

Thirty years later, Paul employed two of the Roman Legion's most prestigious military rites to illustrate the supremacy of Christ's victory.

> You were dead because of your sins and because your sinful nature was not yet cut away. Then God made you alive with Christ, for he forgave all our sins. He canceled the record of the charges against us and took it away by nailing it to the cross. In this way, he disarmed the spiritual rulers and authorities. He shamed them publicly by his victory over them on the cross. (Colossians 2:13-15, NLT)

The Greek historian Plutarch notes that on slaying the enemy general in personal combat (champion warfare), the Roman general stripped his foe's armor, fastened it to the "trunk of a slender oak, straight and tall," and kept it as a war trophy. Called the *spolia opima* ("rich spoils"), it was later offered at the temple of Rome's chief god, *Jupiter Optimus Maximus*, whose name means "Sky Father, the Best and the Greatest."[16] Paul references this rite in verses 14-15 and uses an augmented Greek verb meaning more than just "disarm." He may have coined the term, in fact, which means to "completely strip off."[17] See, historically, a foe was not merely de-weaponized but stripped of all armament and, sometimes, bare—the ultimate sign of defeat.

Notice also that Paul mentions "the rulers and authorities"—plural, the same Greek terms and syntax in Ephesians 6:12, where Christians "wrestle not against flesh and blood but against the rulers, against the authorities… of evil in the heavenly realms." In the grandest paradox, Satan and his demons had no idea that, as they stripped Jesus' body, He was stripping their "armor"—all power to accuse us through "the record of charges against us."[18] Further, as they nailed Him to the Cross, He was forever fastening sin and death to His own "slender, straight, and tall tree."[19] And, as they lifted Him up from the earth in shaming spectacle, His Name would soon be exalted above every other in victory (Philippians 2:6-11)!

In his second illustration, Paul expounds on Satan and his army's utter humiliation using the Greek verb *thriambeuó*, rendered above as the noun "victory." *Helps Word-Studies* defines it: "to display triumph openly; publicly exalting the victor who leads a victory procession—and putting the conquered on display (exhibition, as 'totally defeated')."[20] Originating from the Greek *thriambos*, the root of the verb Paul used above, the Roman *triumphus* was an extravagant parade down the *Via Sacra* ("Holy Road"), the great street of Rome. This parade could span two-plus miles as it included the Roman army, enemy captives, liberated citizens, senators, sacrificial animals, spoils, and the *vir triumphalis* or "man of triumph"—draped in purple and gold and riding in a four-white-horse-drawn chariot.

Originally, the *thriambos* referred to a hymn sung to the Greek deity Dionysus in their victory processions. Similarly, Psalm 68, predicting Christ's triumph at the Cross, sings of Him, "You have ascended on high; you have led captivity captive in your triumphal procession. You have received gifts among men, even from the rebels, that the Lord God may dwell there (v. 18)." Paul cites the first part of this prophecy in Ephesians 4:8, noting that Christ also descended into the lower parts of the earth (v. 9), referring not only to Jesus' burial but reclamation of the captives in "Abraham's bosom"—the ethereal dwelling place of saints before the Cross (Luke 16:22-23).[li] Concerning Jesus' death, Matthew reveals:

> And when Jesus had cried out again in a loud voice, he gave up his spirit. At that moment, the curtain of the temple was torn in two from top to bottom. The earth shook, the rocks split and the tombs broke open. The bodies of many holy people who had died were raised to life. They came out of the tombs after Jesus' resurrection and went into the holy city and appeared to many people. (Matthew 27:50-53, NIV)

Matthew's text is literal. These Old Testament saints rose from their graves and walked about Jerusalem—a manifest token that death's power was shattered. But where did they go afterward? Christ's captive train! Within the four biblical accounts exists the possibility that Jesus ascended not once but twice: the first, shortly after His resurrection (John 20:17); the second, some forty days later at the Mount of Olives after His Great Commission (Mark 16:19).[lii] Perhaps He didn't want Mary Magdalene holding onto Him because He was on His way to gather these resurrected

---

li   *1 Peter 3:18-19*
lii   *Luke 24:51; Acts 1:3, 9-11*

saints and ascend to the Father in His triumphal procession (John 20:17). We can only speculate, of course, but Paul sets forth, arguably, the most profound picture of Christ's victory in all Scripture.

Imagine for a moment standing within the walls of Heaven Itself—the Holy City. Excitement buzzes in the air like electricity. Faces beam with joy. Crowds gather on either side of the true Holy Road—the Great Street of gold (Revelation 21:21). Never has there been such anticipation. Atop the walls, musicians and choirs file into formation. Suddenly, from the highest rampart, a herald cries out. An alarm of trumpets blasts a tune not of warning but celebration—one never heard before. Musicians and choirs break into praise. Outside the walls, we hear a distant thunder rolling toward us, shaking the ground beneath our feet. Then, the giant pearly gates slowly swing open and from a burst of brilliant light a mighty angelic army enters. Marching in perfect cadence, armor and weaponry gleaming like lightning and singing their *paen* war song, they move as one massive unit—the embodiment of strength, righteousness, and discipline. Catching sight of their standard, we realize: this is the legion assigned to aid Jesus throughout His earthly ministry!

The trumpets resound once more, and we turn to see a great multitude approaching with joy and motion like a churning sea. The triumphant words of Psalm 68 ring from their lips. Shouting, singing, and the sound of drums, cymbals, flutes, harps, and other strings fill the air. Their arms stretch toward the sky in every direction; fingers excitedly point toward the myriad of beauties around them. Could it really be? Glory to God—yes! Brimming with the laughter and revelry of hope deferred for thousands of years, the mighty throng of the Redeemed—the captive train of the King of kings—enters Heaven.

Ransomed saints from Adam and Eve to Noah and his family pass before us. Patriarchs, priests, prophets, judges, kings…they're all here—right down to Jesus' earthly father Joseph and his cousin John the Baptist. Not one has been lost! David leaps and dances in their midst. Next to him, laughing and spinning wildly in a bliss beyond words, skips Miriam with her tambourine. Moses, Aaron, and all the prophets shout oracles of blessing, honor, and glory to the Lord, reciting His great works and miracles.

Another flourish of trumpets splits the air, louder than the previous.

Musicians and choirs crescendo into a new song—the most beautiful we've ever heard. Filled with power and mystery, its lyrics and tempo are alive in every sense of the word, conveying the mightiest of loves and most heroic of deeds. The crowd, spanning as far as the eye can see, joins in the song of the holy Lamb of God. And then, there He is! Draped in purple and gold, the leafy laurel crown of victory resting on his brow, and riding in a four-white-horse-drawn chariot, the Man of Triumph—Jesus the Christ, Son of the Living God—rolls through the gates. Arms outstretched in victory, we see the deep nail scars in His wrists. His tunic, resting off His left shoulder, offers a glimpse of the scourge marks across His back as He passes. The signs of Jesus' epic battle are visible to every eye now staring in wonder.

Suddenly, glints and broken rays of light dance across our faces. Simultaneously, every head gazes upward and every mouth falls open. Behind our Lord's grand chariot moves a second car holding his magnificent war trophy. Spattered with blood and decked like a Christmas tree with the dented armament and broken arms of death and hell, towers the Cross—the Cursed Tree. Cherubim and seraphim wisp overhead in streaks of light, soaring high into the sky above; the furious flutter of their wings creates its own percussion, and their very bodies emanate a worship melody to God Most High like the pipes of an organ.

A fourth and final blast of trumpets signals a foreboding tune. We whirl about, and our eyes stop on them...awful them. Trembling in fear, they file slowly under the great archway, trailing for miles like one long river of death. Gray, cadaverous faces hang low in defeat. Paled, leathery bodies, shackled together and stripped bare, trudge forward. The powers of darkness enter the light of Heaven. Princes, powers, rulers, authorities... every last spiritual imp slinks by. Never have they looked so undone. Not a trace of pride shows on their faces; only terror and deep despair. Their wickedness—felt. Their judgment—sealed.

Shortly behind them limps a cloaked skeletal figure whose stench reveals his name. To the Romans, he is *Mors*; to the Greeks—*Thanatos*; and known still by a host of other names. To all, however, he is death. But today he brings no icy chill or even a hint of dread. His presence rings as hollow as his ghostly frame. With a shout of triumph in the distance, Jesus holds the keys of hell and death high for all to see. The power of the pale lord has been broken forever, and the multitude shouts, "Glory to the King of kings, and glory to the Resurrected One who conquered death!" Still, one long, last chain drags behind death.

All celebration stops. Only the drums continue, pounding a singular toll of doom. As one man, the crowd fastens upon the conquered general coming into view. The Adversary, he who accused everyone before God day and night, staggers forward naked, bound, gagged, and stripped of all authority. The king of pride has arrived without pomp. Even his name, held forever in infamy, is unspoken.

All at once, the drums and procession stop. Heaven falls silent. All eyes now fix upon Jesus as He dismounts. Crossing to the car behind Him, He takes up His Cross—His mighty war trophy. Demon shields and breastplates dangle from it. Like a Roman general taking the temple steps of Jupiter, Jesus climbs those of the Heavenly Tabernacle. The powers of darkness, corralled by angelic guardians, groan as He ascends. Reaching the top, Jesus turns toward the crowd and with one decisive motion sets His trophy down. All bow before the Man of Triumph, the Best and the Greatest. That is a semblance of what Paul painted for the Colossian church and the Church of all ages.

In the gladiator chapter, we said that the Sovereignty of God, His providential rule over all the universe, is the foundation of spiritual warfare. *As we now close our study on the legionary, we set forth Jesus Christ and His redemptive work as the cornerstone of our warfare. All authority in Heaven and Earth rests securely upon the shoulders of God's Man of Triumph.* He has delivered all who believe in Him from the domain of darkness and into His Kingdom forever (Matthew 28:18).[liii] Hallelujah!

As soldiers of the Heavenly Legion, we march in what Romans would call His *auspicia*—the supreme authority of our Emperor. We tread upon serpents and scorpions and over all the power of the enemy (Luke 10:19). Satan has no claim upon us (1 John 5:18). We are not ignorant of his schemes (2 Corinthians 2:11). No weapon formed against us will prosper, and every tongue rising against us in judgment shall be condemned (Isaiah 54:17). The gates of hell will never prevail against the Church of the Living God

---

liii   Colossians 1:13

(Matthew 16:18). We are more than conquerors through Him who loved us and always causes us to triumph (Romans 8:37).[liv] "To Him who sits on the throne and unto the Lamb be blessing and honor and glory and power forever and ever (Revelation 5:13)!" Amen.

Tactical Takeaways

1. In the opening, we said: "The Bible's spiritual disciplines are ancient paths to walk with God and equip believers for spiritual combat (Jeremiah 6:16; Ephesians 6:10-20)." We also noted how the disciplines have become confusing and undoable to some because of overcomplexity. So, we pared down the field to four *core disciplines*: meditation, prayer, worship, and fellowship. Do you agree or disagree with this idea? Why or why not?

2. In the meditation section, we discussed three applications to refresh and bolster your walk: daily reading, Scripture reflection (with music), and a rhema arsenal. What areas for personal growth did you identify, and what are your plans here?

3. In the prayer section, we pondered scriptural prayer, agreeing prayer, prayer and fasting, and prayer journaling. Identify growth places here and lay out a plan.

4. Now, do the same for worship and the applications of corporate worship, the hymns, personal playlists, or other ideas you may have. How will you build yourself up in this area?

5. Finally, in the fellowship section we explored applications with the local church, small groups, and special ministry and equipping. What adjustments do you need to make to find healing, grow, and press further into your God-given purpose?

---

liv   *1 Corinthians 15:57*

Conclusion

THE SOLDIER CODE

Those skilled in the art of war permit the Spirit of the Heavens to flow within and without themselves. They do not try to coerce Heaven into thinking in their own favor but seek to do that which they believe and accept to be the correct action of Heaven. The wise and great warlord never goes against Heaven's decrees. Heaven makes itself obvious to the man of wisdom.

—Sun Tzu, The Art of War

And he withdrew from them about a stone's throw, and knelt down and prayed, saying, "Father, if you are willing, remove this cup from me. Nevertheless, not my will, but yours, be done." And there appeared to him an angel from heaven, strengthening him. And being in agony he prayed more earnestly; and his sweat became like great drops of blood falling down to the ground.

—Jesus, Luke 22:41-44

Our trek through the Valley of Soldiers draws to an end. Together, we've sounded the depths of barbarism and cruelty, scaled the heights of prowess and virtue, and now stand atop more than two thousand years of martial tradition. Below us lie six cultures and dozens of countries where we scoured symbols and sacred texts, raked through relics and rituals, and unlocked codes in everything from the Icelandic sagas to medieval church liturgy. Now, let's review some lessons from our journey of a thousand miles.

Way of the Samurai
In the East, Japan's Age of War forged its creation mythos, the archetypal *servant-warrior*—the samurai and his gallant code *bushido* ("the way of the warrior"). His master's call to arms reminded us of our own in the words of James, John, Peter, and Paul. The samurai's daily meditation upon death compelled us to repent of the fatal "civilian mindset" and turn to that of a Kingdom soldier: "Spiritual warfare is not an event but a way of life." And, as millions of casualties marked their day, casualties in everything from pastoral health to declining numbers among believers call us to arms in ours. Most of all, the samurai belief that love is the greatest virtue and laying down one's life the deepest honor challenges us to live as Christ's grain of wheat—"buried in the ground, dead to the world, and ready to serve at a moment's notice (John 12:24-26, MSG)." The way of the samurai and "more excellent way" of Christ's soldiers is love (1 Corinthians 12:31).

Law of the Spartan
At ancient Greece, the reforms of Lycurgus spawned one of antiquity's most devout soldiers: the Spartan. Setting aside each citizen for state service, Lycurgus codified the ideal that "worldly entanglements were beneath a Spartan," corresponding to Christ's command: "No soldier gets entangled in civilian pursuits, since his aim is to please the one who enlisted him (2 Timothy 2:3-4)." Worldly distractions have drawn away many Kingdom soldiers, resulting in catastrophic breaches within our society. Hell has fallen on marriages, families, churches, and more. The stand of the 300 and charge of Spartan mothers "Either with or on this!" urge heavenly *citizen-soldiers* to throw off earthly pursuits, anchor in fellowship, stand

together in prayerful phalanxes, and push back against evil forces in the cultural "shoving match (Romans 12:1-2)."[i] Consecration was Spartan law and is spiritual law for Christian soldiers.

Vow of the Viking

The Northmen flashed into history plundering monasteries and plunging Europe into an era of terror. Like Saul's attack on the first-century Church, however, which led to his salvation and a miracle ministry which shook the Mediterranean world, the Viking invasion turned to a Gospel one as Norsemen encountered the lightning-fisted Christ in sign-wielding saints. Further, as Vikings discovered uncharted lands, raided shores in sleek warcraft, and berserked into enemy lines as a type of *shock trooper*, that same valor soon drove the Gospel into new realms. These lessons remind us: no one is beyond grace, God still works wonders, and His Spirit ever searches for those with lightweight lives, shape-shifting faith, and a heart to plunder hell. Valor was a Viking vow, and it calls Christ's soldiers to "be strong" and berserk for His Kingdom (Joshua 1:7).

Charge of the Knight

As war, famine, and pestilence besieged medieval Europe, the Church "turned Scripture into action" by housing pilgrims and the destitute, restoring institutions of learning, and caring for the elderly and diseased. Kings also enlisted battlefield intercession and psalmody from monks for their campaigns. But, when mounted soldiers began preying on the weak, clerics and theologians drew God's Sword to confront evil, call men to repentance, and lead the charge to create chivalry. From these roots sprung the *martial monk*, a knight who, though often misunderstood today, helped ensure the Church's survival and Europe's emergence from the Dark Ages. Compassion was the order of knights, and Compassion Himself charges every Christian soldier to "give justice to the weak, maintain the right of the afflicted, and rescue the needy (Psalm 82:3-4)."

---

i   *Ephesians 6:13-14*

Oath of the Gladiator

From graveside battles to gruesome spectacles in the Colosseum, we traced the bloody steps of Rome's *fighter-slave*: the gladiator. In his purchase, we saw our redemption in Christ; his oath to endure, our call to suffering; and the red-hot brand marking him as a *lanista's* property, the reminder: we are no longer our own. The *doctor's* skillful training of beast fighters sharpened us to Satan's schemes as the lying serpent, prowling lion, and accusing dragon. Last, the gladiator's life-and-death struggle in the arena unfolded before our eyes and the *editor's*, the "giver" whose turned thumb pointed us to our loving, Sovereign Lord who gives and takes away (Job 1:21). Endurance was the gladiator's oath and, though "pressed, perplexed, hunted down, or knocked down," the Christian soldier's remains the same (2 Corinthians 4:8-9).

Mark of the Legionary

On our final leg, we marched with the ancient world's most proficient conqueror: the Roman legionary, a type of the *heavy infantryman*. His oath reminded us of our confession to Jesus' lordship in salvation; the tattoo on his hand, our eternal security through the Spirit's seal of redemption. The most striking lesson, though, came not from the mark upon his hand but the virtue of his life: *disciplina*, "the training which provides steadiness of character."[1] Vegetius' plea for legionaries to return to discipline teaches us that spiritual discipline is key to becoming "heavily armed." Victorious spiritual combat begins not with warring against the devil but walking with God! This is how we "run with purpose in every step" and throw knockout blows (1 Corinthians 9:26). Discipline was the Legion's mark, and it always marks the lives of God's mightiest soldiers.

A Soldier Synthesis

So, with our spiritual pickaxe we have chiseled out God's "hidden treasures" embedded within the walls of these ancient soldier codes. We've also sifted and examined those findings up close, through the loop of the Bible's original languages, contexts, and cultures. As Solomon says, we have mined for God's "silver" and searched for His "hidden treasures (Proverbs 2:4)." But what have we emerged with? Six precious gems, chief virtues offerings us a code for modern-day Christian soldiers engaged in the good fight: *Love, Consecration, Valor, Compassion, Endurance,* and *Discipline.* When added to our warfare, these qualities give the Christian soldier not only a lethal edge, but checks and balances greatly needed these days.

The warrior typologies of these cultures also hold equal value. Japan's *servant-warrior,* following his master in death, gives us a model to immediately apply in putting to death our pride, sinful desires, and serving God, spouse, leaders, and others with a tender, daring love. Sparta's *citizen-soldier,* guarding the homeland, encourages us to daily be that Thermopylae shield wall for faith and family in a cruel world. Scandinavia's *shock trooper,* breaching enemy lines and expanding borders, beckons us to stop stalling, step out, and follow God on mission to raid the coasts of hell. Medieval Europe's *martial monk,* ministering to the needy and fighting for justice, moves us to shine the light of Christ into our dark age by becoming His hands and feet in practical, life-giving ways. Rome's *fighter-slave,* enduring for the glory of editor and empire, urges us to not quit—to fight on in relationships, ministry, and circumstances where God's face and purpose may be hidden for a season. Last, the mother of nation's *heavy infantryman,* constantly disciplining soul and body to conquer, warns us to not skip our daily "exercises" with God, training with the weapons of our warfare. The hour is too late, and the work of our ancient foe too real! It's time for action, and I want to leave you with three tools to aid you as you march forward.

The Soldier Codex

In the knight's chapter, we noted how "soldiers needed righteous counsels to govern them, honorable causes to guide them, and virtuous codes to guard their conduct." This *Soldier Codex* lays out some key emphases from each warrior chapter. The top half lists "earthly" or historical elements: a rough timeline for the culture's most formative period; the primary catalyst(s) driving martial evolution; the code which developed and ruled conduct; and the key warrior type or model the culture contributed to history. The bottom half highlights our "heavenly" takeaways: a Kingdom cause for believers; an immediate faith application; a biblical type(s) for meditation; a doctrinal focus from Scripture; some spiritual weapons discussed in the chapter; and a biblical text capturing the main theme. Dividing the codex are the six chief virtues we mined from the soldier cultures, virtues bridging the earthly and heavenly realms. Refer back to the codex for guidance, study, prayer points, and more as the Lord leads you.

The Soldier Katas

Your next tool for this new warring season are the six theme Scripture passages from our soldier chapters. Remember in the knight's chapter how we discussed the *rhema-strike,* a specific memory verse to act as a "sword-stroke" for temptation or ministry opportunity (Ephesians 6:17). In part two of the legionary study, we spoke about building a *rhema arsenal,* a set of memory verses for different situations and spiritual foes. Now, I want to add one more dimension to your training by giving you what I call a *spiritual kata.*

In martial arts, a *kata* (Jap., "form" or "pattern") is a sequence of movements a student repeatedly practices to deliver a fast, fluid series of attacks, defenses, or counterattacks. Think of these passages as your "Soldier Katas." Putting them to memory will equip you in ways you never imagined. I can't tell you how often the Lord brings these to my mind in warfare, ministry, and other places. As needs arise, the Holy Spirit will bring a particular kata to your mind, inspiring you with a theme, arming you with a truth, offering you some guiding biblical principle or counsel.

On this note, let me say: as God's soldiers, we need to step up our training in Scripture memory. We don't need soldiers who can just "swing God's Sword." We need spiritual "Benjamites," who can use weapons "with both hands": troops like those of Zebulun who were "equipped for battle with all weapons of war (1 Chronicles 12:2, 33)." In a word, we need biblical "Bruce Lees," believers who can strike the enemy seven times before he knows what hit him!

THE SOLDIER CODEX		
	Samurai	**Spartan**	**Viking**
Timeline	A.D. 701-1877	ca. 750 B.C.-A.D. 195	A.D. 789-1066
Catalyst	*Sengoku Jidai* "The Age of Warring States"	Spartan Social Decline	Homeland Power Struggles
Code	*Bushido* "The Way of the Warrior"	*Megále Rhêtra* "Great Sayings"	Icelandic *Sagas* "The Utterances"
Type	Servant-Warrior	Citizen-Soldier	Shock Trooper
Virtue	Love	Consecration	Valor
Kingdom Cause	The Lord (Luke 10:27)	The Family, God's & Ours (Nehemiah 4:14)	The Lost (Luke 19:10)
Primary Application	Service (Mark 10:42-45)	Fellowship (Acts 2:42-47)	Evangelism (John 3:16-18)
Biblical Type	Ittai (2 Samuel 15:18-22)	Hananiah, Mishael & Azariah (Daniel 3:16-18)	Paul (Acts 26:16-20)
Doctrinal Focus	Mortification of Sin Nature (Colossians 3:5)	Sanctification (Philippians 3:19-21)	The Great Commission (Matthew 28:19-20)
Highlighted Weaponry	Confession to God & Brothers/Sisters (1 Jn. 1:9; Ja. 5:16)	Spiritual Family & Biblical Counsel (Ps. 68:6; Pr. 24:6)	Spiritual Gifts & Active Faith (1 Co. 12:8, 10; He. 11)
Theme Text	John 12:24-26	2 Timothy 2:3-7	Joshua 1:7-9

THE SOLDIER CODEX			
	Knight	**Gladiator**	**Legionary**
Timeline	A.D. 450-1500	264 B.C. -ca. A.D. 445	300 B.C. -A.D. 450
Catalyst	Western Collapse & Eastern Invasion	Hedonism & Brutus Father's Funeral	*Via Romana* "Roman Way"
Code	*Chevalerie* "Horse Soldiery"	*Auctoramentum Gladiatorium* "Gladiator's Wage"	*Sacramentum Militiae* "Military Oath"
Type	Martial-Monk	Fighter-Slave	Heavy Infantryman
Virtue	Compassion	Endurance	Discipline
Kingdom Cause	The Needy (Psalm 82:2-4)	God's Glory (1 Corinthians 10:31)	Godliness (1 Timothy 4:7-8)
Primary Application	Charity (James 2:14-17)	Suffering (Philippians 1:29)	Discipleship (Colossians 2:6-7)
Biblical Type	David (1 Samuel 17:45-47)	Job (Job 1:20-21; 13:15)	John (1 John 2:12-14)
Doctrinal Focus	Good Works in Christ (Ephesians 2:8-9)	God's Sovereignty (Isaiah 46:9-10)	Christ's Victory (Colossians 2:13-15)
Highlighted Weaponry	Prayer, Fasting, & Psalmic Warfare (Mt. 17:21; Ac. 2:42)	Worship, Meditation, & Testimony (Job 1:20; Ps. 1:1-3; Re. 12:11)	Spiritual Disciplines (Ac. 2:42; Eph. 5:18-21; Col. 3:16-17)
Theme Text	Psalm 82:2-4	2 Corinthians 4:8-12	1 Corinthians 9:24-27

Finally, do not say to yourself, "I can't memorize." I've watched grown men and women, the elderly, middle-aged folk with drug-addled pasts, and those with various disabilities and impairments ask the Lord for help in memorization then absolutely crush it. Listen, friend: our Father is not in the habit of giving commands (which Scripture-memory is) and not giving us the power to follow through. Ask Him for help. Believe! Then, do your part and practice, practice, practice. It may come slowly or quickly or some verses easier than others. But, it will come. So, pray, be patient, work hard, and trust the Lord. (Use S.I.M., the pattern of memorization laid out in the second Roman legionary chapter, under "Meditation" and the subheading "Rhema Arsenal.") The Soldier Katas are printed here for quick access, and you can download beautiful pdf versions at **thesoldiercode.com**.

LOVE: THE WAY OF THE SAMURAI

Listen carefully: Unless a grain of wheat is buried in the ground, dead to the world, it is never any more than a grain of wheat. But if it is buried, it sprouts and reproduces itself many times over. In the same way, anyone who holds on to life just as it is destroys that life. But if you let it go, reckless in your love, you'll have it forever, real and eternal. If any of you wants to serve me, then follow me. Then you'll be where I am, ready to serve at a moment's notice. The Father will honor and reward anyone who serves me."

– JOHN 12:24-26, MSG

CONSECRATION: THE LAW OF THE SPARTAN

Share in suffering as a good soldier of Christ Jesus. No soldier gets entangled in civilian pursuits, since his aim is to please the one who enlisted him. An athlete is not crowned unless he competes according to the rules. It is the hard-working farmer who ought to have the first share of the crops. Think over what I say, for the Lord will give you understanding in everything.

– 2 TIMOTHY 2:3-7, ESV

VALOR: THE VOW OF THE VIKING

Only be strong and very courageous, being careful to do according to all the law that Moses my servant commanded you. Do not turn from it to the right hand or to the left, that you may [act wisely] and have good success wherever you go. This Book of the Law shall not depart from your mouth, but you shall meditate on it day and night, so that you may be careful to do according to all that is written in it. For then you will make your way prosperous, and then you will have good success. Have I not commanded you? Be strong and courageous. Do not be frightened, and do not be dismayed, for the LORD your God is with you wherever you go."

— JOSHUA 1:7-9, ESV

COMPASSION: THE CHARGE OF THE KNIGHT

How long will you judge unjustly and show partiality to the wicked? Selah. Give justice to the weak and the fatherless; maintain the right of the afflicted and the destitute. Rescue the weak and the needy; deliver them from the hand of the wicked.

— PSALM 82:2-4, ESV

ENDURANCE: THE OATH OF THE GLADIATOR

We are pressed on every side by troubles, but we are not crushed and broken. We are perplexed, but we don't give up and quit. We are hunted down, but God never abandons us. We get knocked down, but we get up again and keep going. Through suffering, these bodies constantly share in the death of Jesus, so that the life of Jesus may also be seen in our bodies. Yes, we live under constant danger of death because we serve Jesus, so that the life of Jesus will be obvious in our dying bodies. So we live in the face of death, but it has resulted in eternal life for you.

— 2 CORINTHIANS 4:8-12, 1996 NLT

DISCIPLINE: THE MARK OF THE LEGIONARY

Don't you realize that in a race everyone runs, but only one person gets the prize? So run to win! All athletes are disciplined in their training. They do it to win a prize that will fade away, but we do it for an eternal prize. So I run with purpose in every step. I am not just shadowboxing. I discipline my body like an athlete, training it to do what it should. Otherwise, I fear that after preaching to others I myself might be disqualified.

— 1 CORINTHIANS 9:24-27, NLT

The Soldier Code

Last but not least, I leave you a Christian "Soldier Code," which I encourage you to memorize or use as a template to craft your own. Pray and ask the Lord what He might have you do. Aside from the Soldier Katas, if you need additional material for inspiration, look back in the knight's chapter under "God's Sword & the Rhema-Strike" at some of the Bible's chivalric passages or draw ideas or quotations from the historic texts cited in the chapters. However you sense God leading you, listen. Biblically based codes offer valuable paradigms to help navigate difficult circumstances and seasons, along with psychological bulwarks against Satanic attacks, worldly pressures, and fleshly temptations. In a moment, they can remind, refocus, and reinvigorate us. So, build the fort now, soldier. Don't wait for the storm. Become it!

The world around us is spinning further and further out of control, ravaged by sin and our ruthless foe. Never has Western civilization, the Church, and the family needed the Christian soldier more than now. In the battles ahead, you may need to be a tad more Spartan as hell presses against your faith and family. The gladiator within you may need to endure trial a bit longer before breakthrough comes. The Lord may call you into a situation where you must ante up samurai-style with service and sacrifice, dying to yourself in tough ways. Perhaps the Lord has used all of this to push you to a place of decision where you'll finally berserk like a Viking, pressing out into some unknown waters to pursue a vision, reach the lost, or both. Maybe a knight's quest is calling you—the cause of someone (or many) in need: the hungry, lonely, sickly, orphan, or oppressed. Or, maybe it's something as simple yet profoundly important as a more disciplined walk with God, that finally transforms you into a heavily armed legionary, ready for any battle.

Whatever the need, whenever the time should arise, may this code shoot Christ's adrenaline into your soul and remind you of who you are and the Mighty Soldier God revealed in Scripture.

The Soldier Code

I am a Samurai of the Lord of lords,
lovingly following my Master in death;

I am a Spartan of the Lion of Judah,
a consecrated shield for faith & family;

I am a Viking of the only God of thunder,
valiantly plundering the coasts of hell;

I am a Knight of the King of kings,
compassionately rescuing the needy;

I am a Gladiator of the Grand Editor,
enduring for His glory and purpose;

I am a Legionary of the Man of Triumph—Jesus,
the Christ—marching behind Him with discipline;

I am a Christian, a soldier in the Kingdom of God!

ENDNOTES

Prologue: Sun Tzu & Spiritual Warfare

1   Laozi, *Tao Te Ching*, Chapter 64. Circa 6 B.C., the *Tao* is a classical text of Chinese philosophy. Authorship is disputed, but Laozi, who is also referred to as Lao Tzu ("Old Master"), is typically credited. Literally translated, the verse reads: "A journey of a thousand miles begins beneath the feet." "With a single step" is a more modernized, thought-for-thought rendering.

2   Sun Tzu, *The Art of War, translated and with an introduction by Samuel B. Griffith* (New York: Oxford University Press, 1971) 63.

3   A number of studies from secular and religious research centers reveal disturbing trends here. For example, Barna.com's article "Competing Worldviews Influence Today's Christians," from *Research Releases in Culture & Media*, May 9, 2017, "shows that only 17 percent of Christians who consider their faith important and attend church regularly actually have a biblical worldview." Among "practicing Christians," the study found that "61 percent agree with ideas rooted in New [Age] Spirituality, 54 percent resonate with postmodernist views," and "29 percent believe ideas based on secularism." See https://www.barna.com/research/competing-worldviews-influence-todays-christians/.

Not surprisingly, these deviations from biblical orthodoxy ("right belief") have resulted in serious divergences from biblical orthopraxy ("right behavior"), as Pew Research Center's Jeff Diamant notes in his August 31, 2020 article "Half of U.S. Christians Say Casual Sex between Consenting Adults Is Sometimes or Always Acceptable." See https://www.pewresearch.org/fact-tank/2020/08/31/half-of-u-s-christians-say-casual-sex-between-consenting-adults-is-sometimes-or-always-acceptable/.

Pew also notes in its June 17, 2021 article "Key Facts About the Abortion Debate in America," that "[a]ttitudes about whether abortion should be legal vary widely by religious affiliation" under item #3. This research finds that 21 percent of white evangelical Protestants say that abortion "should be legal in at least most instances," 63 percent of non-evangelical white Protestants believe it "should be legal in all or most cases," and 43 percent of Catholics "say it should be legal in all or most cases." See https://www.pewresearch.org/fact-tank/2021/06/17/key-facts-about-the-abortion-debate-in-america/.

These are just a few quick examples. We'll explore more research on beliefs, behaviors, and trends in the coming chapters, which supports this statement.

Introduction: The Soldier Stone

1   1368—*gibbor.* James Strong, *Strong's Exhaustive Concordance of the Bible* (Peabody, MA: Hendrickson Publishers, 1980). Biblehub.com. https://biblehub.com/hebrew/1368.htm (Accessed January 13, 2021). The base definition of *gibbor* is "strong; mighty," and its usage throughout the Old Testament is in a martial context. Some textual examples from David, Isaiah, and Jeremiah are: Ps. 24:8; 45:3; Is. 9:6; 10:21; 42:13; Je. 20:11.

2   Robert Hicks, *The Masculine Journey* (Colorado Springs: Navpress, 1993) 81.

3   *Ibid.,* 81.

4   Patrick M. Arnold, *Wildmen, Warriors and Kings* (New York: Crossroad, 1991) 101, quoted by Hicks, *The Masculine Journey,* 75.

5   Laurence Geller CBE, "Folger Library—Churchill's Shakespeare." International Churchill

Society. https://winstonchurchill.org/resources/in-the-media/churchill-in-the-news/folger-library-churchills-shakespeare (Accessed October 30, 2020).

6   Inazo Nitobe, *Bushido: The Classic Portrait of Samurai Martial Culture* (Boston: Tuttle Publishing, 1969) 122, Brackets Mine.

7   Benjamin Jowett, *Sermons on Faith and Doctrine*, III.II "Greek and Oriental Religions." Christian Classics Ethereal Library. https://ccel.org/ccel/jowett_b/faith/faith.iii.ii.html (Accessed January 13, 2021).

8   Paul's Mars Hill discourse in Ac. 17:22-31 is a textbook example of the usefulness of cultural knowledge to undergird Christian teaching and evangelism. Beginning with an affirmation about the Athenian's spiritual zeal, then accessing their native religion (the idol to the "unknown god," v. 23) and poetry (v. 28), Paul found common ground with his audience and fashioned a captivating weave of illustrations and parallels. Most striking are his quotations of two well-known Greek poems: Epimenides' *Cretica* ("In him we live and move and have our being") and Aeratus' *Phaenomena 5* ("For we are indeed his offspring").

    God used Paul's knowledge and skill with Greek culture to create inroads, which helped convey His message. Paul also quoted Epimenides' *De Oraculis* in Titus 1:12 ("The people of Crete are all liars; they are cruel animals and lazy gluttons") and another Greek poet, Menander, and his *Thais* in 1 Corinthians 15:33 ("Bad company corrupts good character"). The end result of Paul's discourse was that "some mocked" (Ac. 17:32a), some wanted to hear more (Ac. 17:32b), and "some joined him and believed (Ac. 17:34)." Moreover, the Holy Spirit took these examples and moved Luke to record them in His inspired Word. Again then, God has no problem using culture as it suits His purpose.

9   The phrasing of Jeremiah 1:10 appears repeatedly as a theme throughout the book (24:6; 31:28, 40; 42:10; 45:4).

10 Additional biblical references on "pull down's" (Heb., *nathats*) usage in Israel's charge to remove idols in society: De. 7:5; 12:3; Ju. 2:2; 6:28, 30-32; 2 Ki. 10:27; 11:18; 23:7-8, 12, 15; 2 Chr. 23:17; 31:1, 33:3; 34:4, 7; Eze. 16:39.

    Additional references on "pull down's" linguistic use in siege warfare: Ju. 8:9, 17; 9:45; 2 Ki. 25:10; 2 Chr. 36:19; Is. 22:10; Je. 18:7; 31:28; 33:4; 39:8; 52:14; Eze. 26:9, 12.

11 Additional references on the Hebrew *haras*'s use in siege warfare: 2 Sa. 11:25; 2 Ki. 3:25; 1 Chr. 20:1; La. 2:2, 17; Eze. 13:14; 26:4, 12; 36:35.

12 Here is a list of Paul's Greek athletic and Roman military references. Some verses contain more than one term or allusion, which is signified in parentheses: Ac. 20:24; Ro. 6:13; 9:16; 13:12; 15:30; 1 Co. 9:7, 24 (3), 25 (2), 26 (2), 27; 2 Co. 6:7; 10:3, 4 (3), 5 (2); Ga. 2:2; 5:7; Eph. 6:11 (2), 12, 13 (3), 14 (3), 15, 16 (2), 17 (2); Php. 1:27 (2), 30; 2:16; 4:3; Col. 1:29; 2:1; 4:12 (2); 1 Th. 2:2; 5:8 (2); 1 Ti. 1:18 (2); 4:7-8, 10; 6:12 (2); 2 Ti. 2:3-4 (2), 5 (3); 3:10 (*agōgē**) ; 4:7 (3); He. 4:12; 5:14; 11:33-34 (2), 37; 12:1 (2), 4, 11.

    The authorship of Hebrews is contested. Some scholars assert Pauline authorship; others theorize another apostle, such as Barnabas. I mention these references because of their Pauline-style term usage.

    * The etymology of *agōgē* and Paul's use of it is discussed at length in chapter 3 under "The Raising."

13 New Testament occurrences of *agón* as a noun and verb: Lk. 13:24; 22:44; Jn. 18:36; Ro. 15:30; 1 Co. 9:25; Php. 1:30; Col. 1:29; 2:1; 4:12; 1 Th. 2:2; 1 Ti. 4:10; 6:12 (2); 2 Ti. 4:7 (2); He. 11:33; 12:1, 4; Jude 3. The total count of nineteen is reached by the fact that there are two occurrences of *agón* in 1 Timothy 6:12 and two in 2 Timothy 4:7.

14 73—*agón*. *Strong's Exhaustive Concordance of the Bible*. https://biblehub.com/greek/73.htm.

15 Leonard Nimoy, *The First Olympics: Blood, Honor, and Glory*. DVD. Produced by Henry

Schipper (New York: The History Channel, 2004). For those interested, the names of the four Greek events were: *harmatodromía* (chariot racing), *pygmachía* (boxing), *palé* (wrestling), and *pankration* (mixed martial arts).

16 *Ibid.*

17 *Ibid.*, 2004.

18 Dictionary.com. "parable." https://www.dictionary.com/browse/parable (Accessed October 19, 2020).

19 Some Old Testament parables: Ju. 9:7-20; 2 Sa. 12:1-4; 14:1-14; 1 Ki. 20:35-43; Is. 5:1-7; Eze. 17:1-15; 19; 24:1-14

20 3975—*pachúno. Strong's Concordance.* https://biblehub.com/greek/3975.htm (Accessed January 13, 2021).

21 Eugene Peterson, *The Message: The Bible in Contemporary Language* (Colorado Springs: Navpress, 2004) 1151.

22 Sun Tzu, *The Art of War, translated and with an introduction by Samuel B. Griffith* (New York: Oxford University Press, 1971) 77.

23 William Gurnall (1617-1679) is a man most of modern Christendom knows nothing about. His work *The Christian in Complete Armor*, however, was praised by the English pastor John Newton, who gave us the hymn "Amazing Grace" and by the "Prince of Preachers" Charles Spurgeon.

 Gurnall's work, released in three volumes (1655, 1658, and 1662), is an exhaustive exposition of Ephesians 6:10-20. A virtual copy is available through the Christian Classics Ethereal Library at: https://www.ccel.org/ccel/gurnall/armour/files/armour.html (Accessed May 28, 2021).

24 William Gurnall, *The Christian in Complete Armour, Branch Second, Observe First & Second.* The Christian Classics Ethereal Library. https://www.ccel.org/ccel/gurnall/armour/files/gurnal02a.htm (Accessed January 13, 2021).

Book I: Way of the Samurai

1 The *Kojiki* ("Record of Ancient Matters") & *Nihongi* or *Nihon Shoki* ("Chronicles of Japan") are the sacred texts of Japan's oldest native religion, *Shinto* ("way of the gods"). The *Kojiki*, completed in A.D. 712, traces the country's origin to the mid-seventh century through a compilation of fables, songs, poems, genealogies, legends, and partly historical accounts. Its earliest manuscript can be traced to around 1372, but its importance in Japanese history cannot be underestimated as it is held to be its oldest literary work.

 Assembled in A.D. 720, the *Nihon Shoki* catalogues various fables and legends also, but holds important historical information from the early 400s to the late 800s, not the least of which is the country's initiation to Buddhism in the mid-sixth century.

2 Stephen Turnbull, *Samurai: The World of the Warrior* (Great Britain: Osprey Publishing, 2003), 13.

3 *Ibid.*, 14-15.

4 The Onin War (1467-1476) triggered the Age of War *with the destruction of the Japanese capital, Kyoto, and the disgrace of shogun Ashikaga Yoshimasa. The title "Age of War" is an abbreviation of the period's more proper name the Sengoku Jidai: "Age of Warring States." It was adopted from a period in Chinese history pitting state versus state in contrast to Japan's, which centered on clan warfare.*

5 Stephen Turnbull, *The Samurai Sourcebook* (London: Cassell & Co., 1998), 224. In the third siege of Nagashima, daimyo Oda Nobunaga forced the defending *Ikko-ikki* alliance of farmers, Buddhist monks, Shinto priests, and some nobility into their fortress monasteries

of Ganshoji and Nagashima. He then constructed a wooden barricade around the perimeter and set it ablaze, annihilating the structures and their twenty thousand inhabitants, including thousands of women and children.

6   Carol Gaskin & Vince Hawkins, *The Ways of the Samurai* (New York: ibooks, 2003) 115. These findings are based on the Kawanakajima Battlefield Museum, which tolls daimyo Takeda Shingen's losses at 62 percent (12,400) and daimyo Uesugi Kenshin's at 72 percent (12,960). Stephen Turnbull disputes these stats in *The Samurai Sourcebook, 81. In this case, I defer to the onsite source.*

7   Japanese archeology has demonstrated that high samurai death tolls dictated the need for mass battlefield burials, which is what we find at Kamakura Beach (c. 1333)—a site not even from the same era with over four thousand sets of remains. *Warrior Graveyard: Samurai Massacre*, a National Geographic video, explores this finding. Sadly, with Japan's modernization, many sites are buried under current structures.

8   Gaskin & Hawkins, *The Ways of the Samurai, 127.*

9   Turnbull, *The Samurai Sourcebook, 224.*

10 Gaskin & Hawkins, 115.

11 Sekigahara was the *Sengoku Jidai's final battle and the single largest battle ever fought between samurai. Anthony J. Bryant, Sekigahara: 1600, The Final Struggle for Power (Oxford: Osprey Publishing, 1995), notes that over 160,000 warriors were employed in the fighting and places the casualty rate at 40,000.*

12 Taira Shigesuke, *Code of the Samurai: A Modern Translation of the Bushido Shoshinshu,* translated by Thomas Cleary (Boston, MA: Tuttle, 1999) 13, 72.

13 The *panoplía* (from the Greek *pás*, "all," and *hóplon*, "weapon"; hence, "all weapons") was the full set of defensive and offensive armament, which in Ephesians 6 refers to the Roman legionary outfit (Greek hoplites did not wear belts). The Greek verb *histémi* ("stand," v. 11, 13-14) "was a military term meaning to resist the enemy, hold the position, and offer no surrender." (Bruce B. Barton, Philip Comfort, Kent Keller, Linda K. Taylor, David Veerman; series editor: Grant Osborne; editor: Philip Comfort) *Life Application Bible Commentary, Ephesians* (Tyndale House Publishers, Inc.: Wheaton, IL, 1996) 129.

   Analambanó ("take up," v. 13) "is a technical military term describing preparation for battle. The armor is available, but the believer-soldier must 'take it up' in order to be ready (*Ibid.,* 131)." *Anthistémi* ("withstand," v. 13) "was a military term in classical Greek (used by Thucydides, etc.) meaning to 'strongly resist an opponent' ('take a firm stand against')"; it refers to a "180-degree, contrary position" and "to establish one's position publicly by conspicuously 'holding one's ground,' i.e., refusing to be moved ('pushed back')." *Helps Word-Studies* (Helps Ministries, Inc., 2011) Biblehub.com. https://biblehub.com/greek/436.htm.

   Thucydides, whom *Helps* references above, was an Athenian general of the Classical Greek era, and his *History of the Peloponnesian War* is one source among a number of ancient ones where we can trace this military language. His work is a detailed account of the twenty-seven-year war between the Delian League, led by Athens, and the Peloponnesian League, led by Sparta, which Sparta won at the Battle of Aegospotami (405 B.C.).

14 5293—*hupotassó*. James Strong, *Strong's Exhaustive Concordance of the Bible* (Peabody, MA: Hendrickson Publishers, 1980). Biblehub.com. https://biblehub.com/greek/5293.htm (Accessed January 13, 2021).

15 2666— *katapinó. Strong Concordance.* https://biblehub.com/greek/2666.htm (Accessed January 13, 2021).

16 Observations on 1127—*gregoréo* from *Strong's Concordance, Helps Word-Studies, New American Standard Exhaustive Concordance of the Bible with Hebrew-Aramaic and Greek*

Dictionaries (The Lockman Foundation, 1998), and *Thayer's Greek Lexicon,* Electronic Database (Biblesoft, Inc., 2011). Biblehub.com. https://www.biblehub.com/greek/1127.htm (Accessed January 13, 2021).

17 John references the evil one in Revelation thirty-two times using the names: "Satan" (8), "devil" (5), "dragon" (13), "serpent" (5), and "accuser of our brothers" (1).

18 Dr. Richard J. Krejcir, "Statistics on Pastors: 2016 Update." ChurchLeadership.org. http://www.churchleadership.org/apps/articles/default.asp?blogid=4545&view=post&articleid=Statistics-on-Pastors-2016-Update&link=1&fldKeywords=&fldAuthor=&fldTopic=0 (Accessed January 13, 2021).

19 The Barna Group, *Research Release in Leaders & Pastors,* "How Healthy Are Pastors' Relationships?" Barna.com: February 15. 2017. https://www.barna.com/research/healthy-pastors-relationships (Accessed January 13, 2021).

20 Luke Gibbons, "15 Statistics About the Church and Pornography That Will Blow Your Mind." Charismanews.com: September 18, 2018. https://www.charismanews.com/us/73208-15-statistics-about-the-church-and-pornography-that-will-blow-your-mind (Accessed January 13, 2021).

21 Krejcir, "Statistics on Pastors: 2016 Update." ChurchLeadership.org.

22 George Barna, "Survey: Christians Are Not Spreading the Gospel," writing for *American Culture Review.*

I obtained an MS Word document of this research by emailing Dr. Barna on August 17, 2020 at Arizona Christian University's Cultural Research Center (george.barna@arizonachristian.edu). Sources cited by Barna are: 1991-2016 data from the Barna Group (Barna.com) and 2017 data from FullView™ surveys conducted by American Culture & Faith Institute (Culturefaith.com). Culturefaith.com is no longer on the web, hence my correspondence with Barna.

23 The Barna Group, "Signs of Decline & Hope Among Key Metrics of Faith," *State of the Church 2020.* Barna.com: March 4, 2020. https://www.barna.com/research/changing-state-of-the-church (Accessed January 14, 2020).

24 Reach Right Studios, "37 Church Statistics You Need to Know for 2019." Reachright.com. https://reachrightstudios.com/church-statistics-2019 (Accessed February 6, 2019).

25 The Barna Group, "51% of Churchgoers Don't Know of the Great Commission." Barna.com: March 27, 2018. https://www.barna.com/research/half-churchgoers-not-heard-great-commission (Accessed January 14, 2021).

26 The Barna Group, "Almost Half of Practicing Christian Millennials Say Evangelism Is Wrong." Barna.com: February 5, 2019. https://www.barna.com/research/millennials-oppose-evangelism (Accessed January 14, 2021).

27 Yamamoto Tsunetomo, *Hagakure, The Book of the Samurai,* translated by William Scott Wilson (New York: Kodansha International, 1979) 164.

28 This figure is based upon Numbers 1:45-46, which states that all the men in Israel, from twenty years old and upward who were able to go to war, numbered 603,550. This figure would not include women, those too old to go to war, or the Levites who were set aside by the Lord for the priesthood (Numbers 2:33).

Keeping in mind God's judgment for insurrection upon Korah, his house, the false prophets, and the next day's murmuring multitude in Numbers 16, doubling the figure of 603,550 to account for the other people not included in the Fighting-Man Census is still conservative. The real number is likely a bit higher.

29 Tsunetomo, *Hagakure,* 164.

30 Taira Shigesuke, *Code of the Samurai*, 3.
31 *Chakam, NAS Exhaustive Concordance*. Biblehub.com. https://biblehub.com/hebrew/2450. htm (Accessed January 14, 2021).
32 Dr. Arnold Fruchtenbaum, *Psalm 90: An Exposition* (Ariel Ministries: San Antonio, 2005) 10. Ariel.org. http://www.arielcontent.org/dcs/pdf/mbs184m.pdf (Accessed January 14, 2021).
33 Tsunetomo, 45.
34 John Fox, *Fox's Book of Martyrs* (Zondervan Publishing House: Grand Rapids, MI, 1926) 6.
35 *Ibid., 9.*
36 Inazo Nitobe, *Bushido: The Soul of Japan* (Tuttle Publishing: Boston, MA, 1969) 25, 28-29, 31.
37 *Ibid.,* 101.
38 Howard Watson, *Secrets & Lies: Elite Fighting Units, Exposing the Truth Behind History's Most Lethal Fighters* (Metro Books: New York, 2014) 43.
39 Notice how warriors are constantly referred to as "servants" in these references, demonstrating the *servant-warrior* model in Semitic culture. Nu. 14:24; 32:16-32; Jos. 5:13-15; 1 Sa. 17:31-37; 18:30; 20:5-8; 22; 27:5-12; 28:1-3; 29:3, 6-10; 2 Sa. 2:12-17; 3:17-18, 22, 38; 11:9-13; 13:28-29; 14:20-22; 15:21, 34; 16:11; 17:20; 18-19:7; 20:6; 21:15, 22.
40 Observations on 6635—*tsaba* from *Strong's Concordance, NAS Concordance*, and *Brown-Driver-Briggs Hebrew and English Lexicon, Unabridged, Electronic Database* (Biblesoft, Inc., 2006) Biblehub.com. https://biblehub.com/hebrew/6635.htm.
41 By using this turn of phrase, Jesus also signaled to those with "ears to hear" that He was the *Sar Tsaba Yahweh* ("Prince of the Lord's Armies") Joshua had bowed before saying, "What does my Lord [He., *Adonai*] say to his servant (Jos. 5:14)?"
42 The Barna Group, "Church Attendance Trends Around the Country," *Infographics in Cities & States*. Barna.com: May 26, 2017. https://www.barna.com/research/church-attendance-trends-around-country (Accessed January 14, 2021).
43 Miyamato Musashi, *The Book of Five Rings,* translated from the Japanese by Thomas Cleary (Shambhala: Boston, 2003) 68-69.
44 Tsunetomo, 18, 20-21, 23.
45 Bruce B. Barton, Mark Fackler, Linda K. Taylor, David R. Veerman; series editor: Grant Osborne; editor: Philip Comfort, *Life Application Bible Commentary, Matthew* (Tyndale House Publishers, Inc.: Wheaton, IL, 1996) 97.
46 Observations on *idomai* from *Strong's* and *Helps*. https://biblehub.com/greek/2390.htm.

Book II: Law of the Spartan

1 Bernadotte Perrin, *The Parallel Lives by Plutarch, The Life of Lycurgus, 1.1, published in Vol. I, Loeb Classical Library edition* (Cambridge: Harvard University Press, 1914), 205. Bill Thayer's Website. http://penelope.uchicago.edu/Thayer/E/Roman/Texts/Plutarch/Lives/Lycurgus*. html (Accessed January 15, 2021).
2 Paul Cartledge, *The Spartans: The World of the Warrior-Heroes of Ancient Greece* (New York: Vintage Books, 2002) 29.
3 William Smith, *A Dictionary of Greek and Roman Biography and Mythology (Boston: Little, Brown, 1857) 850.*
4 Xenophon, *The Polity of the Lacedaemonians, VII.* An online text of Francois Ollier's 1934 edition, which is in the public domain, is available at Erernow.net. under the title *Spartan Society.* https://erenow.net/ancient/on-sparta/9.php (Accessed May 28, 2021).
    Xenophon's work was divided into two parts. The first half, *The Polity of the Athenians,* discussed Athenian society, Sparta's great enemy; the second, the Lacedaemonians (the

ancient term for Spartans). *Lacedaemon* was the Greek city-state itself; Sparta was the primary township located on the banks of the Eurotas River.

5 Plutarch, *Lives of the Noble Grecians and Romans (Parallel Lives), Lycurgus, 24.1, 3; 25.3,* Parentheses Mine. The University of Adelaide Library. https://ebooks.adelaide.edu.au/p/plutarch/lives/chapter4.html (Accessed February 27, 2019).

The Greek noun simply rendered "camp" in this text, which I have placed "military" next to in brackets, is the compound *stratopedon* in the original language. The root *stratos* is distinct terminology for "army" or "military" and *pedon* refers to a "ground" or "site." *The Parallel Lives by Plutarch, The Life of Lycurgus,* 281 renders 24.1 as: "No man was allowed to live as he pleased, but in their city, as in a military encampment...."

6 Observations on *strateuó* (4754) from James Strong, *Strong's Exhaustive Concordance of the Bible* (Peabody, MA: Hendrickson Publishers, 1980) and *Helps Word-Studies* (Helps Ministries, Inc., 2011). Biblehub.com. https://biblehub.com/greek/4754.htm (Accessed January 15, 2021).

7 Observations on *empleko* (1707) from *Strong's Concordance* and *Helps Word-Studies.* https://biblehub.com/greek/1707.htm (Accessed January 15, 2021).

8 3308—*merimna. Helps Word-Studies.* https://biblehub.com/greek/3308.htm (Accessed January 15, 2021).

9 *Ibid.*

10 Nielsen, "Time Flies: U.S. Adults Now Spend Nearly Half A Day Interacting With Media," July 31, 2018. Nielsen.com. https://www.nielsen.com/us/en/insights/news/2018/time-flies-us-adults-now-spend-nearly-half-a-day-interacting-with-media (Accessed January 15, 2021).

11 Social Media Today, "How Much Time Do People Spend on Social Media?" January 4, 2017. Socialmediatoday.com. https://www.socialmediatoday.com/marketing/how-much-time-do-people-spend-social-media-infographic (Accessed January 15, 2021).

12 Observations on *kúrios* (2962) from *Strong's* and *Helps.* https://biblehub.com/greek/2962.htm (Accessed January 15, 2021).

13 Some examples: Matthew 1:20, 22, 24; 3:3; 4:7, 10; 7:21-22; 8:2, 6, 8, 25; 9:28, 38; 10:24-25; 11:25; 12:8; 18:25, 27, 31-32, 34; 20:8, 30-31, 33; 21:3, 9; Romans 10:9; Philippians 2:11; Jude 1:4.

14 1398—*douleuó. Helps Word-Studies.* https://biblehub.com/greek/1398.htm (Accessed January 15, 2021).

15 Cartledge, *The Spartans,* 29.

16 Pausanias, *Description of Greece, Book 3.16.10 with an English Translation by W.H.S. Jones, Litt. D., and H.A. Ormerod, M.A., in 4 Volumes* (Harvard University Press: Cambridge, MA, 1918). Theoi.com. https://www.theoi.com/Text/Pausanias3B.html (Accessed January 15, 2021). Pausanias was a Spartan regent and general who described their warrior cult ritual of beating called *diamastígosis.*

17 *The Parallel Lives by Plutarch, Lycurgus, 16.2,* 257. http://penelope.uchicago.edu/Thayer/E/Roman/Texts/Plutarch/Lives/Lycurgus*.html (Accessed January 15, 2021).

18 Gamaliel was an elder in the Sanhedrin, the Jewish High Council of Jerusalem, in the first century. He is mentioned twice in the Book of Acts. The first mention in 5:34 references his council office. The second occurs in 22:3 where Paul cites his Mosaic training at his Master Gamaliel's feet.

As demonstrated throughout this book, Paul exhibits a commanding knowledge of Greek language and culture. This caliber of training was readily available in Tarsus, his birthplace, which was known for its philosophy and schools of learning and even outshined Athens and Alexandria, according to the Greek historian and geographer Strabo. See Strabo's *Geographica 14.5.13-14.*

19 Plutarch, *Lycurgus, 19.4,* 267.

20 For more on the biblical pattern of man's unique accountability before God, from the Lord's placement of man in Eden and commands to him about the Forbidden Tree to his charge as provider for the home, see Ge. 2:15-17; 18:17-33; Ps. 106:23; Is. 59:14-16; Je. 5:1; 15:1; Eph. 5:22-33; 6:4; Col. 3:18-21; 1 Ti. 2:8-15; 5:8.

This spiritual truth in no way diminishes a woman's place before God or her great powers in intercession, as the Book of Esther and other parts of Scripture demonstrate. It is simply the revelation of God's order and accountability.

21 Cartledge, *The Spartans*, 119.

22 *Ibid.*, 119.

23 King Xerxes I of Persia or Xerxes "the Great" is the Persian King Ahasuerus in Esther 1:1. In his *Histories, Book VII.60.1*, from *Herodotus, with an English Translation* by A.D. Godley (Cambridge: Harvard University Press, 1920), Herodotus states of Xerxes I's army, "I cannot give the exact number that each part contributed to the total, for there is no one who tells us that; but the total of the whole land army was shown to be one million and seven-hundred thousand." Perseus Digital Library, Tufts University. http://www.perseus.tufts.edu/hopper/text?doc=Hdt.+7.60.1&fromdoc=Perseus%3Atext%3A1999.01.0126

24 *300: The Movie*, directed by Zack Snyder. (Legendary Pictures, Virtual Studios, Atmosphere Entertainment, & Hollywood Gang Productions, 2006) DVD, (Warner Home Video, 2007).

25 See 2 Chr. 32:1-8; Ne. 8:1-3.

26 See De. 16:18-20; 17:8-13; Ru. 4:1-12; 2 Sa. 15:1-6.

27 See Is. 29:21; Je. 17:19-23; 26:10-15; Am. 5:10.

28 See 2 Ki. 23:8; Ac. 14:13.

29 Ps. 1:1-3; 19:7-11; Pr. 20:5; Is. 26:3; 58:6; Jn. 8:31-32; Mt. 17:21; Ro. 12:1-2; 2 Co. 10:3-5; Eph. 4:22-23; 6:18; Php. 4:6-7; Ja. 1:21.

30 The Barna Group, *Research Releases in Family & Kids*, "New Marriage and Divorce Statistics Released," March 31, 2008. Barna.com. https://www.barna.com/research/new-marriage-and-divorce-statistics-released.

31 Got Questions, "Is the Divorce Rate Among Christians Truly the Same As Among Non-Christians." Gotquestions.org. https://www.gotquestions.org/Christian-divorce-rate.html.

32 Plutarch, *Lacaenarum Apophthegmata, published in Vol. III, Loeb Classical Library edition* (Cambridge: Harvard University Press, 1931), 465. In Greek, the saying is: *"Èi tàn èi èpì tàs!"*

This saying also bears the footnote: "Referred to Gorgo [wife of Leonidas] as the author by Aristotle in his *Aphorisms*, as quoted by Stobaeus, *Florilegium*, VII.31, but it is often spoken of as a regular Spartan custom. Compare, for example, the scholium on Thucydides, *History of the Peloponnesian War*, II.39." Brackets mine.

33 Plutarch, *Apophthegmata Laconica, published in Vol. III, Loeb Classical Library edition* (Cambridge: Harvard University Press, 1931), 351. In Greek, the saying is: *"Moⵉn labé!"* ("Come, take [them]!")

34 Cartledge, quoting the Spartan Deineces in Herodotus' *Histories, Book VII.226* (New York: Vintage Books, 2002) 129.

Book III: Vow of the Viking

1 Begun during the reign of Alfred the Great (A.D. 871-899), the *Anglo-Saxon Chronicle* is a series of Old English manuscripts recording the history of the Anglo-Saxons. Though the original is lost, nine partial and complete manuscripts have survived. Written in annal form (year by year), the oldest chronicles begin with the year 60 B.C. and work forward to the

present day of the writing. The *Chronicle* is a vital piece of European history holding information found nowhere else.

2   John Haywood, *The Penguin Historical Atlas of the Vikings* (London: Penguin Books, 1995) 8.

3   *Ibid.*, 9. Haywood notes that it was not uncommon to see Breton, Frankish, Anglo-Saxon, and Slavic warriors in Viking warrior units. Like Norsemen, European men struggled to make a living while others longed for wealth, lands, and adventure.

4   Stephen Allot, *Alcuin of York, c. A.D. 732 to 804—His Life & Letters* (York: William Sessions, Ltd., 1974) 54. This excerpt is from Alcuin's *Letter to King Ethelred of Northumbria*.

5   Magnus Magnusson, *Vikings!* (New York: E.P. Dutton, 1980) 32.

6   Haywood, 51.

7   *Ibid.*, 47.

8   *Ibid.*, 47.

9   Alfred P. Smyth, *Warlords and Holy Men* (London: Edward Arnold, 1984) 142. Smyth quotes *Hofuðlausn* (*"Head's Ransom"*), the Saga of the Icelandic poet and warrior Egill Skallagríms-son, as it celebrates the martial exploits of Eirik Bloodaxe whose name speaks for itself here.

10 Sara Knapton, "Mass Grave of Viking Army Contained Slaughtered Children to Help Dead Reach Afterlife, Experts Believe," *London Telegraph*: February 2, 2018. https://www.telegraph.co.uk/science/2018/02/02/mass-grave-viking-army-contained-slaughtered-children-help-dead (Accessed January 19, 2021).

Knapton writes: "Experts from the University of Bristol have reexamined a huge pit of bones uncovered in the 1970s and 80s in Repton. [N]ew radiocarbon analysis has revealed the skeletons actually belong to soldiers from the Great Viking Army, which drove Burgred, the king of Mercia into exile in 873AD. The excavators also found four youngsters aged between eight and 18 buried together in a single grave with a sheep jaw at their feet, which they dated to the same period. At least two showed signs of traumatic injury suggesting they may have been sacrificed in a ritual to accompany the dead."

11 Magnusson, 61.

12 The proper Old Norse plural of this word is sǫgur. *Saga* is the singular term which, in turn, has been anglicized into our plural "sagas." The term *saga* means an "utterance," "account," or "saying."

13 Snorri Sturluson, *The Sagas of Olaf Tryggvason and of Harold the Tyrant*, translated by Gustav Storm (Original Publisher Unknown, 1899) 34. Gutenberg.org. http://www.gutenberg.org/files/22093/22093-h/22093-h.htm#notes (January 19, 2021).

The *Heimskringla* was Snorri Sturluson's epic history of Scandinavian kings. Sturluson was an Icelandic poet, politician, and historian.

14 Jonathan Clements, *The Vikings: The Last Pagans or the First Modern Europeans?* (Philadelphia: Running Press, 2008) 123.

15 Sturluson, *The Sagas of Olaf Tryggvason and of Harold the Tyrant*, 38.

16 The authenticity of conversions like those of Bluetooth and Tryggvason is sometimes questioned. A main contention is that these men, though Christian, still waged war. This is not problematic, though, when we consider the lives of Israeli kings who believed in Yahweh yet still lived in a land and time of constant war. 2 Samuel 11:1 notes that there were specific times of year when kings went on campaign, saying, "In the spring, at the time when kings go to war...." The Middle Ages was no different, marking a thousand-year period of incessant war, political upheaval, and numerous widespread catastrophes.

We must also consider other evidences. Norse religion held deep roots in Viking society. If Bluetooth's conversion had been mere show, he never would've ordered his father Gorm's body exhumed from its pagan burial mound and reburied in a nearby church. Nor would he have had ordered the Jelling Stones created in tribute to his parents—large stone memorials bearing the inscription: "King Harald bade these memorials to be made after Gorm, his father, and Thyra, his mother. The Harald who won the whole of Denmark and Norway and turned the Danes to Christianity."

A point of argument against Olaf's faith lies in his forcing subjects to convert to Christianity and the tortures inflicted on those who refused. The Frankish King Charlemagne, who also claimed faith and ruled in this period, followed the same rule, as did Alfred the Great who forced the Viking Guthrum, leader of the Danes, to be baptized. This "sword-point conversion," though, was nothing more than the "Christianizing" of a common medieval custom. Kings of all stripes routinely compelled defeated foes to swear fidelity in lieu of their lives and terribly tormented those who resisted. Moreover, the custom can be traced back to empires across ancient history.

The problem of God followers picking up fallen-world customs, though, is certainly observable in Scripture. God warned Israel throughout the Mosaic Law of the temptations awaiting them in Canaan, and the consequences that would follow their rebellion. Nevertheless, from Judges onward we watch Israel swing like a pendulum from fidelity to apostasy with Yahweh. In Judges, for example, Jepthah sacrifices his daughter after making a foolish oath, and one man offers his virgin daughter and a houseguest's concubine when a gang-raping mob, who'd initially come for the male guest, threatens them (Ju. 11:31-40; 19). Yahweh never called for these customs. Pagan custom, however, like the worship of Molech with child sacrifice, and Canaanite culture—where daughters were routinely offered to house guests—had become socially ingrained, and the reason for this was "everyone did what was right in his own eyes (Ju. 17:6b)"—not what God commanded in His Word.

What we can point to in the affirmative for Olaf's conversion are the construction of Christian churches throughout his reign; his steadfastness with the Faith rather than returning to the Norse gods; his desire to unite Scandinavia under Christianity; and baptizing and commissioning disciples like Leif Erikson, who established the first church in North America, whose mother founded Greenland's first church, and whose daughter-in-law founded nunneries in Iceland.

17 For years, controversy has surrounded the end of Mark's Gospel. Bible translations like the ESV note: "Some of the earliest manuscripts do not include verses 16:9-20." But, as James E. Snapp, Jr. states in his essay "Authentic: The Case for Mark 16:9-20," "Out of the over 1,500 existing Greek manuscripts of the Gospel of Mark, only two of them clearly bring the text to a close at the end of 16:8 [the Codices Sinaiticus & Vaticanus]. All the others, unless they have undergone damage in chapter 16, include verses 9 to 20 (p.4, Brackets Mine)."

Snapp further relates that of the "non-Greek manuscripts up to the 700s, only three manuscripts in which the text of Mark is presented do not contain any part of verses 9-20 (p. 19)." Thus, manuscript evidence alone overwhelmingly makes the case for the inclusion of these verses—not their exclusion. Snapp's essay also includes a compelling cross-examination of alleged evidence from leading voices against inclusion from Church Fathers like Eusebius and Jerome, along with fifty-four Patristic Evidences in favor of their inclusion, which voices against continually omit in their analyses.

Finally, Snapp's essay brings both versional and lectionary proofs to the "External Evidence" table and two other sections detailing "Internal Evidence" and "Proposed Solutions." His essay can be downloaded from Academia.edu at: https://www.academia.edu/12545835/Authentic_The_Case_for_Mark_16_9_20.

18 See Matthew 9:6-8; John 4:48-54; 7:31; 9:24-34; 10:25, 37-38; 11:14-45; 12:37, 42; 13:18-19; 14:11-12, 28-29.

19 Dr. Peter Hammond, "How the Vikings Were Won to Christ," *The Ensign Message* (London: The Ensign Trust, 2020). https://ensignmessage.com/articles/how-the-vikings-were-won-to-christ (Accessed January 19, 2021).

20 Cessation theology holds that spiritual gifts like tongues, healing, miracles, and prophecy, seen in Acts and cited in 1 Corinthians 12, ceased with the apostolic age (the time of the apostles). The belief is rooted in an interpretation of 1 Corinthians 13:8-12 asserting that "the perfect" (Gk., *téleios*) the passage speaks of is the completion of the Scriptures, rather than the resurrection of the dead in Christ and regeneration of His living followers, which will occur when He appears, and we finally see Him "face-to-face"—as verse 12 indicates and other key passages confirm (e.g., 1 Corinthians 15; 1 Thessalonians 4).

      Cessationism is also based on an *argument from silence* approach to Bible interpretation, contending that since Paul, for example, mentioned some spiritual gifts in 1 Corinthians 12 (c. A.D. 55) but did not mention them in later epistles, like Ephesians (c. A.D. 61), then these gifts had ceased by that time. An argument from silence works both ways, however, which is why it should remain interpretively off-limits. Just because the Bible is "silent," does not speak on an issue or in a certain place, in no way constitutes evidence for or against a doctrinal position.

      Responsible Bible interpretation works from what God has clearly said in Scripture. Paul specifically warned Corinthians "not to go beyond what is written (1 Co. 4:6)." Modern-day believers should heed the warning also. A fundamental rule of sound biblical interpretation is *exegesis* ("to lead out"), allowing Scripture to speak for itself through its original language, context, culture, and a plain reading of the text versus *eisegesis* ("to lead into"), reading one's own thoughts and experiences into Scripture and seeking support for them.

21 James S. Stewart, *A Faith to Proclaim* (New York: Charles Scribner's Sons, 1953) 102-103.

22 None of the discussion on miraculous healing should be construed as a negation of the medical industry. Acts 28:8-9 offers a balanced, biblical perspective here, noting in verse 8 that Paul laid his hands on Publius, who was sick with dysentery and "healed" him (Gk., *iáomai*), indicating a supernatural healing (https://biblehub.com/greek/2390.htm).

      Verse 9, however, states that after this others from the island came with their infirmities and were "healed" (Gk., *therapeuó*—where we get the English "therapy"). *Strong's Concordance* points out that this word means to serve, cure, attend, treat and, thus, heal. *Helps Word-Studies* adds that *therapeuó* means "heal, reversing a physical condition to restore a person having an illness (disease, infirmity)," and that it "usually involves *natural elements* in the process of healing." This would likely indicate that Paul's physician, Luke, who accompanied him, was involved. A better translation of the Greek here then might be "cured" (https://biblehub.com/greek/2323.htm).

23 Clements, *The Vikings*, 27-28.

24 James Harpur, *Warriors: All the Truth, Tactics, and Triumphs of History's Greatest Fighters* (New York: Atheneum Books, 2007) 15.

25 See Da. 10:1-3; Mt. 8:19-20; Ac. 2:44-45; 4:34-37; 1 Co. 4:11; 8:13; 13:3; 2 Co. 6:3-5, 10; 8:9; 11:23, 25-27.

26 See Ac. 18:1-4; 1 Co. 4:12; 9:12, 15-18; 2 Co. 11:12, 23, 26-28; 12:13-19; 1 Th. 2:9-10; 2 Th. 3:6-16.

27 See Mt. 10:34-39; 12:46-50; 13:53-58; 19:27-29; Lk. 14:33; Jn. 1:11; Ac. 21:12-14; Ga. 1:10.

28 See Mt. 4:18-20; Lk. 5:10; 9:23-26; 14:27, 33; Jn. 1:11; 4:27-34; 12:24-26; Ac. 20:24; 21:13; Ro. 9:1-3; 12:1-2; 14:21; 1 Co. 4:10-13; 2 Co. 4:5; 11:23-28; Ga. 2:20; 6:14; Php. 2:5-8; 3:7-8; 2 Ti. 1:8-12; Jude 22-23.

29 Haywood, 40. Between 1962 and 1969, five Viking ships of varying types were found sunken at Skuldelev Parish in Frederiksborg, Denmark. Haywood describes the eleventh-century

langskip, dubbed by excavators as "Skuldelev 5," at fifty-seven feet long by eight feet wide and holding twenty-six oarsmen. When a replica craft was built and tested, it moved at speeds passing nine knots while drafting just eighteen inches of water.

30 Jason Greenling, *The Technology of the Vikings*, (New York: Cavendish Square Publishing, LLC, 2017) 39.

31 Observations from 4657, *skúbalon*. James Strong, *Strong's Exhaustive Concordance of the Bible* (Peabody, MA: Hendrickson Publishers) and *Helps Word-Studies* (Helps Ministries, Inc., 2011). Biblehub.com. https://biblehub.com/greek/4657.htm (Accessed January 19, 2021).

Book IV: Charge of the Knight

1 In the early second century, the Emperor Trajan expanded the Roman Empire's borders the farthest they'd ever been. Years later, as Rome struggled to recover from two plagues, economic depression, civil war, and invasions, her vast territory proved too much to control. In A.D. 284, Diocletian came to power and posed a unique solution: to divide Roman territory into Eastern and Western Empires. In 293, Diocletian took the east and gave his military ally, Maximian, the west. The solution worked for a time, but became a deciding factor in the fall of the Western Empire.

2 Historians concur that the barbarian invasions of the Western Roman Empire from the third to fifth centuries played a chief role in her demise. An unrelenting press at her borders from multiple foes (Goths, Vandals, Saxons, Suebi, Angles, Bretons, etc.) constantly strained the empire's already failing economy and created an unsustainable burden on the Legion. With every territorial loss, the empire bled funding vital to her widespread military operations, maintenance of a massive infrastructure, and policing of a vast society and trade network spanning from North Africa to Southern France and South Russia. It is a classic study of cause and effect and how intricate operations in complex civilizations can quickly change from an asset to a liability.

3 Before the sack of the Western Empire, Rome suffered two devastating pandemics: The Antonine and Cyprian Plagues. The Antonine Plague struck Rome c. A.D. 165 to 180 and, according to Verity Murphy's article "Past Pandemics That Ravaged Europe" (BBC News: November 7, 2005), took "an estimated five million people" and "killed a quarter of those who caught it." A second outbreak struck between A.D. 251 and 266, taking "some 5,000 people" a day in Rome, matching the timeline for the Cyprian Plague and the statistic noted by Kyle Harper below.

Named after St. Cyprian, a Christian bishop and eyewitness, the Cyprian Plague struck the Roman Empire between A.D. 249 and 270. Dr. Kyle Harper, classical historian and senior vice president and provost at the University of Oklahoma, has written extensively here. As an example of the plague's devastation, he cites a letter of Dionysus of Alexandria and the research of T.G. Parkin in his paper "Pandemics and Passages to Late Antiquity: Rethinking the Plague of c. 249-270 Described by Cyprian" (*Journal of Roman Archeology 28*, 2015), 228. According to these sources, the plague reduced the city of Alexandria's population by 62 percent—just Alexandria.

Harper also mentions contemporary archeological discoveries of mass graves in Egypt and the Catacombs of Marcellinus and Peter (which could be corollary with the Antonine Plague) in his paper (226). Finally, in his article "Solving the Mystery of An Ancient Roman Plague" (*The Atlantic*, November 1, 2017), Harper notes that a period Athenian historian recorded that five thousand people died per day.

4 Beginning with the assassination of the Emperor Severus Alexander in March of A.D. 235

came a period now referred to as the "Crisis of the Third Century." In fifty years, Rome plowed through twenty-six emperors; six of those transitions occurred in just one year (238). A short three-way division came when Gaul, Britannia, and Hispania broke from the empire in 260 to form the Gallic Empire with Syria, Palestine, and Aegyptus seceding to form the Palmyrene Empire in 267. Diocletian ended the crisis when he assumed power in 284.

By this time, however, Rome's Western Empire was very ill. Her massive trade network languishing and currency debased, the empire became more vulnerable to barbarian invasion and civil unrest. The Cyprian Plague, discussed above, fell also in this period. All of these factors proved to be nails in the Western Empire's coffin.

5   The term "Dark Ages" is attributed to the Italian poet and scholar Francesco Petrarch. He bemoaned the loss of Latin literature in the period, a direct result of the Western Roman Empire's fall. The term was later limited by historians to the Early Middle Ages (c. A.D. 500-1000). Some have taken exception to the term entirely.

For this author, the term remains relevant in lieu of many measurable political, social, economic, cultural, and spiritual impacts for Europe such as: a.) the destruction of central government and law enforcement mechanisms resulting in widespread chaos, crime, and death; b.) the disintegration of Rome's immense trade network, which provided substantial revenue, employment, and more favorable living into a much poorer and weaker agrarian system; c.) the deterioration of infrastructure such as roads, bridges, sewers, and aqueducts leading to social isolation, poverty, disease, malnutrition, and famine; d.) the disappearance of medical care, education, and literacy; e.) a substantial rise in superstition, religious persecution, misuse of religious authority, and misapplication of holy texts in the Christian-Muslim Wars, and crimes done in its name; f.) a marked increase in mortality, especially among adolescents, but also in older groupings. Again, the effect of the Western Empire's fall was enormous.

6   Christianity had been spreading throughout the Roman world since its birth. By the early fourth century, it had weathered ten horrible Roman persecutions over some three hundred years, was legalized as a religion by Constantine I with the Edict of Milan (A.D. 313), and later made the state religion by Theodosius I (A.D. 380). Byzantium was the first world empire to do such a thing, blending the powers of state and Church. Not unlike other world empires, however, it was marked by corruption; continued practicing slavery, and often oppressed and persecuted pagans by banning religious practice, destroying shrines, confiscating lands and property, etc. Byzantium was a mix of more and less tolerant emperors regarding paganism.

7   These jaw-dropping global events were documented and corroborated by numerous medieval sources. Procopius, Malalas, Agathias, John of Ephesus, Girgis Bar Hebraeus, Scholasticus, Theophanes, John of Nikiu, Giovanni Lido, Zachariah of Mitylene, *The Chronicle of 819*, *Chronicle of 1234*, *The Annals of Ulster*, and *The Annals of Inisfallen* are but a handful of sources relating this Revelation-type series of catastrophes. When these events are placed beside the plagues, dearth, violence, and warfare characterizing the age, it's not hard to see why many felt they were living in the end times.

8   Sbeinati, M.R.; Darawcheh, R. & Mouty, M. (2005). "The Historical Earthquakes of Syria: An Analysis of Large and Moderate Earthquakes from 1365 B.C. to 1900 A.D.," *Annals of Geophysics, Vol. 48, N.* June 3, 2005: 355-60. Researchgate.net. https://www.researchgate.net/publication/27771958_The_Historical_Earthquakes_of_Syria_An_Analysis_of_Large_and_Moderate_Earthquakes_from_1365_BC_to_1900_AD (Accessed January 19, 2021).

9   Ryad Darawcheh, Mohamed Reda Sbeinati, Claudio Margottini, Salvatore Paolini, "The 9 July 551 AD Beirut Earthquake, Eastern Mediterranean Region," *Journal of Earthquake*

Engineering, Vol. 4, No. 4, October 2000: 403-14. Researchgate.net. file:///C:/Users/User/Downloads/DarawchehJEE_0404_P403.pdf (Accessed January 19, 2021).

10 Tom Streissguth, *Extreme Weather*, Michael E. Mann—Consulting Editor (Detroit: Green Haven Press, 2011) 46.

11 Editors Sam White, Christian Pfister, and Franz Mauelshagen, *The Palgrave Handbook of Climate History* (London: Palgrave—Macmillan, 2018) 447-93. Academia.edu. https://www.academia.edu/37246847/The_Climate_Downturn_of_53650_in_S._White_C._Pfister_and_F._Mauelshagen_eds._The_Palgrave_Handbook_ of_Climate_History_Palgrave_London-don_2018_pp._447-493 (Accessed January 19, 2021).

12 Lester K. Little, *Life and Afterlife of the First Plague Pandemic*. In: Little LK, editor. *Plague and the End of Antiquity: The Pandemic of 541—750*. (Cambridge: Cambridge University Press, 2007) 9. Academia.dk. http://www.academia.dk/MedHist/Sygdomme/Pest/PDF/Plague_and_the_End_of_Antiquity.pdf (Accessed January 19, 2021).

13 William Rosen, *Justinian's Flea: Plague, Empire, and the Birth of Europe* (New York: Viking Press, 2007) 3.

14 Jerome (A.D. 347-420) was a contemporary historian, theologian, and Doctor of the Church. "Doctor of the Church" was a title created by the Catholic Church and awarded to saints seen as notable contributors to doctrine and theology through their works. Among Jerome's significant works were his translating the Hebrew and Greek Scriptures into Latin, *The Vulgate* (382-405), a number of original Old and New Testament commentaries, and the line he drew between canonic and non-canonic books of Scripture. The title *Vulgate* comes from the Latin *vulgatus*, which means "common," referring to Latin as a common language of the period.

15 Jerome, *Commentary on Ezekiel, Preface to Book III*, from "Jerome: Letters and Select Works" in *Nicene and Post-Nicene Fathers of the Christian Church, Series II, Volume 6* by Philip Schaff (Grand Rapids, MI: William B. Eerdmans Publishing Company, 1985) 500. Cornell University Library. https://ia800208.us.archive.org/16/items/cu31924096463470/cu31924096463470.pdf (Accessed January 19, 2021).

16 Jerome, *Commentary on Ezekiel, Preface to Book VII, Ibid.*, 500.

17 The Islamic doctrine of *jihad* (Arb., "battle") is expressed in numerous verses in the Qur'an, and in its earliest interpretations and applications, medieval Europe specifically, enjoined Muslims to armed conflict to spread their faith and the rule of Allah. As Israeli diplomat Dore Gold noted, it was not until "the ninth century, as two centuries of Muslim holy wars and territorial expansion ended, [that] Muslim theologians broadened the meaning of *jihad*, emphasizing armed struggle and, under the influence of Sufism (Islamic mysticism), adopting more spiritual definitions," (*Hatred's Kingdom*, DC: Regnery Publishing, 2003) 7-8.

Author Charles Phillips, speaking on the modern interpretations of *jihad*, says, "Mainstream Islam teaches that *jihad* is intended to be carried out by fighting against sin. Traditionally, there are four types of *jihad*: in the heart, with the tongue, by hand and using the sword. *Jihad* in the heart is interpreted as meaning fighting evil in one's inner self, *jihad* by tongue and hand are usually said to mean avoiding wickedness and promoting righteousness. *Jihad* by the sword involves waging war against enemies of Islam. A key idea behind *jihad* is that the world is divided into two, one that belongs to Allah, and the other subject to chaos; it is the Muslim's duty to combat the rule of chaos by extending submission to Allah's will, within the self but also in the world." See *The Illustrated History of Knights & Crusades* (London: Lorenz Books—Anness Publishing, 2010) 184.

Here are a handful of passages (*suras*) from the Qur'an expounding on *jihad* in various settings, its parameters, and more. Surrounding verses which provide context are included:

2:190-194; 3:149-151, 165-171; 4:47, 71-76, 84, 95-96; 5:33, 35; 8:15-19, 38-40, 59-62, 65-69, 72-75; 9:5, 29, 123; 22:39-41, 78; 49:9-10.

18 Qur'an 4:24; 8:67-69. The *Hadith* are a collection of traditional utterances from Muhammad, recorded and released later in the Islamic tradition. Theologically, they are held as secondary to the Qur'an, but provide moral and spiritual law and instruction. The Hadith discusses *gazhwa* conquest and raiding activities extensively.

19 Qur'an 9:29. *Jizya* is only mentioned in the Qur'an once. The *Hadith* contains numerous exhortations on it.

20 Charles Phillips, *The Illustrated History of Knights & Crusades* (London: Lorenz Books—Anness Publishing, 2010) 184.

21 Qur'an 3:110, *The English Translation of the Meaning of Al-Qur'an, The Guidance for Mankind, Second Edition,* translated by Muhammad Farooq-i-Azam Malik (Houston: The Institute for Islamic Knowledge, 1997) 161.

  Italics are from the text. The term "people of the Book" is distinct to Islam. It refers to the Orthodox Jew's belief in the *Tanakh*, the Jewish name for the Hebrew Scriptures (the Christian Old Testament) and to a Christian's belief in the Catholic Bible, which would include the *Apocrypha* (Gk., for non-canonical books), or the Protestant Bible, that is, the Old and New Testaments. The term is also used to distinguish Jews and Christians as non-Muslims for lack of belief in the Qur'an.

22 *Ibid.,* 178.

23 Qur'an 9:5, *The Holy Qur'an*, translated by Abdullah Yusuf Ali, Ed. (Hertfordshire: Wordsworth Editions Ltd., 2000). Tufts University, Perseus Digital Library. https://www.perseus.tufts.edu/hopper/text?doc=Perseus%3Atext%3A2002.02.0004%3Asura%3D9%3Averse%3D5 (Accessed January 19, 2021).

24 Qur'an 9:29-30, Malik, 260-61.

25 Patrick Franke, *Holy Wars: In the Name of Christ, Episode I.* Film Editing by Katrin Suhren (Seattle: Prime Video, 2017).

  Usama ibn Munqidh was a Muslim author, ambassador, and knight of the Middle Ages. His most famous work, referenced here by Franke is the *Kitab al-I'tibar* ("Book of Meditation"), a collection of musings presented as a gift to Saladin, the sultan and commander of the Muslim army in its campaign for the Crusader East. In it, he says, "When one comes to recount cases regarding the Franks, he cannot but glorify Allah (exalted is he!) and sanctify him, for he sees them as animals possessing the virtues of courage and fighting, but nothing else; just as animals have only the virtues of strength and carrying loads." Like some *surahs* from the Qu'ran, the passage is an important snapshot into the mentality, which animated Islamic imperialism and led directly to the Crusades.

26 Adnan Husain, *The Dark Ages: The Fall of Civilization, the Rise of a New World Order*, directed by Christopher Cassel (A & E Home Video, 2007), DVD, (The History Channel, 2007).

27 Paul K. Davis, *100 Decisive Battles: From Ancient Times to the Present* (New York: Oxford University Press, 1999) 104.

  Davis notes that Muslim forces, which depended entirely upon looting to survive, numbered "some 80,000." Prior to the battle, their general, Abd er-Rahman, split his army for raiding and foraging. At Tours, it was six days before Muslim forces engaged the Franks, which seems to indicate that Rahman was waiting for the remainder of his forces to return from pillaging in order to begin his attack.

28 *Ibid.,* 104.

29 Raymond Ibrahim, "Today in History: The Battle of Tours." CBN.com. https://www1.cbn.com/ibrahim-58 (Accessed January 19, 2021).

30 Davis, 104; Davis quoting the contemporary Latin historian and Christian bishop Isidorus Pacensis. His *Mozarabic Chronicle of 754* or *Continuatio Hispana* is considered the most detailed account of the Battle of Tours, which is also known as the Battle of Poitiers.

31 John H. Haaren & A.B. Poland, *Famous Men of the Middle Ages*, 98. Gutenberg.org. http:// www.gutenberg.org/files/3725/3725-h/3725-h.htm (Accessed January 19, 2021).

32 Jim Nelson Black, *When Nations Die* (Illinois: Tyndale House Publishers, 1994) xix-xx.

33 Some scriptures on the Bible's Inspiration & Inerrancy: De. 4:2; 8:3; Ps. 19:7-9; Pr. 30:5-6; Is. 40:8; Mt. 24:35; Jn. 12:48; 17:17; 1 Co. 2:13; 2 Co. 3:17-18; 1 Th. 2:13; 2 Ti.3:16; He. 4:12; 2 Pe. 1:20-21.

34 Katherine Allen Smith, *War and the Making of Medieval Monastic Culture* (Woodbridge: The Boydell Press, 2011) 9-10. Brackets Mine.

35 *Ibid.*, 30.

36 *Ibid.*, 29.

37 *Ibid.*, 29.

38 1411—*dúnamis.* James Strong, *Strong's Exhaustive Concordance of the Bible* (Peabody, MA: Hendrickson Publishers, 1980). Biblehub.com. https://biblehub.com/greek/1411.htm (Accessed January 19, 2021).

39 A number of modern Bible versions omit Matthew 17:21, where Christ, referencing the demon expelled from the boy, said, "But this kind never comes out except by prayer and fasting." A similar omission occurs in Mark 9:29. This is not because the Bible translation in question is "satanic" as some allege, but because of a disagreement between scholars about how the manuscript evidence should be interpreted. Our earliest, best Greek manuscripts, namely, the *Codex Vaticanus* and *Codex Sinaiticus* (c. A.D. 325-350 and 330-360, respectively) do not contain the verse. The verse does, however, appear as a later scribal correction in the *Sinaiticus'* margin. Understandably, the margin notation is problematic to some scholars, as it could demonstrate a later alteration on the text. However, the note could also be a correction to the text as the evidence below suggests.

  1.) Pseudo Clement (c. 100-200), the unknown author of the phony fiction allegedly written by Pope Clement I (A.D. 88-97), quotes the verse some two hundred years before the *Vaticanus* in 2 *Clement, 16.* 2.) The verse appears in the *Diatesseron*, a harmony of the Four Gospels dating between A.D. 160 and 175, placing it around 150 years before the *Vaticanus.* 3.) The Early Church Father Tertullian (c. A.D. 220) references it as the words of Jesus in his *Against the Physics*, saying, *"After that, he prescribed that fasting should be carried out without sadness. For why should what is beneficial be sad? He also taught to fight against the fiercer demons by means of fasting. For is it surprising that the Holy Spirit is led in through the same means by which the sinful spirit is led out?"* Thus, his citation happens about one hundred years before the fact. 4.) The Early Church Father Origen's Commentary on Matthew (*Book VIII, 7*), dating in the mid-third century, also contains the verse—placing it some seventy-five to eighty years prior. 5.) Matthew 17:21 is also found in most early and late Latin manuscripts, including the *Codex Vercellensis* (A.D. 350), aur, b, c, d, f, ff2, g1, l, n, q, and r1—placing it right in the *Vaticanus* and *Sinaiticus* window. 6.) The verse is quoted by many Latin Fathers in the time period or within fifty years of it, including Asterius (c. A.D. 340), Hilary (c. 355), Basil (c. 370), Athanasius (c. 375) Ambrose (c. 385), Chrysostom (c. 395), Jerome (c. 400), and Augustine (430). 7.) Matthew 17:21 is also found in the majority of the Greek manuscripts dating from the late fourth and up to about the tenth century, namely: C, D, E, F, G, H, K, L, M, O, S, U, V, W, X, Y, Gamma, Delta, Pi, Sigma, Phi, and Omega, with W dating in the fourth century and making it yet another contemporary with *Vaticanus* and *Sinaiticus.* 8.) Last, Matthew 17:21 is found in the Syriac (2nd cent., p h), the

Vulgate (5th-8th), Harklean (c. A.D. 616), some Coptic Boharic (mae bo-pt) and Ethiopic, and the Armenian (c. 434), Georgian (B), and Slavonic versions.

40 A.F. Kirkpatrick, *The Cambridge Bible for Schools and Colleges, Psalms* (Cambridge: Cambridge University Press, 1902) Appendix. Cited by Jesuswalk.com. http://www.jesuswalk. com/psalms/psalms-NT-quotations.htm (Accessed January 19, 2021).

41 Clayton Kraby, "Why Pray the Psalms? Our Psalm-Saturated Savior." Reasonabletheology. org. https://reasonabletheology.org/pray-psalms-psalm-saturated-savior (Accessed January 19, 2021).

42 Smith, *War and the Making of Medieval Monastic Culture*, 23-24.

43 *Ibid.*, 29.

44 See Ps. 24:10; 46:7, 11; 48:8; 59:5; 69:6; 80:4, 7, 19; 84:3. 8, 12; 89:8. In her footnoted biblical references, Smith cites the Latin Psalter whose chapter and verse numbering system differs from Protestant translations. I have adjusted her references here and in footnotes 45 and 46 to reflect their corresponding Protestant Bible verses. I have also added references for study and documentation.

45 See Ps. 24:8.

46 See Ps. 7:12-13; 17:13; 35:1-3; 44:4-7; 68:17; 104:3; 144:1-2.

47 Smith, 24-25.

48 Philip Daileader. *The Dark Ages: The Fall of Civilization, the Rise of a New World Order,* DVD.

49 John of Salisbury, *Politicratus, Book VI, Cambridge Texts in the History of Political Thought,* edited and translated by Cary J. Nederman (Cambridge: Cambridge University Press, 1990) 115. Archive.org. https://archive.org/details/JohnOfSalisburyPolicraticusJohnOfSalisbury (Accessed June 29, 2020).

50 Charles Phillips, *The Illustrated History of Knights & Crusades*, 43.

51 Lech Marek, "The Blessing of Swords: A New Look Into Inscriptions of the Benedictus Type," *Acta Militaria Mediaevalia X* (Krakow—Sanok—Wroclaw: 2014) 9, republished on Academia.edu. https://www.academia.edu/13386318/THE_BLESSING_OF_SWORDS_A_ NEW_LOOK_INTO_INSCRIPTIONS_OF_THE_BENEDICTUS_TYPE_Acta_Mili- taria_Mediaevalia_Vol_10_pp_9_20.

The Latin inscription reads: *"Benedictus, Dominus Deus meus qui docet manus meas ad prælium, et digitos meos ad bellum."* Rendered in English, it reads: "Blessed be, the Lord my God who teaches my hands to war and my fingers to fight."

52 *Ibid.*, 12.

53 *Ibid.*, 15.

54 *Ibid.*

55 John of Salisbury, *Politicratus, Book VI*, quoted in *The Kingdom of Heaven* Newmarket Pictorial Moviebook (New York: Newmarket Press, 2005) 34.

56 John of Salisbury, *Politicratus, Book VI*, edited and translated by Cary J. Nederman, 116.

57 A great example of this is an oath taken by Robert II, king of the Franks from A.D. 996-1031, which combined elements from the Peace of God (*Pax Dei*) and Truce of God (*Treuga Dei*) movements. The oath swore nobles and warriors off harming churches, hurting priests and peasants, destroying and stealing property, etc., with some seasonal exceptions.

58 Scriptures where Jesus speaks of hell's actual existence: Mt. 5:29-30; 10:28; 11:20-24; 13:24-30, 36-43, 47-50; 22:1-14; 23:15, 33; 25:14-46; Mk. 9:43, 45, 47; Lk. 10:15; 12:5; 16:23.

59 Scriptures where Jesus speaks of hell's eternal nature: Mt. 18:8; 25:41, 46.

60 Scriptures where Jesus speaks of hell's incomprehensible torment: Mt. 5:22; 7:23; 8:12; 13:40-42, 50; 18:8-9; 22:13; 24:51; 25:30, 41; Lk. 13:28.

61 Scriptures where Jesus commanded repentance and warned of the day of judgment: Mt. 4:17; 10:14-15; 11:20-24; 12:35-37, 40-42; Mk. 1:14-15; Lk. 5:31-32; 10:13-15; 11:29-32; 13:1-5; 15.

62 Ramon Llull, *The Book of the Order of Chivalry*, translated by William Caxton, 10. Mythologyteacher.com. http://www.mythologyteacher.com/documents/TheBookoftheOrderofChivalry.pdf (Accessed January 19, 2021).

A mathematician, polymath, philosopher, writer, and Franciscan tertiary (a third order created by St. Francis for recognized contributors and authorities outside the monastic pale), Llull wrote *The Book of the Order of Chivalry* (its English title) in the mid-1270s. Even as Latin clergy sought to rehabilitate the institution of knighthood from its pagan and criminal ways through their liturgies and social reform movements like the Peace and Truce of God, Llull aimed to take it one step further by creating, essentially, a bible on knighthood.

A brilliant, pioneering endeavor, for which he also had the forethought of penning in the more common Catalan language instead of the clerically confined Latin, the work identified and expounded on the qualities and responsibilities of the ideal knight. Not long after his passing, Llull's vision was realized as the book circulated among knights and clergy across Europe.

63 Author Unknown, "Fleur De Lis Symbol, Its Meaning, History and Origins." Mythologian.net. https://mythologian.net/fleur-de-lis-symbol-its-meaning-history-origins (Accessed September 28, 2020).

64 Other crusades were waged in Northern Europe to conquer pagan lands or other Christian sects.

65 Timothy S. Miller, "The Knights of Saint John and the Hospitals of the Latin West." *Speculum, Vol. 53, No. 4* (October, 1978) 709. Jstor.org. https://www.jstor.org/stable/2849782 (Accessed June 29, 2020).

66 *Ibid.*, 719.

67 *Ibid.*, 722.

68 *Ibid.*, 718, 732.

69 *Ibid.*, 719.

70 *Ibid.*, 722.

71 Phillips, *The Illustrated History of Knights & Crusades*, 302.

72 *Ibid.*, 295.

73 Frank Harber, *Reasons for Believing* (Arizona: New Leaf Press, 1998) 149.

Book V: Oath of the Gladiator

1   Period sources supporting this belief are Valerius Maximus' *Factorum et Dictorum Memorabilium* ("Collection of Words & Deeds"), *Book II.4.7*, and Titus Livius' (Livy's) *History of Rome From Its Beginning, Book XVI.6*. Maximus' account cites the names of both brothers; Livy's only Decimus. Much of Livy's work is lost to the ages.

Citations like this originate from the *Periochae*, a large sampling of the work. A virtual Latin text of the *Memorabilium* is available at: http://penelope.uchicago.edu/Thayer/L/Roman/Texts/Valerius_Maximus/2*.html#4.7.

A virtual English translation of the *Periochae* by Jona Lending, *Books 16-20*, may be found at: https://www.livius.org/sources/content/livy/livy-periochae-16-20/#16.1.

2   Alan Baker, *The Gladiator: The Secret History of Rome's Warrior Slaves* (Cambridge: Da Capo Press, Perseus Books Group, 2002) 10-19, 29.

3   Tacitus, *Annals 13.42*, translated by Colin Wells, *The Roman Empire* (Stanford: Stanford University Press, 1984), 277, quoted in Shannon E. French, *The Code of the Warrior: Exploring Warrior Values Past & Present* (Maryland: Rowman & Littlefield Publishers, Inc., 2003) 86.

4   Elyssa Bernard, "Ten Fascinating Facts About the Roman Colosseum." Romewise.com. https://www.romewise.com/facts-about-the-roman-colosseum.html (Accessed January 19, 2021).

5   Hope Babowice, "You Wanted To Know: How Many Gladiators Died In The Colosseum." Chicago Daily Herald: August 4, 2010. https://www.dailyherald.com/article/20100804/news/308049980/ (Accessed July 17, 2020).

6   By the end of the Roman Republic (55-31 B.C.), the gladiatorial scene had shifted drastically. According to Baker, "about half of all gladiators were volunteers" at this point (p. 21). The volunteer shift came for many reasons, from a desire for adventure and achievement to meaning and purpose in life. Gladiators commanded a martial respect among the people, rivaling that of the Roman Legion, and this fact did not escape young men. What also didn't escape their view was the glory of the arena. Still others had lost their money, gone into debt, and were looking for basic assurances like food and lodging, despite the risks that came with it. Lanistas took excellent care of their gladiators, who were even allowed to keep their winnings.

7   Baker, *The Gladiator: The Secret History of Rome's Warrior Slaves,* 29.

8   Rupert Matthews; Philip Steele, Consultant; *100 Things You Should Know About Gladiators* (New York: Barnes and Noble, 2005) 30.

9   Archeology has yet to unearth an actual text recording the precise wording of the gladiatorial oath: the *Auctoramentum Gladiatorium.* Gaius Petronius Arbiter's *Satyricon, 117* is the closest we get through an incidental mention, which says, "We took an oath to obey Eumolpus; to endure burning, bondage, flogging, death by the sword, or anything else that Eumolpus ordered. We pledged our bodies and souls to our master most solemnly, like regular gladiators. When the oath was over, we posed like slaves and saluted our master...."

    This quote is taken from *Petronius,* with an English translation by Michael Heseltine: *Seneca, Apocolocyntosis, with an English translation by W.H.D. Rouse* (London: William Heinemann Ltd., New York: G. P. Putnam's Sons, 1913) 248-49. Tufts University, Perseus Digital Library. http://www.perseus.tufts.edu/hopper/text?doc=Petr.+117&fromdoc=Perseus%3Atext%3A2007.01.0027.

    Seneca, in his *Letters, 37: On Allegiance to Virtue* gives credence to Petronius, stating, "The word of this most honourable compact are the same as the words of that most disgraceful one, to wit: 'Through burning, imprisonment, or death by the sword.' From the men who hire out their strength for the arena, who eat and drink what they must pay for with their blood, security is taken that they will endure such trials even though they be unwilling; from you, that you will endure them willingly and with alacrity." "Seneca: Letters from a Stoic," October 13, 2015. Lettersfromastoic.net. https://www.lettersfromastoic.net/letter-37-on-allegiance-to-virtue (Accessed January 19, 2021).

10 2 Corinthians 11:22-28, *New Living Translation* (Wheaton, Il: Tyndale House Publishers, Inc., 1996) 941.

11 Jeremy Hart, "Blood of Sheep Protects Against Tongue of Viper." The Independent: February 8, 1994. https://www.independent.co.uk/life-style/health-and-families/health-news/health-blood-of-sheep-protects-against-tongue-of-viper-there-may-be-no-rattlesnakes-in-wales-but-1392764.html (Accessed January 20, 2021).

12 Antivenom is also commonly referred to as antivenin.

13 *Ibid.,* Feb. 8, 1994.

14 Author Unknown, "Tsavo, What's In A Name." Tsavo West National Park website. http://www.african-horizons.com/SAFARI_WEB/UK/destination-detail-Tsavo%20West%20National%20Park-Kenya-Parks_Reserves_and_Conservancies.awp (Accessed January 20, 2021).

15 "Tsavo Man-Eaters," Wikipedia. https://en.wikipedia.org/wiki/Tsavo_Man-Eaters (Accessed January 20, 2021).

16 The death toll accrued by the Tsavo lions is disputed. In his personal account, Patterson claimed the number was 135 men. Modern research employing a twofold approach of caloric estimates and stable isotope analysis have estimated that the Ghost and the Darkness (the lions) killed only 34 men between them. But, the isotope analysis cannot account for multiple victims who were completely devoured, nor does this dualistic methodology make allowances for men who were slain yet not consumed, like Patterson and many laborers noted.

17 "You" in Luke 22:31's original Greek is plural. Thus, Jesus warned Peter that Satan desired to sift all the disciples, not just him.

18 "Facts and Statistics: Did You Know?" Anxiety and Depression Association of America. ADAA. org. https://adaa.org/about-adaa/press-room/facts-statistics (Accessed January 20, 2021).

19 Hannah Ritchie and Max Roser, "Mental Health: Anxiety Disorders." Our World in Data: April, 2018. https://ourworldindata.org/mental-health#anxiety-disorders (Accessed January 20, 2021).

20 "Major Depression," National Institute of Mental Health. NIMH.gov. https://www.nimh. nih.gov/health/statistics/major-depression.shtml (Accessed January 20, 2021).

21 Ritchie and Roser, "Mental Health: Prevalence of Depressive Disorders." https://ourworld-indata.org/mental-health#anxiety-disorders (Accessed January 20, 2021).

22 *Ibid.*, citing data from the World Health Organization.

23 *Ibid.*

24 3309—*merimnaó. Helps Word-Studies* (Helps Ministries, Inc., 2011). https://biblehub.com/greek/3309.htm.

25 "Prayer Can Reduce Levels of Depression and Anxiety in Patients, According to Research," *Nursing Times:* February 12, 2009, citing the *Journal of Clinical Nursing (2009), 18:637-651.* Nursingtimes.net. https://www.nursingtimes.net/archive/prayer-can-reduce-levels-of-de-pression-and-anxiety-in-patients-according-to-research-12-02-2009/

26 Traci Pederson, "New Study Examines the Effects of Prayer on Mental Health," *Psych Central:* July 8, 2018. Psychcentral.com. https://psychcentral.com/blog/new-study-examines-the-effects-of-prayer-on-mental-health/.

27 *Ibid.* The research Pederson cites by Lisa Miller, professor of clinical psychology at Columbia University, may be found on Science Daily at https://www.sciencedaily.com/releases/2014/01/140116084846.htm.

28 Chittaranjan Andrade and Rajiv Radhakrishnan, "Prayer and Healing: A Medical and Scientific Perspective On Randomized Controlled Trials," *Indian Journal of Psychiatry:* October-December, 2009. Ncbi.nlm.nih.gov. https://www.ncbi.nlm.nih.gov/pmc/articles/PMC2802370/(Accessed June 1, 2021).

29 Observations on 1225, *diaballó,* and 1228, *diábolos,* compiled from James Strong, *Strong's Exhaustive Concordance, Helps Word-Studies* (Helps Ministries, Inc., 2011), *NAS Exhaustive Concordance of the Bible with Hebrew-Aramaic and Greek Dictionaries* (The Lockman Foundation, 1998), and *Thayer's Greek Lexicon,* Electronic Database (Biblesoft, Inc., 2011). Biblehub.com. https://biblehub.com/greek/1225.htm. https://biblehub.com/greek/1228.htm. (Accessed January 21, 2021).

30 2725—*katégoros. Strong's Exhaustive Concordance.* https://biblehub.com/greek/2725.htm (Accessed January 21, 2021).

31 Lord of the Rings Fandom Wiki, "Smaug," citing *The Hobbit:* "Inside Information," chapter twelve. https://lotr.fandom.com/wiki/Smaug (Accessed January 21, 2021).

32 Walsh, Fran, Philippia Boyens, Peter Jackson, and Guillermo del Torro. *The Hobbit: The*

Desolation of Smaug. DVD. Los Angeles: New Line Cinema, Metro-Goldwyn-Mayer, and Wingnut Films, 2013.

33 The Barna Group, "Most American Christians Do Not Believe that Satan or the Holy Spirit Exist," *Research Releases in Faith & Christianity:* April 13, 2009. Barna.com. https://www.barna.com/research/most-american-christians-do-not-believe-that-satan-or-the-holy-spirit-exist (Accessed January 21, 2021).

34 The typical custom of Bible translations is to render the Hebrew noun *satan* in English as the name "Satan." *Satan* means "adversary." Thus, it is a title, not a name. He exists as the ultimate adversary of God and His people.

35 The Greek adjective *diábolos* is customarily rendered as "devil" in English Bible translations. Literally translated, *diábolos* means "slanderous" or "accusing falsely." Hence, in his relationship to God and mankind, the devil is The Slanderer or "Slanderous One." If this word was translated into modern Bible texts like other words, would it, perhaps, help modern-day believers understand more of how the devil works, by calling him what he is—The Slanderer?

36 Rupert Matthews; Philip Steele, Consultant; *100 Things You Should Know About Gladiators,* 38-39.

37 Baker, *The Gladiator: The Secret History of Rome's Warrior Slaves,* 183-84.

38 Alison Futrell, *The Roman Games* (Massachusetts: Blackwell Publishing, 2006) 88.

39 Matthews; Philip Steele, Consultant; *100 Things You Should Know About Gladiators,* 38.

40 Baker, 184.

41 Matthews, 39.

42 Baker, 184.

43 *Ibid.,* 84.

44 Matthews, 27.

45 The term rendered in English as "sons of God" occurs five times in the Old Testament: Ge. 6:2, 4; Job 1:6; 2:1, 38:7. Without exception, each citation uses the term to refer to holy angels of God. The oldest extra-biblical source material (c. third century B.C. and forward) from apocryphal to historical texts such as the *Book of Enoch,* the *Genesis Apocryphon,* the *Jubilees, Histories* of Josephus, as well as Early Church Fathers like Justin Martyr, Clement of Alexandria, Origen, and Eusebius also follow this same line of interpretation. This is an important note when it comes to biblical interpretation because, generally, sources closer to the time of writing are considered most reliable.

46 An account similar to the Lord's throne room conversation with Satan is found in 1 Ki. 22 and 2 Chr. 18. Here, God converses with demons before His throne to orchestrate judgment on the wicked King Ahab. "I will go out, and will be a lying spirit in the mouth of all his [Ahab's] prophets," a demon says to God, who replies, "You are to entice him, and you shall succeed; go out and do so (v. 22)." The principle is clear then: ultimately, Satan doesn't even exercise command his own army.

47 When Job asked, "Shall we accept good from God and not *evil* also (2:10)?" he was not offering a personal opinion about what happened to him and his family. It was a factual statement about God and his Sovereignty breathed out by the Holy Spirit (1 Co. 2:13; 2 Ti. 3:16; 2 Pe. 1:21), namely, that whatever God allows to happen in His universe—good or evil—ultimately comes from Him. 42:11 confirms this. After God restored to Job twice of all that had been taken from him, the verse says, "Then came to him all his brothers and sisters…. And they showed him sympathy and comforted him for all the *evil* that the *Lord* had brought upon him…." Thus, in allowing Satan to perpetrate the evil he did, God takes responsibility for it. He's not like man, who plays politics, semantic word games, and

dodges controversy by "plausible deniability." As an all-powerful deity, God takes ownership for whatever happens in His universe.

Also, God always calls evil what it is. The original Hebrew *rá* rendered in Job 2:10 and 42:11 as "evil" is typically rendered so in Scripture, like "the tree of the knowledge of good and *evil* (Ge. 2:9)." It's also rendered as "wicked" and "evil" in verses like, "The Lord saw that the *wickedness* of man was great in the earth, and that every intention of the thoughts of his heart was only *evil* continually (Ge. 6:5)." In Genesis 13:13, the Scriptures, describing their moral depravity, says, "The men of Sodom were exceedingly *wicked*." *Rá* is sometimes rendered in Scripture as "calamity," "trouble," "bad," "adversity," etc., but this is merely stylistic—not a change in its meaning.

Rá is always used in a negative sense in Scripture, and the major theme of Job is that God is running every aspect of His universe, superintending all its affairs in the finest detail. No, God Himself does not perpetrate evil (See Ja. 1:17; 1 Jn. 1:5), but He does allow it as it serves His glory and purposes. This is part of the Mystery of God and Faith (De. 29:29; Ro. 11:33-36; 1 Ti. 3:9; 6:13-16).

48 God invites His sons and daughters to reason, wrestle, and debate with Him in Scripture. In Isaiah 1:18, He uses the Hebrew verb *yakah*, a legal term that's been rendered as "let us reason together" in a number of Bible translations (KJV, NKJV, NASB, RSV, etc.). The word's meaning, however, is better understood when rendered "let us debate our case in court," according to the *Theological Wordbook of the Old Testament*, edited by R. Laird Harris, Gleason L. Archer, Jr., and Bruce K. Waltke (Chicago: Moody Press, 1980) 377.

The Passion Translation in its marginal notes concurs, noting the verse could also be worded, "Come now and let us argue it out together." It further notes that *yakah* "has clear judicial overtones with an implication of a verdict in court." See footnote "a.," *The Passion Translation* (BroadStreet Publishing Group, LLC, 2017) biblegateway.com. https://www.biblegateway.com/passage/?search=Isaiah+1%3A18-19&version=TPT (Accessed January 21, 2021).

Yakah occurs seventeen times in Job, indicating he recognizes that he's in the midst of some sort of divine trial and longs to plead his case like a defendant before God as the Great Judge (Job 5:17; 6:25 (2), 26; 9:33; 13:3, 10 (2), 15; 15:3; 16:21; 19:5; 22:4; 23:7; 32:12; 33:19; 40:2).

49 Released originally in pamphlet form under the title "The Heavenly Vision" in 1918 England, the hymn by Helen Howarth Lemmel that would later be known as "Turn Your Eyes Upon Jesus" made its way to America in 1924 with a collection of other hymns called "The Gospel Truth in Song." God Tube Staff, "The Heavenly Vision (Turn Your Eyes Upon Jesus)." Godtube.com. https://www.godtube.com/popular-hymns/the-heavenly-vision-turn-your-eyes-upon-jesus-/(Accessed January 21, 2021).

50 Observations on 4994—*na*, compiled from: *NAS Exhaustive Concordance* and *Brown-Driver-Briggs Hebrew and English Lexicon, Unabridged, Electronic Database* (Biblesoft, Inc. 2006). https://biblehub.com/hebrew/4994.htm (Accessed January 21, 2021).

51 C. Suetonius Tranquilus, *The Lives of the Twelve Caesars*, translated by A.S. Kline, *Book Five: Claudius (later deified), XXI, His Public Entertainments* (A.S. Kline, 2010) 171. Worldlibrary.net. http://uploads.worldlibrary.net/uploads/pdf/20121106193837suetoniuspdf_pdf (Accessed July 17, 2020).

Fox's Book of Martyrs notes that this same saying, *"Ave, Caesar, morituri te salutant!"* (*"Hail, Caesar, those about to die salute you!"*) was uttered by gladiators as they stood before Emperor Honorius (c. A.D. 393-423), just after the *pompa* had circled the arena and prior to the games' commencement. John Fox, *Fox's Book of Martys, A History of the Lives, Sufferings and Triumphant Deaths of the Early Christian and Protestant Martyrs,* edited by William Byron Forbush, D.D. (Grand Rapids, MI: Zondervan Publishing House, 1926) 36.

Book VI: Mark of the Legionary, Pt. I

1   Saint Jerome used the title "mother of nations" for Rome in his *Commentary on Ezekiel, Preface to Book III*. See "Jerome: Letters and Select Works" in *Nicene and Post-Nicene Fathers of the Christian Church, Series II, Volume 6* by Philip Schaff (Grand Rapids, MI: William B. Eerdmans Publishing Company, 1985) 500. Internetarchive.org. https://ia800208.us.archive.org/16/items/cu31924096463470/cu31924096463470.pdf (Accessed January 21, 2021).

2   Sigourney Weaver, *Empires: The Roman Empire in the First Century*, directed by Lyn Goldfarb and Margaret Koval (Boston: PBS Distribution, 2001). DVD.

3   Flavius Vegetius Renatus, *Epitoma Rei Militaris, Book I, translated from the original Latin by Lieutenant John Clarke* (W. Griffin: London, 1767). Digitalattic.org. http://www.digitalattic.org/home/war/vegetius/index.php#b100 (Accessed January 21, 2021).

4   Vegetius' treatise is also known as *Rei Militaris Instituta* ("The Military Institutions") and more simply *De Rei Militari* ("Regarding the Military"). Rome ignored Vegetius' work, and her Western Empire fell in A.D. 476. There is continuing debate as to whether Rome's fall could have been prevented at this point.

5   Raoul McLaughlin, *Rome and the Distant East: Trade Routes to the ancient lands of Arabia, India and China* (New York: Continuum US, 2010) 173.

6   For more information on the plagues which devastated Rome and her Legion, see chapter five's note #3.

7   Christine A. Smith, "Plague in the Ancient World: A Study from Thucydides to Justinian," *The Student Historical Journal, Volume 28, 1996-1997*. J. Edgar & Louise S. Monroe Library, Loyola University. http://people.loyno.edu/~history/journal/1996-7/Smith.html#19 (Accessed January 21, 2021).

8   Raoul McLaughlin, *Rome and the Distant East*, 218—footnote 273.

9   *Ibid.*, 175.

10 *Ibid.*, 174-75.

11 In March of A.D. 235, the Roman Legion assassinated Emperor Severus Alexander triggering the "Crisis of the Third Century." Over the next fifty years Rome cycled through twenty-six emperors, many being generals. In 238, Rome saw the rise and fall of six emperors alone, three of whom were assassinated because of corruption and incompetence. Overall, about half of these emperors died by assassination. Others fell in battle or to "mysterious causes." A couple died by plague, one by suicide, and another by lightning.

    A short three-way division of the empire came when Gaul, Britannia, and Hispania broke away in 260 to form the Gallic Empire with Syria, Palestine, and Aegyptus seceding to form the Palmyrene Empire in 267. The crisis came to an end in 284 when Diocletian, a general himself, came to power. But, the final twenty-five-year crisis period (260-284) proved too much for the Western Empire. With her immense trade network deteriorating and currency debased, Rome became more anemic to civil strife and barbarian threats. The Cyprian Plague, noted above, also struck in this time, and all of these events climaxed into the fall of the West.

12 McLaughlin, *Rome and the Distant East*, 176.

13 Vegetius, *Epitoma Rei Militaris, Book II.3*. http://www.digitalattic.org/home/war/vegetius/index.php#b202 (Accessed January 21, 2021).

14 *Ibid., Book II.4*. http://www.digitalattic.org/home/war/vegetius/index.php#b203 (Accessed January 21, 2021).

15 Some scriptures demonstrating the pattern of repentance and faith in Gospel preaching: Acts 2:38-39; 3:19-20; 5:30-31; 17:30-31; 20:21; 26:19-20; 2 Timothy 2:24-26; Hebrews 6:1; 2 Peter 3:9.

16 Observations on 4982—*sózó*, compiled from James Strong, *Strong's Exhaustive Concordance of the Bible* (Peabody, MA: Hendrickson Publishers, 1980), *Helps Word-Studies* (Helps Ministries, Inc., 2011), *NAS Exhaustive Concordance of the Bible with Hebrew-Aramaic and Greek Dictionaries* (The Lockman Foundation, 1998), and *Thayer's Greek Lexicon,* Electronic Database (Biblesoft, Inc., 2011). Biblehub.com. https://biblehub.com/greek/4982.htm (Accessed January 21, 2021).

17 4972—*sphragízo. Helps Word-Studies* (Helps Ministries, Inc., 2011). https://biblehub.com/greek/4972.htm (Accessed January 21, 2021).

18 The *mos maiorum* (Lat., "custom of ancestors"), essentially an unwritten social compact of all Roman citizens, had been cultivated and passed down for generations. It was a core philosophy and companion to Roman law.

19 R.H. Barrow, *The Romans* (London: Penguin, 1949) 22-23. Stephenson Library. http://bard. edu/library/arendt/pdfs/Barrow_Romans.pdf (Accessed January 21, 2021).

20 Vegetius, *Epitoma Rei Militaris, Book I.* http://www.digitalattic.org/home/war/vegetius/ index.php#b100 (Accessed January 21, 2021).

21 Josephus, *A History of the Jewish War, 3.71-97,* cited by French, *The Code of the Warrior,* 76-77, who cites Jo-Ann Shelton, *As the Romans Did: A Sourcebook in Roman Social History* (New York: Oxford University Press, 1988) 260.

22 Vegetius, *Rei Militaris, Book I.* http://www.digitalattic.org/home/war/vegetius/index. php#b100 (Accessed January 21, 2021).

23 *Ibid.*

24 1743—*endunamóo. Strong's Exhaustive Concordance.* https://biblehub.com/greek/1743.htm (Accessed January 21, 2021).

25 1411—*dúnamis. Ibid.* https://biblehub.com/greek/1411.htm (Accessed January 221, 2021).

26 Harold W. Hoehner, *Ephesians: An Exegetical Commentary* (Grand Rapids: Baker Publishing Group, 2002) 820.

27 1746—*endúo. Ibid.* https://biblehub.com/greek/1746.htm (Accessed January 21, 2021).

28 Lewis Sperry Chafer, *Major Bible Themes,* revised by John F. Walvoord (Michigan: Zondervan Publishing House, 1974) 163.

29 Richard Foster, *Celebration of Discipline* (San Francisco: Harper Collins Publishers Inc., 1998) 1.

30 Frank Newport, Gallup: *Polling Matters,* "Church Leaders and Declining Religious Service Attendance." Gallup.com: Sept. 7, 2018. Gallup.com. http://news.gallup.com/opinion/ polling-matters/242015/church-leaders-declining-religious-service-attendance.aspx (Accessed January 21, 2021).

31 Reach Right Studios, "37 Church Statistics You Need to Know for 2019." Reachright.com. reachrightstudios.com/church-statistics-2019 (Accessed January 21, 2021).

32 George Barna, *Research Releases in Culture & Media,* "Competing Worldviews Influence Today's Christians." Barna.com: May 9, 2017. Barna.com. http://barna.com/research/competing-worldviews-influence-todays-christians/(Accessed January 21, 2021).

33 Barna, *Articles in Faith & Christianity,* "Almost Half of Practicing Christian Millennials Say Evangelism Is Wrong." Barna.com: Feb. 5, 2019. *Ibid.* barna.com/research/millennials-oppose-evangelism (Accessed January 21, 2021).

34 R.G. Grant, *Warrior: A Visual History of the Fighting Man* (New York: DK Publishing, 2007) 36.

35 Josephus, *The Jewish War, Book III* from *Josephus; with an English Translation by H. St. J. Thackeray, in Nine Volumes, Volume II* (Cambridge: Harvard University Press, 1956) 605. Thackeray was a remarkable scholar specializing in Koine Greek (the language of the New Testament), Josephus, and the *Septuagint,* the earliest Greek translation of the Hebrew Old Testament, which also contains additional works important to both biblical and

Church history. Ryan Baumann, Loebolus. https://ryanfb.github.io/loebolus-data/L203.pdf (Accessed January 21, 2021).

36 Vegetius, *Rei Militaris, Book II.* http://www.digitalattic.org/home/war/vegetius/index. php#b216 (Accessed January 21, 2021). Vegetius also mentions iron hooks called "wolves," but I have not listed that here because of Josephus' citation of the bill-hook. Most likely, these were the same instrument.

37 *Amas, NAS Exhaustive Concordance* (Lockman, 1998). Biblehub.com. https://biblehub.com/ hebrew/6006.htm. Examples of this beast of burden-type usage can be found in Ge. 44:13 and Ne. 13:15.

38 4335—*proseuché, Helps Word-Studies* states "*proseux* (from 4314/*prós,* "towards, exchange" and 2171/*euxe,* "a wish, prayer")—properly, exchange of wishes; prayer." https://biblehub.com/ greek/4335.htm (Accessed January 21, 2021).

Book VII: Mark of the Legionary, Pt. II

1   1128—*gumnazó, Helps Word-Studies* (Helps Ministries, Inc., 2011) Biblehub.com. https:// biblehub.com/greek/1128.htm.

2   An extensive endnote on questions concerning Matthew 17:21 can be found in Book IV's endnote #39.

3   4335—proseuché. Ibid. https://biblehub.com/greek/4335.htm (Accessed January 21, 2021).

4   For more, see Book IV's Endnote #39.

5   Author Unknown, "222 Prayers of the Bible." Hopefaithprayer.com, citing the work of Finis Dake in *Dake's Annotated Reference Bible.* Hopefaithprayer.com. https://www.hopefaith-prayer.com/prayernew/222-prayers-of-the-bible (Accessed January 21, 2021).

6   Barna.com, "Signs of Decline & Hope Among Key Metrics of Faith," *State of the Church 2020.* Barna.com: Mar. 4, 2020. https://www.barna.com/research/changing-state-of-the-church (Accessed January 21, 2021).

7   4744—*miqra.* James Strong, *Strong's Exhaustive Concordance of the Bible* (Peabody, MA: Hendrickson Publishers, 1980). https://biblehub.com/hebrew/4744.htm (Accessed January 21, 2021).

8   4864—*sunagógé.* Ibid. https://biblehub.com/greek/4864.htm (Accessed January 21, 2021).

9   1058—*bakah. NAS Exhaustive Concordance of the Bible with Hebrew-Aramaic and Greek Dictionaries* (The Lockman Foundation, 1998). https://biblehub.com/hebrew/1056.htm & https://biblehub.com/hebrew/1058.htm (Accessed January 21, 2021).

10 1577—*ekklésia. Helps Word-Studies.* https://biblehub.com/greek/1577.htm (Accessed January 21, 2021).

Conclusion: The Soldier Code

1   R.H. Barrow, *The Romans* (London: Penguin, 1949) 22-23. A virtual copy is available from the Stephens Library at: www.bard.edu/library/arendt/pdfs/Barrow Romans.pdf.